"Developing the idea famously set out by W. E. B. Du Bois, Stuart Hall suggested that living with difference would be the problem of the twenty-first century. Instances all across the world provide evidence of this and this insightful book, centred on the Nordic countries, adds powerfully to a body of critical scholarship on race and ethnicity that shows how entangled they are within repressed histories of internal and external colonisation and imagined nationhood. By considering the treatment of indigenous minorities alongside migrant communities, the editors and contributors impressively advance understandings of the ways in which difference is imagined and represented. Moreover the essays in this book skilfully analyse the peculiarity of claimed ethnic homogeneity. By linking the role of this myth to the influential model of the social democratic welfare state, they show that Hall's 'fateful triangle' of ethnicity-race-nation requires a fourth pillar, namely the state. Here is a book that may seem to be mainly of relevance to Nordic scholars but will I hope be read well beyond there and by all those interested in ethnicity, migration and the state, for its critical, engaged and engaging, unmasking of assumed homogeneity as well as its search for the possibilities of solidarity across difference."
—*Karim Murji, Co-editor of* Current Sociology, *University of West London, UK*

"This collection is a welcome addition to the ongoing discussion on politics of difference in Europe. Offering a Nordic perspective, it combines a historical deconstruction of national myths of homogeneity (questioning notions of exceptionality, denials of colonialism/racism and claims of innocence) with policy level analysis (securitization), individual narratives and group negotiation strategies. Particularly insightful is its inclusion of diverse exclusionary discourses in one volume. This strategy highlights the similarities between discourses concerning different disadvantaged groups that are often presented and discussed separately (Samis and Romas but also migrants and asylum seekers). Discussing the interconnected nature of these exclusionary structures through a historical perspective provides a strong foundation for joint struggles from below and for co-creating new politics of solidarity."
—*Halleh Ghorashi, VU Amsterdam, The Netherlands*

"This wide-ranging and engaging collection underlines the historical and political labour involved in producing homogeneity as a state of innocence under perpetual threat. With its emphasis on histories and practices of nation-building, bordering and race-making, the chapters not only contest the political and affective investments in Nordic homogeneity that are so pronounced in the region, and transnationally, they also foreground the reality and potential of forms of solidarity forged against and beyond homogeneity's coercive fictions."
—*Gavan Titley, author of* The Crises of Multiculturalism.
Maynooth University, Ireland

Undoing Homogeneity in the Nordic Region

This book critically engages with dominant ideas of cultural homogeneity in the Nordic countries and contests the notion of homogeneity as a crucial determinant of social cohesion and societal security. Showing how national identities in the Nordic region have developed historically around notions of cultural and racial homogeneity, it exposes the varied histories of migration and the longstanding presence of ethnic minorities and indigenous people in the region that are ignored in dominant narratives. With attention to the implications of notions of homogeneity for the everyday lives of migrants and racialised minorities in the region, as well as the increasing securitisation of those perceived not to be part of the homogenous nation, this volume provides detailed analyses of how welfare state policies, media, and authorities seek to manage and govern cultural, religious, and racial differences. With studies of national minorities, indigenous people and migrants in the analysis of homogeneity and difference, it sheds light on the agency of minorities and the intertwining of securitisation policies with notions of culture, race, and religion in the government of difference. As such it will appeal to scholars and students in social sciences and humanities with interests in race and ethnicity, migration, postcolonialism, Nordic studies, multiculturalism, citizenship, and belonging.

Suvi Keskinen is Professor and an Academy Research Fellow in the Centre for Research on Ethnic Relations and Nationalism (CEREN) at the University of Helsinki, Finland. She is the co-editor of *Complying with Colonialism. Gender, Race and Ethnicity in the Nordic Region*.

Unnur Dís Skaptadóttir is Professor of Anthropology at the University of Iceland, Iceland. She is the co-editor of *Mobility to the Edges of Europe; The Case of Iceland and Poland*.

Mari Toivanen is an Academy of Finland Post-Doctoral Researcher at the Swedish School of Social Science, University of Helsinki, Finland. She is the co-editor of *Methodological Approaches in Kurdish Studies. Theoretical and Practical Insights from the Field*.

Studies in Migration and Diaspora

Studies in Migration and Diaspora is a series designed to showcase the interdisciplinary and multidisciplinary nature of research in this important field. Volumes in the series cover local, national and global issues and engage with both historical and contemporary events. The books will appeal to scholars, students and all those engaged in the study of migration and diaspora. Amongst the topics covered are minority ethnic relations, transnational movements and the cultural, social and political implications of moving from 'over there', to 'over here'.

Series Editor: Anne J. Kershen, Queen Mary University of London, UK

Color that Matters
A Comparative Approach to Mixed Race Identity and Nordic Exceptionalism
Tony Sandset

Lives in Transit
An Ethnographic Study of Refugees' Subjectivity across European Borders
Elena Fontanari

Migration, Work and Home-Making in the City
Dwelling and Belonging among Vietnamese Communities in London
Annabelle Wilkins

Home States and Homeland Politics
Interactions between the Turkish State and its Emigrants in France and the United States
Damla B. Aksel

Undoing Homogeneity in the Nordic Region
Migration, Difference, and the Politics of Solidarity
Edited by Suvi Keskinen, Unnur Dís Skaptadóttir and Mari Toivanen

Wellbeing of Transnational Muslim Families
Marriage, Law and Gender
Edited by Marja Tiilikainen, Mulki Al-Sharmani and Sanna Mustasaari

For more information about this series, please visit: https://www.routledge.com/sociology/series/ASHSER1049

Undoing Homogeneity in the Nordic Region
Migration, Difference, and the Politics of Solidarity

Edited by
Suvi Keskinen, Unnur Dís Skaptadóttir and
Mari Toivanen

LONDON AND NEW YORK

First published 2019
by Routledge
2 Park Square, Milton Park, Abingdon, Oxon OX14 4RN

and by Routledge
52 Vanderbilt Avenue, New York, NY 10017

Routledge is an imprint of the Taylor & Francis Group, an informa business

© 2019 selection and editorial matter, Suvi Keskinen, Unnur Dís Skaptadóttir and Mari Toivanen; individual chapters, the contributors

The right of Suvi Keskinen, Unnur Dís Skaptadóttir and Mari Toivanen to be identified as the authors of the editorial material, and of the authors for their individual chapters, has been asserted in accordance with sections 77 and 78 of the Copyright, Designs and Patents Act 1988.

All rights reserved. No part of this book may be reprinted or reproduced or utilised in any form or by any electronic, mechanical, or other means, now known or hereafter invented, including photocopying and recording, or in any information storage or retrieval system, without permission in writing from the publishers.

Trademark notice: Product or corporate names may be trademarks or registered trademarks, and are used only for identification and explanation without intent to infringe.

British Library Cataloguing-in-Publication Data
A catalogue record for this book is available from the British Library

Library of Congress Cataloging-in-Publication Data
Names: Keskinen, Suvi, editor. | Unnur Dâis Skaptadáottir, editor. | Toivanen, Mari, editor.
Title: Undoing homogeneity in the Nordic region : migration, difference and the politics of solidarity / edited by Suvi Keskinen, Unnur Dâis Skaptadâottir and Mari Toivanen.
Description: Abingdon, Oxon ; New York, NY : Routledge, 2019. | Series: Studies in migration and diaspora | Includes bibliographical references and index.
Identifiers: LCCN 2019004645 (print) | LCCN 2019015432 (ebook) | ISBN 9781315122328 (ebk) | ISBN 9781351347372 (web pdf) | ISBN 9781351347365 (epub) | ISBN 9781351347358 (mobi/kindle) | ISBN 9781138564275 (hbk)
Subjects: LCSH: Cultural pluralism--Scandinavia. | Assimilation (Sociology)--Scandinavia. | Ethnicity--Scandinavia. | Nationalism--Scandinavia. | Solidarity--Scandinavia. | Scandinavia--Emigration and immigration--Social aspects.
Classification: LCC HN540.Z9 (ebook) | LCC HN540.Z9 M8486 2019 (print) | DDC 303.48/20948--dc23
LC record available at https://lccn.loc.gov/2019004645

ISBN: 978-1-138-56427-5 (hbk)
ISBN: 978-1-315-12232-8 (ebk)

Typeset in Times New Roman
by Taylor & Francis Books

Printed and bound in Great Britain by
TJ International Ltd, Padstow, Cornwall

Contents

List of contributors ix
Series editor's preface xiii

1 Narrations of homogeneity, waning welfare states, and the politics of solidarity 1
   SUVI KESKINEN, UNNUR DÍS SKAPTADÓTTIR AND MARI TOIVANEN

PART 1
Histories of homogeneity and difference 19

2 Forgetting diversity? Norwegian narratives of ethnic and cultural homogeneity 21
   TEEMU RYYMIN

3 Myths of ethnic homogeneity: The Danish case 35
   GARBI SCHMIDT

4 Finnish media representations of the Sámi in the 1960s and 1970s 50
   NIINA SIIVIKKO

PART 2
Governing and negotiating differences 67

5 Knowledge about Roma and Travellers in Nordic schools: Paradoxes, constraints, and possibilities 69
   JENNI HELAKORPI

6 Problematising the urban periphery: Discourses on social exclusion and suburban youth in Sweden 88
   MAGNUS DAHLSTEDT

7 Welfare chauvinism at the margins of whiteness: Young unemployed Russian-speakers' negotiations of worker-citizenship in Finland 103
DARIA KRIVONOS

8 Starry starry night: Fantasies of homogeneity in documentary films about Kvens and Norwegian-Pakistanis 119
PRISCILLA RINGROSE AND ELISABETH STUBBERUD

PART 3
Questioned homogeneity and securitisation 139

9 From welfare to warfare: Exploring the militarisation of the Swedish suburb 141
SURUCHI THAPAR-BJÖRKERT, IRENE MOLINA AND KARINA RAÑA VILLACURA

10 "Living in fear": Bulgarian and Romanian street workers' experiences with aggressive public and private policing 162
MARKUS HIMANEN

11 A 'Muslim' response to the narrative of the enemy within 179
SHARAM ALGHASI

12 Being unknown: The securitisation of asylum seekers in Iceland 195
HELGA KATRIN TRYGGVADÓTTIR

Index 209

Contributors

Sharam Alghasi is Associate Professor at Kristiania Collage in Oslo, Norway. His research includes a wide range of issues linked to migration in Norway and Europe. In particular he is preoccupied with the question of migration in relation to media. His PhD dissertation from 2009 deals with the relation between Iranian-Norwegian media consumption and their construction of identity, and strategies of adaption in Norwegian society. In this regard, Alghasi focuses as well on the questions of religion of Islam, and nationalism in identity work among migrants with Muslim background. Alghasi has published several edited books, as well as journal articles in, for example, *Nordicom, Social Semiotics,* and *Journal of Migration Research.*

Magnus Dahlstedt is Professor in Social Work at Linköping University, Sweden. His research interests include citizenship, marketization of welfare, critical social work, and civil society. He is currently conducting research on youth in urban peripheries, sports as a means of social intervention, and adult education targeting newly arrived refugees. Dahlstedt has published a range of articles and books, among these *The confessing society: Foucault, confession and practices of lifelong learning* (with Andreas Fejes), *International migration and ethnic relations – critical perspectives* (edited with Anders Neergaard) and *Adult education and the formation of citizens – a critical interrogation* (with Fejes, Olson, and Sandberg).

Jenni Helakorpi is a doctoral student in the Nordic Centre of Excellence Justice through Education, at the Faculty of Educational Sciences, University of Helsinki. In her PhD dissertation she studies the policies and practices that aim to promote the basic education of Roma and Traveller minorities in Finland, Norway, and Sweden. Her research interests also include critical studies on race and whiteness in education, gender in education, and special education.

Markus Himanen (M.Soc.Sc in political science) is a doctoral student in sociology at the University of Helsinki and researcher in the project "The Stopped – Spaces, Meanings and Practices of Ethnic Profiling" (2015–2018, Kone foundation). Himanen's dissertation focuses on immigration policing and ethnic profiling in Finland. He analyses how discriminatory practices of immigration law enforcement undermine equal citizenship, and the fundamental rights associated with it. He has published journal articles and book chapters in Finnish; as well as several non-academic articles concerning migration, borders, citizenship, and the labour market.

Suvi Keskinen is Professor in Ethnic Relations and Nationalism at the Swedish School of Social Science, University of Helsinki in Finland. During 2014–2019, she holds the Academy Research Fellow position. Her research interests include post/decolonial feminism, critical race and whiteness studies, nationalism, political activism, and Nordic colonial/racial histories. She currently leads a research project on post-ethnic minority activism and another project on intersectional border struggles and disobedient knowledge in activism. Earlier Keskinen has studied right-wing populism, media and political debates on migration and racism, gendered violence and youth in racialised residence areas. She has published several books and edited Special Issues, as well as journal articles in, for example, *Social Politics, Ethnicities, Journal of Youth Studies, Nordic Journal of Migration Research, Critical Social Policy, Social Identities* and *Journal of Intercultural Studies*.

Daria Krivonos is a doctoral candidate in Sociology at the University of Helsinki. Her research interests include migration, critical race and whiteness studies, labour, gender, and racialisation. Her ethnographic research deals with racialisation of young Russian-speaking migrants in Finland, which she has analysed from the perspective of legal status, whiteness, coloniality, gender, and racialisation.

Irene Molina is Professor of Human Geography at the Institute for Housing and Urban Research, Uppsala University, Sweden. She is also affiliated to the Center for Multidisciplinary studies on Racism, CEMFOR, at Uppsala University, where she is the Research Director, as well as to the Department of Social and Economic Geography, at the same university. Her research areas are all related to the spatialities of power, particularly exploring the intersections between racism, sexism, and neoliberalism, looking both at mechanisms of oppression and forces of resistance. Among her recent publications is the chapter "Planning for Patriarchy? Gender Equality in the Swedish Modern Built Environment", published in *The Routledge Companion to Modernity, Space and Gender* (2018)

Priscilla Ringrose is Professor of Gender Studies and of French Literature at the Norwegian University of Science and Technology. Her research interests include migration and gender, education and integration, paid domestic labour, Islamic fundamentalisms, and postcolonial francophone literature. She currently leads a Research Council of Norway funded project *Language, Integration, Media: A majority-inclusive approach to integration relating to citizen and non-citizen adolescents*. She has edited and published several books and journal articles, including the co-edited *Paid*

Migrant Domestic Labour in a Changing Europe (Palgrave MacMillan 2016), and contributed to *Journal of Scandinavian Cinema, Feminist Media Studies* and *International Journal of Communication*.

Teemu Ryymin is Professor in Modern History at the Department of Archaeology, History, Cultural Studies and Religion, University of Bergen, Norway. His research interests include history of minorities, history of health and medicine, use of history as well as historiography, and historical research methodology. Ryymin has edited and published several books and numerous journal articles. Among his latest publications are *Historie og politikk. Historiebruk i norsk politikkutforming etter 1945* (Universitetsforlaget, Oslo 2017) and *Historikerens arbeidsmåter* (with Leidulf Melve, Universitetsforlaget, Oslo 2018).

Garbi Schmidt is a Professor of Cultural Encounters at Roskilde University in Denmark. Over the last decades, her research has focused on migration, transnationalism, Muslim minorities in Europe and the United States, and social cohesion. In her most recent research, she has included a both historical and anthropological perspective on the contribution of migrants to the Danish capital Copenhagen, in particular to the two neighbourhoods Nørrebro and Østerbro.

Niina Siivikko is a PhD student in Cultural History at the University of Turku, Finland. She is currently working on her PhD thesis on representations of the Sámi people in Finnish media in the second half of the 20th century. Her research interests include Sámi history, indigenous studies, representations, minorities, and media history. She is of Northern Sámi origin.

Unnur Dís Skaptadóttir is Professor of Anthropology at the Faculty of Sociology, Anthropology and Folkloristics at the University of Iceland. Her research interests include transnationalism, gender, nationalism, and questions of borders and boundaries. She has conducted research among various migrant groups in Iceland. Skaptadóttir co-coordinates the Centre of Excellence: *Mobilities and Transnational Iceland* (2016–2019). She has published book chapters in edited books and in journals such as *Journal of Immigrant & Refugee Studies, Nordic Journal of Migration Research, NORA – Nordic Journal of Feminist and Gender Research*. She has recently co-edited the book *Mobility to the Edges of Europe: The Case of Iceland and Poland* (Gdansk: SCHOLAR).

Elisabeth Stubberud has a PhD in gender research, and is currently a postdoctoral research fellow at the Department of Education and Lifelong Learning at the Norwegian University of Science and Technology. She is currently working on a research project on historical and contemporary coastal cultures in Northern Norway, focusing in particular on local knowledge, identity, migration, and belonging. Over the past years Elisabeth has also worked with and published on issues relating to youth, gender and sexuality, gendered violence, discrimination, and hate speech. Her research interests include feminist and decolonial methodologies, migration and belonging, and queer theory.

Suruchi Thapar-Björkert is docent and senior lecturer at the Department of Government, University of Uppsala in Sweden. Her research falls in four specific areas: Gendered Discourses of Colonialism and Nationalism, Gendered Violence, Ethnicity, Social Capital and Social Exclusion and Deliberative Democracy, Riots and the Suburb. She has published widely in journals such as *Ethnic and Racial Studies, Feminist Review, Feminist Theory, Sociological Review,* and *Interventions*. She is currently working on the following funded projects: *Civil Society and Deliberative Democracy, The paradoxes of empowerment in India; Gender, Biopolitics and Neo-liberalism in Indian Commercial Surrogacy,* and *Understanding Racism in Healthcare.*

Mari Toivanen currently works as a Postdoctoral Researcher in an Academy of Finland project, at the Swedish School of Social Science, University of Helsinki. She has written scientific articles on diaspora activism and political participation, media representations, identity, belonging and racialisation in the Nordic context in *Ethnic and Racial Studies, Nordic Journal of Migration Research, Kurdish Studies Journal, Middle East Journal of Culture and Communication,* and recently co-edited the book *Methodological Approaches in Kurdish Studies* (Lexington). She holds a PhD in Social Sciences from the University of Turku and is an affiliated member of the School for Advanced Studies in Social Sciences (EHESS) in Paris.

Helga Katrin Tryggvadóttir was a PhD student of Anthropology at the Faculty of Sociology, Anthropology and Folkloristics at the University of Iceland. The title of her doctoral dissertation was "The Politics of Eligibility: A Research on the Asylum Determination Process in Iceland", which was part of a bigger Project of Excellence *Mobilities and Transnational Iceland*. Helga had already begun to publish articles and a book chapter on her research when she passed away in the July of 2018. Besides academic writing Tryggvadóttir applied her knowledge on refugee and environmental issues in writing in public media. She worked with a number of volunteer and activist organisations in Iceland.

Karina Raña Villacura has a master's degree in Geography from Stockholm University. She is currently affiliated to Uppsala University and Stockholm University as a research assistant. She is particularly interested in the spatial dimension of securitisation and racism intertwined with the politics of late capitalism and various forms of resistance. Her latest publication "An intersectional perspective for addressing the global phenomenon of racism" (co-authored with Irene Molina), was published in the journal *Actuel Marx-Intervenciones* (2017, in Spanish).

Series editor's preface

In the first two decades of the 21st century, the countries which are the geographic focus of this book changed their policies towards immigrants from Welfare to Warfare, what has been called the 'crimmigration of migration'. This was particularly aimed at those from the non-Western world. For those for whom the politics of solidarity and securitisation in the Nordic Region are little known, this book provides a revelatory insight into the policies that Denmark, Finland, Norway, Iceland, and Sweden have adopted towards outsiders, particularly those whom they label as 'undeserving others'. Historically, not all the securitising policies have been directed towards non-nationals. In Sweden, indigenous misfits were perceived as a threat to the nation's societal homogeneity. Wishing to maintain its image of morality and harmony of behaviour and appearance, from 1906 until 1975 it operated a policy of sterilising 'misfits'; these were mostly women whose 'difference' ranged from apathy and promiscuity to dyslexia and cleft palates. These past policies help explain current strategies undertaken in order for the Nordic Region's nation-states to maintain their image as homogeneous societies.

The editors remind us that certain of the Nordic nations were themselves colonisers and that this has influenced those countries' reaction to the minority presence and multiculturalism. For example, the original inhabitants of the region, the Sámi, are now identified as indigenous peoples; they have had their histories silenced and now occupy a middle place in contemporary society.

Significantly, the studies in this book combine both historic and more recent—post 1960—responses to the presence of those who do not conform to the required cultural and social characteristics which reflect the national identity. The temporal range of essays thus enables the reader to compare and contrast Nordic nations' attitudes and policies towards difference. And whilst certain benevolent acts towards immigrants have taken place—in 2015 Sweden admitted 163,000 asylum seekers—a manifest oversight in anticipating the impact of the migrant presence has resulted in many incomers remaining on the margins and, as such, becoming a perceived threat to the security and identity of the nation, and accordingly victims of recent securitisation policies.

What becomes apparent when reading this insightful and highly informative volume is the way in which public and political attitudes have changed towards immigrants who do not readily conform to the Nordic icon. Whiteness and non-whiteness have come to play an increasing part in determining access to welfare and several chapters highlight the ways in which the provision of welfare has now become racialised and neighbourhoods virtually segregated. In response, some migrants and their children are now taking action to 'make their voices heard'. However, this does little to encourage and ensure cultural uniformity within nations that, as one contributor suggests, look upon homogeneity and whiteness as a binary.

As the editors point out in their introduction, this book is not intended as a hagiographical account of the policies that countries in the Nordic region are currently adopting in order to restore and ensure their nations' images of solidarity and cohesion through their cultural sameness. Rather, the chapters set out to deconstruct the securitisation strategies adopted as a means of re-imposing the stereotypical Nordic identity by exposing the use of the policing of those whose presence undermines the traditional image of Nordic homogeneity by means of their colour, race, ethnicity, or religion. There are five main Nordic nations and their policies of securitisation and provision of welfare to outsiders vary. What does not vary is the clear intent to maintain their nation's image of a homogenous cultural identity by means of restricting those who are other and endanger the icon.

Whilst this book is very specific in its spatial and national foci it sends a message to all those who readily accept national images and identities. It calls on those concerned about the treatments of those who are other, different, and misfits to deconstruct the public face, look beneath the social rubric and unearth the actual national composition and identity. For this reason and for the originality and scholarship of its contributions, it should be required reading for all those engaged in researching and understanding nations, nation building, and national responses to migration and difference within their society.

Anne J Kershen
Queen Mary University of London
Winter 2019

1 Narrations of homogeneity, waning welfare states, and the politics of solidarity

Suvi Keskinen, Unnur Dís Skaptadóttir and Mari Toivanen

Cultural heterogeneity, and grounds for a politics of solidarity that would connect the "imagined communities" (Anderson 2006) of today's nation-states, have become core questions in European politics. Across Europe and including the Nordic region, we have witnessed the rise of right-wing populism that builds its political agenda on ideals of cultural homogeneity, claims of diminished social cohesion, and security threats posed by migrants and racialised minorities. The emphasis on problems of difference and demands for stricter policies relating to immigration and integration, have by no means been restricted to the far right. Scholars have identified a "crisis of multiculturalism" discourse (Lentin and Titley 2011) or a "backlash against multiculturalism" (Vertovec and Wessendorf 2010), circulating among large sections of the political centre-right and parts of the left, as well as among many prominent journalists and intellectuals. The shift towards (demands of) cultural homogeneity, neo-assimilatory politics, and security measures would not have been possible without the active participation and rebranding of political rhetoric by the broader political field. As Lentin and Titley (2011) argue, public debates about multiculturalism and cultural differences are often ways to address questions of race, power, and privilege in a hidden way, in times when racism is treated as an outdated and awkward topic not to be explicitly engaged with. In this book, we investigate the historical and societal context within which the claims of the far-right parties become understandable—instead of viewing them as totally alien or exceptional phenomena, we see them as radicalised extensions of more accepted and normalised ways of thinking and acting. We also argue that new configurations of solidarity are needed in European politics, which would replace ideas around homogeneity/sameness and reformulate notions of social justice to include migrants and racialised minorities that are today increasingly portrayed as the "undeserving Others". New politics of solidarity needs to acknowledge the histories and currents of colonialism and depart from an understanding of social justice that incorporates and seeks to repair the experiences of cultural and economic injustices.

This book provides a critical approach to the narratives of cultural homogeneity and social cohesion that are usually taken for granted in the understandings of societal security in the Nordic region. The perception of the Nordic countries as exceptionally homogeneous in relation to culture and population is widespread in academic, administrative, and public discussions (Alghasi, Eriksen, and Ghorashi 2009; Keskinen et al. 2009; Loftsdóttir and Jensen 2012; *Ryymin* and *Schmidt* in this volume[1]). Cultural homogeneity is often portrayed as one of the central reasons for the Nordic countries' high level of social cohesion[2] and—by extension— the high level of societal security in the region. Societal security in this sense refers to society's capability to preserve its essential characteristics in the face of actual or imagined threats. National and regional identities have become central to understandings of societal security, the maintenance of which is seen to depend on the preservation of experienced social cohesiveness and togetherness, that in turn legitimise the welfare state.

In this book, we trace the historical emergence of narratives of exceptional homogeneity and examine how governing of differences relates to the securitisation of migration in the Nordic region—a tendency interconnected with common trends in Europe (e.g. Guild 2009; d'Appolonia 2012), but with contextual specificities within the countries studied here. The contributors illuminate how normative understandings of cultural homogeneity neglect the histories of transnational migration and ethnic minorities within the region, as well as bypassing the colonial appropriation of land, and the assimilation policies towards the indigenous peoples in the Arctic. The book aims to answer the following questions:

- How are national identities in the Nordic countries developed around notions of cultural homogeneity, and what kinds of histories have created such understandings?
- What are the (ethnicised and racialised) presumptions of the idea that cultural homogeneity promotes societal security?
- How do welfare state policies and practices seek to manage and govern cultural/religious/racial differences?
- Which differences are seen as (cultural, economic, political) threats and become security problems, while others do not?
- How are migrants, minorities, and targeted local actors resisting securitisation processes, and creating alternative narratives from their viewpoints?

Compared to earlier studies on cultural homogeneity and migration in the Nordic region, this book elaborates three new perspectives. First, we not only investigate the historical trajectories of taken-for-granted notions of cultural homogeneity across the Nordic countries, but also detect how these are intertwined with ideas of race and racial homogeneity as part of nation-state formation. Second, the book deconstructs ideas of cultural homogeneity by focusing on indigenous peoples and ethnic minorities with a long-term presence in the region, *together with* post-1960s migrants and their descendants. This contrasts with previous research that has discussed (the governing and perspectives of) these groups separately. Third, we understand the histories and current societal processes of the Nordic countries to be shaped by (post) colonial relations. In contrast to dominant discourses, the Nordic countries participated in colonial endeavours in many ways, outside Europe and within the region (Keskinen forthcoming; Kuokkanen 2007; Loftsdóttir and Jensen 2012; Körber and Volquardsen 2014). These ignored histories continue to affect relations between the indigenous populations and the Nordic nation-states, as well as the perceptions and exclusionary processes encountered by migrants from the non-'Western' world, and their children, in today's Nordic societies.

Ideas of exceptional homogeneity, nation building, and race

Historical narratives of the post-1960s transnational migration that presuppose initial homogeneity as a central characteristic of the Nordic countries are prone to depicting growing migration as a potential threat. Embedded in such narratives—either implicitly or explicitly—is the idea that the national sovereignty and cultural identities of the Nordic states are being eroded by a greater level of cultural diversity, that is then seen to be undermining the countries' level of social cohesion, and consequently their societal security. If (cultural) homogeneity is seen as a foundation for, or a precondition of, a well-functioning welfare system, then increased migration—by leading to greater cultural, ethnic, and racial heterogeneity—logically threatens that system, or at least is a problem that has to be dealt with.

However, all Nordic countries have been diverse in many ways, as documented in the growing body of historical research and literature on multiculturalism (e.g. Kivisto and Wahlbeck 2013; Skaptadóttir and Loftsdóttir 2009; Sandset 2019), as well as the chapters in this volume. The social, cultural, and ethnic heterogeneity of Nordic societies was readily acknowledged in the late nineteenth and early twentieth century nation-building processes and policies. It was considered to be something that threatened the societal integrity of the nation-states, and thus was to be overcome through diverse assimilatory and/or integrative policies. This was not least evident in the building of the welfare systems, designed to overcome class and regional differences through equalisation.

The idea of ethnic and cultural homogeneity is thus more a product of nation-building processes, than a description of actual existing conditions. As David Theo Goldberg (2002, p. 33) argues, "ethnoracial, cultural and national homogeneity is sustained throughout modernity, not because it is the natural condition", but because it is the ideal kept alive and imposed on heterogeneous groups of people "through repression, occlusion and erasure, restriction and denial, delimitation and domination". For Goldberg, homogeneity is part of the ordering of the modern state, notably about the regulation of social, economic, and cultural relations, and the governing of populations defined in racial terms (ibid., p. 110). Modern states have also, in varying ways, managed and sought to secure the conditions for economic production, expansion of capital, and reproduction of labour. The processes of homogenisation are thus as much about power over resources and distribution of wealth, as they are about cultural hegemony and normative understandings of the 'people' and ways of living.

Nation-state building in the Nordic region differs to some extent among the individual countries. While Sweden and Denmark have been the region's dominant states for centuries, having ruled over what is today known as Norway, Finland, and Iceland, the latter three countries gained independence in the wake of the nationalist movements of the nineteenth and early twentieth centuries. Nevertheless, as the contributions in this book show, all Nordic countries have promoted ideas of being exceptionally homogeneous, ignoring and denying assimilatory and repressive state actions towards indigenous people and ethnoracially defined minorities.

The nation-states in the region have historically sought to manage and deal with existing differences in multiple ways. The appropriation of land, and subsequent erosion of livelihoods, have seriously affected the indigenous Sámi and Inuit people, while expulsion, restriction of movement, and interventions into family life have targeted the Roma and Traveller minorities (*Helakorpi*). Racial and ethnic categorisations—including racial biology—have been used to define and inferiorise indigenous people and several minorities. Compared to these, assimilation policies may seem less severe, but they have resulted in the silencing of identities and local histories, as well as cultural and linguistic erasure (*Siivikko, Ringrose, and Stubberud*). Since the 1970s, Norway, Sweden, and Finland have adopted multicultural policies in their efforts to respond to cultural heterogeneity that has become hard to ignore (*Ryymin*). Since the 1960s and 1970s, indigenous people and ethnic minorities have organised to struggle for their cultural and land rights, both in dialogue and in conflict with different state policies. The post-1960s migrants and their children have also mobilised in civil society to make their voices heard.

Notions of "exceptionalism" also refer to the perceived outsider position that the Nordic countries are often thought to have in relation to colonialism (Keskinen et al. 2009; Loftsdóttir and Jensen 2012; Sawyer and Habel 2014). However, recent research has shown that Danish colonialism stretched from the Caribbean to West Africa, East Asia and the Arctic (Jensen 2015; Körber and Volquardsen 2014), while Sweden had minor colonies in North America, the Caribbean, and West Africa. The colonisation of Sápmi, the land of the Sámi people, crosses the national borders of Norway, Sweden, and Finland. While Iceland was not in possession of colonies, it has strongly identified with

European history and modernity (Loftsdóttir 2017). Compared to the British, French, or Dutch empires, the Nordic countries may have been "small time actors" (Naum and Nordin 2013) in overseas colonialism, but they actively participated in and benefited from the unequal economic, political, and cultural relations developed during European colonialism—a position that has been described as "colonial complicity" (Vuorela 2009; Keskinen et al. 2009). When these histories are combined with knowledge of Nordic colonialism in the Arctic, it becomes clear that the Nordic countries were in multiple ways involved in colonial endeavours, both as "accomplices", but also as active colonial powers (Keskinen, forthcoming).

The chapter in this book by Teemu Ryymin uses social science texts to examine how and when the notion of Norway as a particularly homogeneous society was established. Ryymin detects the rise of a narrative that portrays a dramatic shift from an ethnically homogeneous country, to increasing diversity following labour migrations of the early 1970s, and refugee migrations since the 1980s. Ryymin shows how claims of exceptional homogeneity are at odds with the historical experiences of cultural, linguistic, ethnic, religious, and social diversity in Norway. The chapter analyses the silencing of the histories of Sámi people and several ethnic minorities, due to Norwegian assimilation policies, and the social democratic welfare state project that sought to equalise class differences from a universalist standpoint. Moreover, Ryymin discusses the impact of racialisation, when distinctions are made towards migrants from non-'Western' countries.

Garbi Schmidt analyses the 'myth' of ethnic homogeneity from a local perspective, focusing on two neighbourhoods in Copenhagen. She investigates the history of Danish national symbols, and the stories that hold together the notion of a "homogeneous" nation. Contrasting the narrative of homogeneity with the actual diversity in these two neighbourhoods at the turn of the nineteenth and twentieth centuries, Schmidt argues that Denmark and its citizens were engaged in networks of communication that exceeded the space of the nation-state. Ethnic and cultural homogeneity cannot be evaluated by investigating only the number of immigrants; instead, a broader view that addresses the transnational social, political, financial, and cultural connections of the country is needed. The chapter further examines perceptions of homogeneity and heterogeneity in the two neighbourhoods today, showing that such understandings are deeply racialised, and that homogeneity is conflated with whiteness.

In her chapter, Niina Siivikko examines Sámi representations in the Finnish media during the 1960s and 1970s. The chapter focuses on a period called the "Sámi Renaissance", referring to the revival of Sámi culture after harsh assimilation policies that nearly led to the extinction of Sámi culture in Finland. It is not coincidental that the Sámi defended their cultural and land rights during a time when many other indigenous peoples and racialised minorities were involved in similar struggles around the world. Siivikko examines mainstream Finnish newspapers, arguing that the role of the Sámi within the nation was ambiguous. At times, the Sámi people were treated as part of the Finnish nation, while they were otherwise thought to be in the process of becoming part of the nation. Sometimes, they were even considered to not want to become Finnish. The "Sámi Renaissance" meant the voice of Sámi cultural activists became stronger, and a new identity politics was developed that built on a spirit of solidarity to provide greater visibility to Sámi demands.

Priscilla Ringrose and Elisabeth Stubberud analyse how two documentary films about old and new minority groups in Norway position themselves in relation to the Norwegian "national fantasy". The documentaries explore issues of national identity and belonging in relation to the Kven and the Norwegian-Pakistani communities. Both films reflect on the assimilationist policies of the Norwegian nation-state towards ethnic and racial minorities, but adopt different ways of positioning themselves to majoritarian and minoritarian perspectives. The documentaries revolve around family stories, bringing to the fore questions of gender, generation, and Norwegian state interventions in the arena of family life. Ringrose and Stubberud interpret the two films as being in dialogue with each other, suggesting that the Kven documentary contains both a symbolic warning and a promise to its Norwegian-Pakistani counterpart.

Nordic welfare model and social cohesion

The link between social cohesion and cultural/ethnic homogeneity in different societies, and the long-term consequences of migration, have been widely explored in recent research literature. Putnam's 2007 article 'E Pluribus Unum' created a controversy when it suggested that there are negative effects within ethnic diversity resulting from migration to "Western" societies (Putnam 2007; Morales 2013). The last decade has witnessed a heated debate among scholars, and a growing body of research has evaluated the "threat" hypothesis put forward by Putnam. Indeed, one of the central questions in this literature has been whether the increased ethnic and cultural heterogeneity resulting from migration to a given society leads to the erosion of social cohesion in that society. Scholars have examined, for instance, the relationship between increased ethnic/cultural diversity and its potentially weakening effect on reciprocity, participation in volunteering, social capital, social trust, and solidarity in different societies (Koopmans, Lancee, and Schaeffer 2015; van der Meer and Tolsma 2014 for a summary of these studies). Whereas some have confirmed (to a certain extent) Putnam's hypothesis, others have shown that racial inequalities, segregation, and economic and social precariousness are more consequential for social cohesion and trust, than ethnic diversity (see ibid; Uslaner 2012).

The debates in Nordic research have been similar to those in the United States and continental Europe, in that they have also included contrasting views on whether the link between social cohesion and increased diversity resulting from migration is negative or positive (Delhey and Newton 2005; Larsen 2013; van der Meer and Tolsma 2014; Goldschmidt 2017). The studies have also examined, for instance, the attitudes of the white majority towards government-funded welfare to migrants living in the Nordic welfare states, known for their universalistic approach to social policies. The majority population's willingness to accept migrant and minority groups as legitimate members of the welfare community has been considered to be central to the social cohesion of that society (Goldschmidt 2017). Whereas the Nordic countries may share some elements of their welfare models, they have had quite different approaches concerning immigration and integration policies. These have ranged from more restrictive models of inclusion in Denmark, to more liberal approaches in Sweden (Brochmann and Hagelund 2012), and somewhere in-between for Norway, Finland, and Iceland. However, in recent years, the policies have converged towards stricter measures in all countries. Furthermore, the Nordic countries have in the past decade witnessed increasing political and public debate about who is deserving of social welfare benefits, and who is not. Keskinen, Norocel, and Jørgensen (2016) discuss how welfare chauvinistic claims—that is, how the white majority population is seen to deserve welfare benefits, more so than migrants and racialised minorities—have become policy matters, influencing welfare practices in the aftermath of the 2008 global recession.

What seems to be characteristic of debates (and research) on social cohesion, both in the Nordic countries and elsewhere, is the conflation between heterogeneity and migration: the heterogeneity of a given society is framed in terms of an increased number of racialised migrant groups, without reference to indigenous people or existing national minorities. This can lead to the often-implicit assumption that national societies before 1970s migrations were more or less culturally homogeneous. This can also come with a certain level of normativity, when social cohesion that is associated with an alleged lack of ethnic diversity is considered to be a desirable state of affairs. Increasing heterogeneity through migration has been approached as a potential problem and threat for the societal and political order, to be resolved through the integration of the migrant 'Others'. Indeed, Hickman, Mai, and Crowley (2012) suggest that the phenomenon of social cohesion should not be approached through the normative and functionalist models of social cohesion that contain an essentialist understanding of what constitutes a "good society". Instead, the authors show that "local hierarchies of social entitlement and mobility, the acknowledgement of transnational affiliations, belongings and histories of diversity and/or homogeneity are all constitutive of social cohesion" (p. 10).

Another underlying premise in social cohesion literature seems to be that only the nation-state is the basis of social cohesion and the provider of resources (see Delanty 2000). In other words, cultural homogeneity, social cohesion, and the "problem of integration" have been approached through the nation-state frame, both in policymaking and research (see Wimmer and Glick-Schiller 2003). Migrants, although coming from outside the national space, could not be excluded from the emerging welfare systems in Europe in the post-Second World War period, since the emergence of the welfare systems was closely linked to the labour market the migrants became part of (ibid, p. 310). Post-war immigration studies, especially in Europe, focused upon the consequences of immigration to national welfare systems, and how this related to the question of integration. Indeed, Bommes and Thränhardt (2010) suggest that the way migration is conceptualised and the "problem of migration and integration" is rearticulated, is rooted in the different histories of nation building. They argue that "paradigms of migration research" are "rather scientific re-articulations of nation-state specific ways to constitute international migration-related problem constellations" (ibid, p. 29).

Therefore, it is important to question the normative understandings of cultural homogeneity and social cohesion—and to problematise the implicit assumption of the nation-state as their frame of reference. Similarly, in debates that conflate cultural homogeneity with social cohesion, difference/heterogeneity needs to be approached in a way that does not overlook the histories of transnational mobility, indigenous people, and ethnic minorities. And finally, there is a need to critically examine the implicit link between social cohesion and cultural homogeneity, particularly in Nordic societies where cultural/ethnic/racial homogeneity has been part of the historical and present-day narratives of national identity.

The development of the welfare state in the Nordic region was tightly connected to the nation-state and notions of homogeneity. From the 1930s, Sweden led the way in developing what became known as the Nordic or the social democratic welfare model (Esping-Andersen 1990), combining redistribution policies, comprehensive welfare benefits, and social services, in order to enhance class and regional equality. The Swedish social democrats made the notion of *folkhemmet*—literally, the people's home—the basis of their political ideology. *Folkhemmet,* originally a social-conservative nationalist idea, presented the Swedish people as a unified and homogenous entity under the shared familial roof (Norocel 2013, p. 139). From the beginning, kinship ties and common origins were thus part of the welfare state ideology, the aim of which was to create social cohesion and reduce class differences understood as the root of conflict.

The "golden era" of the Nordic welfare states gave way to neoliberal policies from the 1980s onwards. The economic recession of the following decade provided grounds for politicians who argued for welfare cuts and privatisation in the name of competitiveness, efficiency, and reducing welfare costs (Pyrhönen 2015, pp. 24–25; Keskinen, Norocel, and Jørgensen 2016). With the shrinking welfare state came the reduction of available political means, and the will, to decrease social divisions and govern economic fractures. The economic crisis of 2008 led to austerity politics, especially in Iceland and Finland. The welfare state that developed as a national project to reduce economic differences and promote class solidarity now seems to be a threatened project—this is due to neoliberal policies, but also waning class solidarity when the economic redistribution element no longer benefits lower income groups, and the support from the middle class simultaneously hovers. While the idea of the welfare state still receives broad popular support in the Nordic countries, in practice, privatisation policies and increasing socio-economic divisions have become characteristic for these societies (e.g. Schierup, Hansen, and Castles 2006; Kamali and Jönsson 2018).

In this political and economic climate, migration from non-"Western" countries in particular has become perceived as an economic threat. At the same time, migrants and racialised minorities form a large part of the low-paid workforce essential for the Nordic economies and welfare states. While migrants from post-socialist countries face certain advantages in comparison to groups racialised as "non-white Others", they can still lack employment opportunities, and be inferiorised in relation to the majority population (*Krivonos*). Even today, social exclusion and economic inequalities are treated as challenges to social cohesion, but now they include a clearly ethnicised and racialised angle. In public debates, the threat is located in racialised residential areas, and especially in their young non-white residents (*Dahlstedt*). The Roma and Traveller minorities—who have a long history in the Nordic region—also suffer from economic disadvantages but are largely defined in public through cultural difference (*Helakorpi*). In dominant discourses, economic threats thus seem to be connected more to the post-1960s migrants and their children, than to older minorities or indigenous peoples.

In this book, Jenni Helakorpi examines the ways in which professionals identifying as Roma and Travellers working to promote the basic education of these groups, make sense of the practice of "provision of knowledge about Roma and Travellers". This chapter challenges the view that providing knowledge about minoritised groups would be enough to promote justice in education; instead, a more thorough institutional transformation that includes continuous interrogations of power relations is needed. Helakorpi argues that although professionals seek to use their knowledge about Roma and Travellers to problematise ingrained processes of racialisation, they are not able to totally avoid contributing to the very same discourses. The chapter connects the production of knowledge about Roma and Traveller minorities to state policies and public discourses about Roma people more generally, which differs across the three studied Nordic countries. Recent state recognition of historical atrocities seems to provide space for narratives of discrimination and abuse to be included in basic education knowledge.

The chapter by Magnus Dahlstedt focuses on the problematisations of suburban youth in racialised residential areas in Sweden. In media coverage, suburban youth are seen to pose a serious threat to the social cohesion of Swedish society: stories of burning cars and stones thrown at police and rescue vehicles present the urban peripheries as the locus of social disorder and disintegration. Dahlstedt's analysis departs from the local level, investigating the views of local authorities and the youth themselves. Dahlstedt shows that the authorities view the "area of exclusion" and its inhabitants as causing the problems of social exclusion. On the other hand, the youth in these racialised suburbs focus on the mechanisms of social exclusion, and the interventions that would be needed for change. New articulations of social exclusion emerge when the suburban youth challenge others' perceptions, and call for societal responsibility in tackling exclusion.

Daria Krivonos analyses how Russian-speaking migrants positioned as unemployed draw on a racial grammar to legitimise their place in the Finnish welfare system. Krivonos relates these processes to the Finnish context, where welfare chauvinist and neoliberal ideas of "deservingness" and "undeservingness" are widely circulating in the public sphere. Krivonos argues that the boundaries of deservingness and entitlement for welfare benefits are racialised and interconnected with the idea of whiteness. Her analysis suggests that through the reproduction of notions of non-white Others as workshy, young unemployed Russian-speaking migrants construct not only their whiteness but also their belonging to a form of neoliberal citizenship that has stigmatised unemployment.

Securitisation policies and crimmigration

After the end of the Cold War and initial optimism about the opening of borders, a growing emphasis has been placed on security and military concerns in Europe. At the same time, the notion of security went through a transformation, where the constitution of threat and security measures were redefined and expanded. Whereas hostile states and communism were formerly viewed as primary security threats to national territory, mobile populations and racialised minorities are now regarded as threats requiring the policing of borders (Fassin 2011; Ibrahim 2005). The focus has thus moved from the state to the individual, reinforcing the connection between security and migration/migrants. With global neoliberal capitalism and the declining welfare state, securitisation has become a central way to deal with perceived differences within nation-states. While formerly perceived to be beneficial for the expansion of capitalism, migrants have now come to be regarded as a threat to the conceived homogeneity of the population and the maintenance of the welfare state (Fassin 2011; Ibrahim 2007; Faist 2004). These transformations are reflected in various policies characterised by the strengthening of border controls, transnational surveillance networks, and internal security measures that include the surveillance of minority populations. In the aftermath of 9/11 in 2001, the so-called migration–security nexus was reinforced and, as part of this, societal security was even more strongly connected to cultural, religious, and political issues. Perceptions of migrants as a threat to cultural identity or as criminals are not entirely new, but such discourses have been reinforced and expanded in the past two decades (Togral 2011; Aas 2011; Faist 2004).

According to the Copenhagen School, securitisation refers to a discursive practice. Something becomes understood as a security threat when it is claimed by the state or a dominant actor to be a threat that needs to be tackled, regardless of whether it is a real threat. Thus, securitisation is seen as the successful discursive construction of an issue as a threat, which validates what measures are taken against it (Floyd and Croft 2011; Diez and Huysmans 2007; Buzan, Wæver, and de Wilde 1998). On the other hand, the Paris School defines an understanding of securitisation focused on discourses to be insufficient, and instead emphasises the necessity of also encompassing bureaucratic practices—the effects of security technology, and professional security knowledge. For these critics, securitisation consists of different policy issues that enable the conveying of security knowledge, skills, and technology (Diez and Huysmans 2007). Following Foucauldian ideas, surveillance is understood as a form of governmentality. In the chapters of this book, we can see how *both* discourses on migrants as a threat to the Nordic homogenous societies *and* policies and practices related to such notions affect the way racialised minorities are treated (see *Thapar-Björkert et al., Dahlstedt, Alghasi, Himanen*, and *Tryggvadóttir*).

Nordic and European migration policies are institutionally linked to crime and criminality. This is reflected in policies and transnational cooperation in relation to asylum and immigration, and in national policies and institutions such as the criminal justice system. The intertwining of crime control and immigration control is an important part of contemporary surveillance networks, not only of borders, but also within nation-states (Aas 2011; Fekete and Webber 2010). This merging of crime and immigration (crimmigration) in law and in crime and migration control, is also revealed in public debates and practices of police on migration, and in transnational border surveillance networks (Aas 2011). Surveillance and security discourses are connected to citizenship, belonging, and global privilege, as well as social exclusion, and Othering of migrants and minorities. This is reflected in recent research depicting how the policing of minorities and racialised groups—such as undocumented migrants, asylum seekers, and Roma migrants—are linked to crime control and immigration control regimes (Aas and Bosworth, 2013; Fekete and Webber, 2010). Thus, although migrants and their descendants are the main targets of contemporary security systems and databases, these measures are also extended to other minority groups, such as the Roma, "whose standing as full citizens is in doubt" (Aas 2011, p. 339; *Himanen*). In the Nordic countries, the indigenous Sámi and the Roma people have extensive experience of racialisation and securitisation, as depicted by this book's chapters by Siivikko and Helakorpi. Roma people, in particular, seem to be portrayed in relation to crime and security, even today.

Ibrahim (2005) shows how these security discourses are racist discourses. Connecting migrants with forms of cultural difference that threaten existing ways of life (including being a burden on the health and welfare system), and lead to social breakdown, is in fact a modern form of racism, as it becomes a criterion for exclusion. The resulting discriminatory actions towards migrants and minorities based on ideas of danger is racism. Migrants and racialised minorities have increasingly become scapegoats for economic problems and crimes in the Nordic countries. This is reflected in public debates, in which the connection is made between migration and criminality, and the ethnic, racial, or religious background of the perpetrator functions as an explanation of crime (Keskinen, 2014; Loftsdóttir 2017).

In their chapter, Suruchi Thapar-Björkert, Irene Molina, and Karina Raña Villacura examine how a shifting political discourse—from welfare to warfare—has led to the increasing securitisation of Swedish suburbs with a high proportion of racialised minorities. This has occurred in the context of growing neoliberalism and cuts in welfare services, while the penal sector, surveillance, and racial profiling has been strengthened. The chapter shows how crimmigration has taken place in the suburbs the authors investigate, leading to a rising perception of the inhabitants as potentially dangerous. The police are increasingly present, and body searches without motives are becoming more common. The authors describe how the participants in their study respond to the security discourse, and the demonisation of their neighbourhoods in the media discourse.

Markus Himanen examines criminalisation of immigration, through focusing on the public and private policing of vulnerable and marginalised people from Romania and Bulgaria, living as street workers in Finland. The chapter also contributes to research on the position of the Roma minority, to which many of the interviewees belong. Moreover, the study is based on interviews with police officers and third-sector experts. Himanen shows how the street workers are commonly met with criminalising and securitising policies. They experience ethnic profiling; arbitrary surveillance; being stopped by the police and security guards on a regular basis; as well as being frequently evicted from public spaces. This leads to stress and humiliation among the street workers. The police frame them as a threat to the general public's feeling of safety, and in terms of criminality, linking mobility and criminality.

Sharam Alghasi analyses the changing debates about migration in Norway in the aftermath of the 9/11 attack, with new narratives about Islam in which Muslims have come to represent the potential enemy within. This discourse is repeated in the many terrorist-related stories about Muslims that have dominated the Norwegian media. He interviews participants with Muslim backgrounds in his study, examining their responses to these narratives as represented in a film about radical Muslims. He shows how the participants distance themselves from violent and reactionary portrayals of Islam and Muslims in the documentary, the media, and society at large. They perceive media practices related to Islam and Muslims as reductionist, and express being surrounded by a state of stigma and Islamophobia in their everyday lives. Moreover, they reject the reductionist image of being a Muslim that excludes other dimensions within their identities.

Helga Tryggvadóttir examines the securitising discourse on asylum seekers arriving in Iceland, arguing that the media discourse about them is both racialised and gendered. Although asylum seekers are few, they are seen as arriving in large numbers, while being undocumented and unknown. As demonstrated in the chapter, securitisation discourse of asylum seekers in Iceland seeps into public and political discussions, in which the discourse of criminality, cultural clashes, and potential terrorism intertwine. Tryggvadóttir examines how statements in the media, and official reports, link asylum seekers to terrorism, focusing on the threat they present (for example, because of a lack of identification papers, which is framed as a sign of criminality), while negating the risks asylum seekers face. Tryggvadóttir depicts how authorities spread dubious "knowledge" about asylum seekers, invoked by racialised images. On the other hand, asylum seekers attempting to become "known" in this society can also wield this notoriety as a strategy, to contest the authorities' decisions about their cases.

Towards a new politics of solidarity

This book provides a critical approach to the notions of cultural homogeneity, social cohesion, and societal security that circulate in the Nordic societies. Through historical analyses, the contributions show how the idea of exceptional cultural homogeneity was developed through activities by social scientists, nationalist politicians, journalists, and cultural actors, among others. This process has, however, not been univocal nor without challenges. The production of a "homogeneous nation" was achieved through repression and assimilation of indigenous peoples and ethnoracially defined minorities living within the nation-state borders. While we emphasise the need for historically and contextually specific analyses of such processes, it is evident that there are continuities between the past ways the indigenous peoples, the Roma, and other minorities were treated, and the situations the post-1960s migrants and their descendants face today in the Nordic nation-states. Likewise, these differences relate to the histories of colonisation, differential categorisations in racial hierarchies, and changes in political economies. Nevertheless, an examination of *both* indigenous people (such as the Sámi) and "old" ethnic minorities (such as the Roma, Travellers, and Kvens) *and* the post-1960s migrants and their descendants, is useful in exposing the heterogeneity of the "people", as well as the homogenisation processes through which states and political movements seek to control, regulate, and exclude such heterogeneities.

These questions have become especially pressing in the wake of the waning welfare states and neoliberal policies that erode the fiscal basis of redistributive policies and services, but also the (class) solidarity project that has carried the welfare state and formed the basis for its "social cohesion". That migrants and their children—notably those racialised as "non-white Others"—are increasingly blamed for the erosion of the welfare state (which in fact is a result of several decades of neoliberal policies), can be interpreted as a sign of an exclusionary form of politics of solidarity (Ålund, Schierup, and Neergaard 2017). It seeks to reserve welfare only for those perceived as "deserving" and "white enough" to belong to the core group, to which solidarity is restricted. Those not perceived to belong to this core group to which solidarity applies, are targeted by securitising policies, surveillance methods, and punitive measures. Such groups include recent migrants and asylum seekers, but also the racialised populations living in poor suburban city areas, and ethnic minorities within and across borders, such as the Roma.

The current societal condition in the Nordic region, and more broadly in Europe, calls for other kinds of politics of solidarity—solidarities that are not based on expectations of cultural, ethnic, or racial homogeneity and their related exclusions; solidarities that acknowledge the histories and currents of colonialism; and solidarities that depart from an understanding of social justice that incorporates and seeks to repair the experiences of cultural and economic injustices, be they the result of unequal global power relations, policies towards indigenous or minority groups with a long residence within the Nordic region, or class structures. This means taking distance from functionalist views on "social cohesion" that build on essentialising notions of shared ethnic, cultural, or racial backgrounds, and instead approaching the togetherness needed in current societies through a politics of solidarity. The contributions in this book provide space for narratives that build on the histories and experiences of indigenous people, ethnoracially defined minorities, migrants, and asylum seekers (*Siivikko, Helakorpi, Dahlstedt, Ringrose and Stubberud, Thapar-Björket et al., Himanen, Alghasi, Tryggvadóttir, Schmidt*). They also raise questions about solidarities across cultural, ethnic, and racial divides. A careful reading shows moments, movements, and collaborations in which new forms of the politics of solidarity can, and are, taking shape.

Notes

1 In the following, we use italics to refer to contributions in this book.
2 Social cohesion is most commonly understood as a sense of togetherness and of common social norms (Demireva 2012).

Acknowledgements

This book is a result of the Nordic network *Multiculturalism, Cultural Homogeneity and Societal Security* (NordHOME), funded by the Nordic Joint Committee for Nordic Research Councils in the Humanities and Social Sciences (NOS-HS) in 2016 to 2018. We thank NOS-HS for the possibility to organise the exploratory workshops that provided the grounds for this publication. Suvi Keskinen (projects 275032 and 316445) and Mari Toivanen (project 287667) also wish to thank the Academy of Finland, whose funding made the work with this book possible. Unnur Dís Skaptadóttir expresses her acknowledgements to the Icelandic Research Fund (Rannis, project 163350–053). We also thank all those who gave lectures and presented papers at the NordHOME-workshops for inspiring thoughts and discussions. Most of all, we miss Helga Tryggvadóttir, who passed away at the late stage of the preparation of this book. We remember her as a thoughtful, intellectually ambitious, and kind colleague, who did not fear to take part in public discussions on migration and migrants' rights.

References

Aas, K.F. (2011). '"Crimmigrant" Bodies and Bona Fide Travelers: Surveillance, Citizenship and Global Governance'. *Theoretical Criminology* 15(3), pp. 331–346.
Aas, K.F. and Bosworth, M. (2013). *The Borders of Punishment: Migration, Citizenship and Social Exclusion*. Oxford: Oxford University Press.
Alghasi, S., Eriksen, T.H., and Ghorashi, H. (eds.) (2009). *Paradoxes of Cultural Recognition*. Farnham: Ashgate.
Ålund, A., Schierup, C., and Neergaard, A. (eds.) (2017). *Reimagineering the Nation. Essays on Twenty-First-Century Sweden*. Frankfurt Am Main: Peter Lang.
Anderson, B. (2006). *Imagined Communities: Reflections on the Origin and Spread of Nationalism*. Revised edition. London: Verso.
Bommes, M. and Thränhardt, D. (2010). 'Introduction: National paradigms in Migration Research', in *National Paradigms in Migration Research*, M. Bommes and D. Thränhardt (eds.), Göttingen: V&R Unipress, pp. 9–38.
Brochmann, G. and Hagelund, A. (2012). *Immigration Policy and the Scandinavian Welfare State*. Basingstoke: Palgrave Macmillan.
Buzan, B., Wæver, O., and de Wilde, J. (1998). *Security: A New Framework for Analysis*. Boulder: Lynne Rienner Publishers.
d'Appolonia, A.C. (2012). *Frontiers of Fear: Immigration and Insecurity in the United States and Europe*. Ithaca, NY: Cornell University Press.
Delanty, G. (2000). 'Social Integration and Europeanization: The Myth of Cultural Cohesion', in *Yearbook of European Studies*, 14, pp. 221–238.
Delhey, J., and Newton, K. (2005). 'Predicting Cross-National Levels of Social Trust: Global Pattern or Nordic Exceptionalism?'. *European Sociological Review*, 21(4), pp. 311–327.
Demireva, N. (2012). *Briefing. Immigration, Diversity and Social Cohesion*. University of Oxford: The Migration Observatory. http://migrationobservatory.ox.ac.uk/wp-content/uploads/2016/04/Briefing-Immigration-Diversity-and-Social-Cohesion.pdf [Accessed 8 October 2018].
Diez, T. and Huysmans, J. (2007). *Migration, Democracy and Security (midas). Research report on the ESRC-funded research project The Socio-Political Effects of Securitising Free Movement: The Case of 9/11*. Birmingham: University of Birmingham.
Esping-Andersen, G. (1990). *The Three Worlds of Welfare Capitalism*. Cambridge: Polity Press.
Faist, T. (2004). 'The Migration-Security Nexus. International Migration and Security Before and After 9/11'. *Willy Brandt Series of Working Papers in International Migration and Ethnic Relations 4/3*. Malmö:Malmö University.
Fassin, D. (2011). 'Policing Borders, Producing Boundaries. The Governmentality of Immigration in Dark Times'. *Annual Review of Anthropology*, 40, pp. 213–226.
Fekete, L. and Webber, F. (2010). 'Foreign Nationals, Enemy Penology and the Criminal Justice System'. *Race & Class* 41(4): pp. 1–25.
Floyd, R. and Croft, S. (2011). 'European Non-Traditional Security Theory: From Theory to Practice'. *Geopolitics, History and International Relations*, 3 (2), pp. 152–179.

Goldberg, D.T. (2002). *The Racial State*. Malden: Blackwell.
Goldschmidt, T. (2017). *Immigration, Social Cohesion, and the Welfare State: Studies on Ethnic Diversity in Germany and Sweden*, PhD Thesis, University of Stockholm.
Guild, E. (2009). *Security and Migration in the 21st Century*. Cambridge: Polity Press.
Hickman, M., Mai, N., and Crowley, H. (2012). *Migration and Social Cohesion in the UK*. Basingstoke: Palgrave Macmillan.
Ibrahim, M. (2005). 'The Securitization of Migration: A Racial Discourse'. *International Migration*, 43(5), pp. 163–187.
Jensen, L. (2015). 'Postcolonial Denmark: Beyond the Rot of Colonialism?' *Postcolonial Studies*, 18(4), pp. 440–452.
Kamali, M. and Jönsson, J. (eds.) (2018). *Neoliberalism, Nordic Welfare States and Social Work*. London: Routledge.
Keskinen, S. (2014). 'Re-Constructing the Peaceful Nation. Negotiating Meanings of Whiteness, Immigration and Islam in Media and Politics after a Shopping Mall Shooting'. *Social Identities*, 20(6), pp. 471–485.
Keskinen, S. (forthcoming, 2019). 'Intra-Nordic Differences, Colonial/Racial Histories and National Narratives: Re-Writing Finnish History'. *Scandinavian Studies*.
Keskinen, S., Tuori, S., Irni, S., and Mulinari, D. (eds.) (2009). *Complying with Colonialism. Gender, Race and Ethnicity in the Nordic Region*. Farnham: Ashgate.
Keskinen, S., Norocel, O.C., and Jørgensen, M.B. (2016). 'The Politics and Policies of Welfare Chauvinism under the Economic Crisis'. *Critical Social Policy*, 36(3), pp. 321–329.
Kivisto, P., and Wahlbeck, Ö. (2013). *Debating Multiculturalism in the Nordic Welfare States*. Basingstoke: Palgrave Macmillan.
Koopmans, R., Lancee, B., and Schaeffer, M. (eds.) (2015). *Social Cohesion and Immigration in Europe and North America. Mechanisms, Conditions and Causality*. New York/London: Routledge.
Körber, L. and Volquardsen, E. (eds.) (2014). *The Postcolonial North Atlantic: Iceland, Greenland, and the Faroe Islands*. Berlin: Nordeuropa Institut der Humboldt Universität.
Kuokkanen, R. (2007). 'Saamelaiset ja kolonialismin vaikutukset nykypäivänä, in *Kolonialismin jäljet. Keskustat, periferiat ja Suomi*', edited by J. Kuortti, M. Lehtonen, and O. Löytty. Helsinki: Gaudeamus, pp. 142–155.
Larsen, C.A. (2013). *The Rise and Fall of Social Cohesion. The Construction and Deconstruction of Social Trust in the US, UK, Sweden and Denmark*. Oxford: Oxford University Press.
Lentin, A. and Titley, G. (2011). *The Crises of Multiculturalism*. London: Zed Books.
Loftsdóttir, K. (2017). 'Being the "Damned Foreigner": Affective National Sentiments and Racialisation of Lithuanians in Iceland'. *Nordic Journal of Migration Research*, 7(2), pp. 70–78.
Loftsdóttir, K. and Jensen, L. (eds.) (2012). *Whiteness and Postcolonialism in the Nordic Region*. Farnham: Ashgate.
Morales, L. (2013). 'Assessing the Effects of Immigration and Diversity in Europe: Introduction to the Special Issue'. *Journal of Elections, Public Opinion and Parties*, 23(3), pp. 241–254.
Naum, M. and Nordin, J. (eds.) (2013). *Scandinavian Colonialism and the Rise of Modernity. Small Time Agents in a Global Arena*. New York: Springer.
Norocel, O.C. (2013). *Our Family—A Tight-Knit Family Under the Same Protective Roof. A Critical Study of Gendered Conceptual Metaphors at Work in Radical Right Populism*. Helsinki: University of Helsinki.

Putnam, R.D. (2007). '"E Pluribus Unum": Diversity and Community in the Twenty-First Century: The 2006 Johan Skytte Prize Lecture'. *Scandinavian Political Studies*, 30(2), pp. 137–174.

Pyrhönen, N. (2015). *The True Colors of Finnish Welfare Nationalism*. SSKH Skrifter 38. Helsinki: University of Helsinki.

Sandset, T. (2019). *Color that Matters. A Comparative Approach to Mixed Race Identity and Nordic Exceptionalism*. London: Routledge.

Sawyer, L. and Habel, Y. (2014). 'Refracting African and Black Diaspora through the Nordic Region'. *African and Black Diaspora: An International Journal* 7(1), pp. 1–6.

Schierup, C., Hansen, P., and Castles, S. (2006). *Migration, Citizenship, and the European Welfare State*. Oxford: Oxford University Press.

Skaptadóttir, U.D. and Loftsdóttir, K. (2009). 'Cultivating Culture? Images of Iceland, Globalization and Multicultural Society', in S. Jakobsson, (ed.) *Images of the North, Histories, Identities, Ideas*. Amsterdam/New York: Rodopi, pp. 205–216.

Togral, B. (2011). 'Convergence of Securitization of Migration and "New Racism" in Europe: Rise of Culturalism and Disappearance of Politics', in G. Lazaridis (ed.), *Security, Insecurity and Migration in Europe*. Surrey: Ashgate, pp. 219–237.

Uslaner, E.M. (2012). *Segregation and Mistrust: Diversity, Isolation, and Social Cohesion*, New York: Cambridge University Press.

van der Meer, T. and Tolsma, J. (2014). 'Ethnic Diversity and Its Effects on Social Cohesion'. *Annual Review of Sociology*, 40(1), pp. 459–478.

Vertovec, S. and Wessendorf, S. (eds.) (2010). *The Multiculturalism Backlash*. Abingdon: Routledge.

Vuorela, U. (2009). 'Colonial Complicity: The Postcolonial in a Nordic Context', in *Complying with Colonialism. Gender, Race and Ethnicity in the Nordic Region*, edited by S. Keskinen, S. Tuori, S. Irni, and D. Mulinari, Farnham: Ashgate, pp. 19–33.

Wimmer, A. and Glick-Schiller, N. (2003). 'Methodological Nationalism, the Social Sciences, and the Study of Migration: An Essay in Historical Epistemology'. *The International Migration Review*, 37(3), pp. 576–610.

Part 1
Histories of homogeneity and difference

2 Forgetting diversity? Norwegian narratives of ethnic and cultural homogeneity

Teemu Ryymin

Introduction

Historical narratives of post-1960s transnational migration that presuppose initial homogeneity as a central characteristic of the receiving country are prone to depicting growing migration as a potential future threat—particularly in relation to specific welfare models. If homogeneity is seen as a precondition of a functioning welfare system, then increased migration that leads to greater ethnic and cultural heterogeneity logically threatens it. Social scientists have tried to ascertain whether migration actually is a problem in the context of, for instance, the Norwegian welfare system, inspired by claims by Alesina and Glaeser (2004) that greater ethnic heterogeneity is the main reason for the much smaller welfare system in the United States compared to Europe. Others, such as Putnam (2007), have claimed that immigration and ethnic diversity tend to reduce social solidarity and social capital, at least in the short term. However, results are inconclusive (Hatland 2011).

While most historically oriented welfare researchers carefully avoid stating that ethnic and cultural homogeneity was indeed a foundation of the Norwegian welfare system—talking rather about homogenisation processes in the post-WWII decades when the system was given its classic design—such notions may nevertheless be found in recent research literature. A 2013 analysis of immigrant electoral participation in Norway took as its point of departure that Norway in the late 1960s was "a markedly homogeneous country with the exception of a Sámi minority"; within this context, global migration had from the 1970s made a "noticeable impact" on Norwegian society (Bjørklund and Bergh 2013, p. 12).[1] A 2017 historical discussion of immigration, development aid, and state policy in Norway posited that early 1960s Norway "was one of the thinnest populated and most ethnically and culturally homogeneous countries in the world"—a state of affairs radically altered by subsequent overseas labour migration (Tvedt 2017, p. 111).

While acknowledging the diversity of social science and historical research, and by no means claiming that global migration was or is without noticeable impact on Norwegian society, I argue that postulating such notions of "marked homogeneousness" as an accurate characteristic of 1960s Norwegian society, is at odds with the historical experiences of cultural, linguistic, ethnic, religious, and social diversity in Norway (cf. e.g. Kjeldstadli 2003; Kjeldstadli 2008). It is also at odds with the current state of politically acknowledged historical ethnic and cultural diversity in Norway. The state of Norway had acknowledged in the 1980s that the Sámi had historically been present in the area when the Norwegian state was established, and the ratification of the ILO Convention No 169 concerning indigenous and tribal peoples in independent countries in 1990 confirmed the status of indigenous people for the Norwegian Sámi (cf. Aarseth 2006). In 1998, the Norwegian Parliament also acknowledged the presence of five national minorities in Norway: the Kvens, Jews, Roma, Romani, and Forest Finns.[2] In addition to self-identification by the minorities themselves, the acknowledgement of these groups as distinct minorities was also premised historically: all five minorities had been present in Norway for more than one hundred years. The Kvens, for instance, were descendants of eighteenth- and nineteenth-century migrants to Northern Norway from Finnish-speaking areas of today's Northern Sweden and Finland; the Forest Finns descend from migrants of the border area between Southeastern Norway and Sweden, arriving in the early seventeenth century.[3] In addition to these acknowledged minorities with a long historical presence in Norway, the country has also received immigrants from other countries before the 1970s. However, compared to the aforementioned minorities, the immigrant population—who were mostly of European origin—was not made visible, for example, in the censuses from the nineteenth and early twentieth centuries, as they were not seen as sufficiently different to be counted as something other than Norwegians.[4] We might thus talk about a statistical assimilation of everyone considered to share a 'European culture' or 'race'.

Despite this, the notion of a society which at some point in the historical past was very ethnically and/or culturally homogeneous, and which subsequently has become increasingly heterogeneous through (mainly) overseas immigration, seems to be a particularly persistent myth in Norway. Such myths also persist in other Nordic countries (cf. Hagerman 2006; Tervonen 2014). In the following, I will first discuss how and when the notion of Norway as an especially homogeneous society was established, particularly in texts related to social science research. Second, I will put forth some reasons for why notions presupposing a homogeneous Norway were particularly visible in the late 1960s. Finally, I offer some thoughts as to why such notions still persist, despite both recent scholarship, and policies to the contrary.

The goal of a homogeneous population

The notion of Norway—and Norwegians—as particularly homogeneous has long roots. In 1882, Anders Nicolai Kiær, Director at Statistics Norway [*Det Statistiske Centralbureau*] since 1876, stated in a presentation of population statistics: "The population of Norway is uncommonly homogenous".[5] Just what this statement meant is, however, not straightforwardly clear. Kiær continued by adding: "Besides the Norwegians and those sparse elements of foreign origin that are absorbed in them, there are but two particularly distinguished Tribes, namely the Lappish and the Finnish".[6] They were not many in number—30,878 or 1.7 percent of the total population—but even so, the two groups were clearly regarded by Kiær as an exception from the image of Norwegian homogeneity. In parts of the country, for instance in Finnmark, the Sámi (who were at the time called "Lapps"), were in fact the majority in 1845, consisting of more than 50 percent of the country's population; the Finns—or Kvens, as they are called today—were counted as more than 10 percent. In 1900, they numbered 29 percent and 16 percent, respectively. The defining difference that sat the Sámi and the Kvens apart from the Norwegians proper, was however not their numbers or foreign origin, but *race*, according to Kiær.[7]

The image of uncommon homogeneity of the population of Norwegians was thus, for Kiær, not affected by the presence of ethnic minorities. Not only were the Sámi and the Kvens seen as irrelevant in this respect, they were also considered by many as belonging to a lower position on the evolutionary ladder. The supposedly 'primitive' Sámi were commonly placed on the lowest rung of the ladder, the Kvens in the middle, and the Norwegian population on top (cf. e.g. Ryymin 2007). Neither did the presence of (European) foreigners in Norway affect the image of homogeneity. When comparing the percentage of "foreign-born" persons in Norway to other countries, Kiær found that Norway was very near the European average: 1.99 percent of the resident population in Norway in 1875 was "foreign-born", while the average percentage in Scotland, England, Switzerland, Denmark, France, Belgium, Ireland, Greece, the Netherlands, Germany, Hungary, Italy, Sweden, and Spain was in fact only 1.8 percent.[8] Compared to the United States, with 14.3 percent "foreign-born" in 1870, the European numbers were of course very low. The fact that Norway had slightly more resident foreign-borns than the European average, was by Kiær turned into an expression of "uncommon" homogeneity because most of those "foreign-born" were in fact Swedes (about 77.6 percent of the total of the "foreign-born"). For Kiær, such "sparse elements of foreign origin" as Swedes were obviously similar enough in racial terms to Norwegians that they were easily absorbable into that category. While Kiær did not discuss this, Norway and Sweden were in a personal union until 1905, so perhaps this also made it easier for him to subsume the Swedes. Thus, despite the presence of "two distinguished Tribes" and relatively more "foreign-born" than in many other European countries, the population of Norway was still characterised by Kiær as "uncommonly" homogeneous.

We might best interpret Kiærs' statement of "uncommon homogeneity" as an expression of a wish or a goal for how the population of Norway *should* be—that is, "racially" and nationally unified. Such a goal was of course not particular to Kiær—or to Norway. The desirability of a monocultural, homogeneous nation was a sentiment shared by the immensely powerful nineteenth-century Norwegian nationalist movement. The realities of the nation's nineteenth-century population did not, however, concur with such a sentiment. While Kiær acknowledged the presence of the Sámi and the Kvens, he did not mention that there existed yet another minority not registered in the population censuses: the Romani, who were registered separately and thus made statistically invisible (Niemi 2003, p. 162). Even so, their presence counteracted the image of a homogeneous Norway. In 1854, the founding father of Norwegian social research, Eilert Sundt, received a grant from Parliament to study the *Fanteproblem*, that is, the Romani problem, resulting in several reports to Parliament suggesting ways to deal with the challenge of itinerant Romani (cf. Midbøe 1968). Sundt perceived the Romani as an ethnic group—but additionally saw them as problematic and uncivilised, in need of being "uplifted" and ultimately assimilated into the Norwegian majority, a task the Norwegian state took upon itself to finance (cf. Minken 2009, pp. 101–111; Niemi 2003, pp. 147–174; Haave 2017). From the mid-nineteenth century, the Sámi and Kven presence was similarly acknowledged as a political and national challenge, giving rise to a sustained state policy of Norwegianisation. Through various means, the state strived for the minorities to change their language(s) to Norwegian, and to become assimilated into the majority culture (Niemi 2017). Also, in Sweden, Statistics Sweden upheld an image of a very homogeneous population—exceptions, such as ethnic minorities, simply did not matter.[9]

In the early twentieth century, particularly after the first world war, heterogeneity in the form of the presence of ethnic minorities in Norway was acknowledged—they were counted in censuses as separate categories—and perceived by researchers and politicians as highly problematic (Lie and Roll-Hansen 2001, pp. 146–150; Kjeldstadli 2010, p. 24). Different minorities, however, represented different problems in the eyes of the authorities. The Kvens were seen as a potential fifth column, first for Imperial Russia, and after 1917 for an allegedly expansionist Finland. The Sámi were considered by many as a remnant of a primitive, non-developable culture and race that was destined to die. The "wandering" Romani were perceived as a threat to the bourgeois social order. Jews—who in the nineteenth century were generally seen as a religious rather than an ethnic minority—were banned from the country by the constitution of 1814 until 1851 (for overviews of Norwegian minority policy in this period, see Kjeldstadli 2003 and Brandal et al. 2017). The search for solutions to the perceived problem of ethnic heterogeneity culminated, at least in terms of radicalism, during the Second World War. The constitutional ban of Jews from Norway was reintroduced in 1942, at the same time that 772 Norwegian Jews were deported to Nazi extermination camps in accordance with *die Endlösung* [the Final Solution] (Tjelmeland 2003, pp. 27–35; Bruland 2010; Banik 2017). In 1944, the national socialist collaboration regime also presented a plan to eradicate the Romani (*Hanheide-utvalget*) through segregation and forced sterilisation (Tjelmeland 2003, pp. 37–38).

Thus, it is reasonable to state that in late nineteenth and early twentieth century nation-building processes and policies, the ethnic heterogeneity of Norwegian society was acknowledged as a problem, as something that had to be overcome through assimilatory and/or integrative measures. During the Second World War, even genocidal measures were launched and contemplated. The ethnic and cultural homogeneity of the Norwegian population was therefore held forth as a goal, having gained tremendous momentum via the Norwegian nationalist movement since the mid-nineteenth century. However, such 'homogeneity' was by no means a precise description of the country's population.

Describing homogeneous Norway

While different ethnic and religious groups had thus been problematised on a regular basis until the end of the Second World War, a radical break occurred after 1945: Norway was increasingly seen as, and described to be, a homogeneous country in terms of ethnicity and culture. For instance, the national census of 1946 did not register the Sámi or Kvens at all; in the 1950 census, only information on the use of Sámi and Finnish languages was registered. The non-acknowledgement of the Sámi and the Kvens in 1946 was justified by Statistics Norway because of the "experiences of war" (Lie and Roll-Hansen 2001, p. 150). Other representatives of the authorities were of the same persuasion in the immediate post-war years. In his 1947 plan for rebuilding the Norwegian public health system, the highly influential General Director of Health, Karl Evang, could state that the future prospects for such an undertaking were good. Among others, one reason for this was that Norway had a "homogeneous population" (Evang 1947, pp. 96–97). This assessment was also based on "experiences of war", namely Evang's knowledge of the United States and United Kingdom obtained during his wartime exile (cf. Nordby 1989). Compared to those countries, particularly the United States, Norway indeed seemed homogeneous in terms of nationality and race: there was no "Negro Problem" in Norway, even though some Norwegian scientists saw the Sámi in Norway as a parallel (Andresen 2016, pp. 414–415). Evang did not pay much heed to the Sámi; even though he was fully aware of their presence, their linguistic and cultural differences from the Norwegian majority population were largely irrelevant in his eyes. For the ardent social democrat Evang, the only differences that made a difference were social and geographical; class and regional differences were to be ameliorated through universalist health and welfare policies (cf. Ryymin and Andresen 2009).

However, the acknowledgement of the presence of the Sámi was an exception to a growing conviction among many observers that Norway *was* indeed a homogeneous country in the post-WWII decades. From the late 1940s, the Sámi were again visible both in policymaking—in particular concerning language and cultural issues—and in research by leading linguists, ethnologists, and ethnographers as a specific problem demanding political action.

However, the goal of the new Sámi policy developed in the late 1950s and early 1960s was not to assimilate the Sámi, and eradicate their language(s) or culture(s). It was rather to strengthen and develop what was seen as Sámi culture, as stated during the 1963 Parliamentary debate on the proposal for a new Sámi policy by the so-called Sámi Committee (Aarseth 2006, pp. 67–70; Andresen 2016).

But the Sámi exception was just that—an exception. Even though the Sámi were acknowledged, they alone came to represent diversity—and this had no impact on the overall characterisation of Norwegian society as "uncommonly homogeneous". Rather, one could argue that ethnicity was increasingly perceived as an irrelevant or marginal societal category in the post-war decades. In his influential 1964 book *Sosiologi*, sociologist Vilhelm Aubert stated that the Sámi were but a marginal presence in some isolated rural peripheries of Northern Norway. A "sami element" could be found in many villages in Northern Norway, and that did have some significance for individual social identity, but it "seldom leads to a genuine minority problem. The ethnic criteria are too unclear for that"[10] (Aubert 1964, p. 190). Other ways of perceiving social differences, such as class and geography, were seen as far more relevant by many—including many of those who otherwise could have been classified as belonging to an ethnic minority. A case in point here is the negative local reception of the Sámi Committee's proposal to strengthen Sámi language and culture in the schools of Finnmark. The so-called "Easter Resolution" passed in a local popular meeting in Karasjok in 1960, stating that the Sámi did not want any positive, affirmative action aimed at them *as Sámi*—they regarded themselves as Norwegians (Andresen 2016, pp. 428–429; Selle et al. 2015, pp. 54–61).

While the Sámi were politically acknowledged, the *other* ethnic minorities in Norway were rendered more or less invisible. For instance, silence reigned regarding the Kvens, in both policy and research (Niemi 2010). More generally, no official minority policy dealing with other minorities than the Sámi was formulated until the 1970s. And in some social science research, the notion of an "unusually" homogeneous Norway was strengthened towards the end of the 1960s.

In 1968, the social scientist Johan Galtung observed that Norway was indeed "an unusually homogeneous country, regarding both race and ethnic relations (particularly language)" (Galtung 1968, p. 459). Compared to many other states in the world, "practically everyone in Norway are Norwegians and most Norwegians are in Norway (...)", wrote Galtung, thus echoing the director of Statistics Norway from 1882 (Galtung 1968, p. 453). These characteristics were chiefly based on statistics from the *World Handbook of Political and Social Indicators* (Russett et al. 1964), from which Galtung chose three indicators: the percentage of the population that spoke the dominant language in a country or identified as Roman Catholic or Muslim. Amazingly enough, the *World Handbook* placed Norway at the top of the list regarding speakers of dominant language, as 99.7 percent of the population allegedly spoke "Norwegian" (Russet et al. 1964, p. 134, Table 39). This was stated despite the fact that "Norwegian" indeed consists of *two* languages, as Galtung himself also fleetingly mentioned. Nevertheless, Norway was on top here, closely followed by East and West Germany (99.5 percent each, with German as the dominant language), Madagascar (99.0 percent, Malagasy), Austria (98.7 percent German-speaking), and the Dominican Republic (98.0 percent Spanish). And Norway was pretty low on religious diversity—only 0.2 percent of the population were Roman Catholics, giving Norway a rank of 110 among 118 countries—with Japan, Sweden, and Pakistan just above, with 0.3 percent (Russet et al. 1964, pp. 249–251, Table 73). According to the *World Handbook*, there were no Muslims, statistically speaking, in Norway in 1950—making Norway one of 44 other countries with a similar count, out of a total of 103 (Russet et al. 1964, pp. 255–257, Table 75). The connection between "race and ethnic relations", and the percentage of Norwegian speakers, and of Roman Catholics and Muslims, was not explicated by Galtung. Nevertheless, according to him this "unusual" linguistic and religious "homogeneity" explained the notable lack of organised violence between population groups in Norway, as well as the country's "current very low rates of immigration and emigration" (Galtung 1968, p. 453). To put it mildly, the foundation for Galtung's notion of the "unusual" homogeneity of Norway was thus rather flimsy, and he did not even consider the presence of the Sámi, the Kvens, or other ethnic minorities in Norway as relevant in his assessment.

Galtung did however cite population statistics from a number of countries regarding the number of "foreign-born" in a country. Norway's 1.7 percent "foreign-born" of the population was "low, but not extreme", according to Galtung: it was far less than the 16.9 percent in Australia, 14.7 percent in Canada, or 7.4 percent in France (Galtung 1968, p. 457, and Table 12.5). Switzerland, Sweden, Turkey, Great Britain, Brazil, and Thailand also had a somewhat higher percentage than Norway in this regard; only Finland (0.7 percent) had less—as well as the United States (0.5 percent), which, however, had no less than 19 percent of its population registered as of "foreign stock". All in all, Norway could, according to Galtung, be described as a country that had achieved "extreme peacefulness and equality with the help of homogeneity, anti-pluralism, and congruence" (Galtung 1968, p. 468).

These observations by Galtung were set forth in a highly influential 1968 publication, *Det norske samfunn*, presenting an overview of current scientific sociological knowledge of Norway—and they have had a long-lasting impact. The aforementioned social scientists discussing immigrant electoral participation in Norway in 2013, explicitly cited Galtung's contribution in *Det norske samfunn* as proof for the claim that Norway indeed *had* been a "markedly homogeneous country" in the late 1960s. Historian Terje Tvedt's recent assertion of Norway as one of the world's most culturally and ethnically homogeneous countries in the early 1960s was based on the tiny number of African, Asian, or Latin American-born individuals in the country at the time. According to him, 99.9 percent of the country's population in 1963 consisted of "ethnic Norwegians" (Tvedt 2017, pp. 111–112). The Sámi, the Kvens, and the other minorities had seemingly vanished into thin air.

Forgetting diversity: Possible reasons for the late 1960s amnesia

On this basis, it seems that the historian Knut Kjeldstadli has made a valid point in stating that by the late 1960s, the previously acknowledged historical ethnic diversity of Norwegian society was "forgotten" (Kjeldstadli 2008, p. 50). Several possible reasons for this "amnesia" may be put forth: first, the relative success of long-standing assimilation policies, resulting in lower visibility of ethnic minorities than before. This cut both ways—many belonging to the majority were less prepared to see ethnicity as a relevant identity category, but also many among those who could have categorised themselves as Sámi, for instance, chose—or felt compelled—not to do so (cf. also below). To the extent the minorities were visible in the politicians' and scientists' gaze, they were often seen as a social problem—for instance, as particularly poor, marginalised groups that had not been able to participate in growing post-war affluence and welfare. Examples of this way of looking at the Sámi can be found among sociologists (e.g. Aubert 1968; Aubert 1973), and for the Roma, also among the political authorities (cf. Holme 2015, pp. 22–39).

This connects to the second reason, namely the general success of the social democratic project, focusing on the equalisation of social (class) and geographical differences—disregarding cultural and ethnic difference. In some ways, the late 1960s represented the completion of the social democratic integration project, manifested in the "crowning" of the social welfare system with the Social Security Act in 1966, giving occasion to the notion of "the happy moment of social democracy" (Sejersted 2005, pp. 291–292). The extent to which this development also led many of those who otherwise might be categorised as belonging to an ethnic minority to rather identify in terms other than ethnic, as in Karasjok in 1960, is immensely difficult to assess. It seems reasonable that this indeed was the case, pointing to what latter-day scholars of a more ethno-political bent have described as "ethnic self-denial" among, for instance, the Sámi (cf. Ryymin 2015, pp. 35–36).

Third, the "new" social sciences such as sociology—which gained influence in the post-war decades—focused mainly on societal aspects other than ethnicity and culture. The extent to which ethnic minorities such as the Sámi or Roma (who at the time were called "Gypsies") were investigated in social science research until the late 1960s/early 1970s were, as mentioned, often discussed in terms of social policy, social deprivation, and poverty in peripheral areas. Perhaps the tendency to invoke global comparisons—of considering Norway in relation to countries such as the United States, Canada, or Australia—also contributed to the impression that Norway indeed *was* exceptionally homogeneous in cultural and ethnic terms. Compared to these countries, with their history of colonisation and migration, such a conclusion was plausible—even though it was misleading.

A fourth—admittedly somewhat speculative—reason for the 1960s tendency to regard the population in Norway as particularly homogeneous in *ethnic* terms, may lie in the then prevailing way of constructing ethnic difference as a matter of race and skin colour. In the early 1960s, many Norwegians obviously considered skin colour as a main indicator of ethnic difference, and the overwhelming "whiteness" of the population may thus easily have strengthened an understanding of the country's population as essentially homogeneous. That race or skin colour was seen as significant was infamously expressed in the newspaper *Aftenposten*, reporting on the opening of the railway line to the city of Bodø in Northern Norway in 1962: the 2 February, 1962 headline stated "First passenger train to and from Bodø today—Negro on board" (cf. Tvedt 2017, p. 111). The tendency to racialise difference was of course nothing new, as Kiær's view of the homogeneity of the Norwegian population from 1882 shows. Moreover, this tendency has by no means disappeared—as amply demonstrated by the use of the cited *Aftenposten* example by Tvedt in 2017 as *proof* of Norway's exceptional homogeneity in the 1960s.

Growing awareness of ethnic diversity in research and policy

However, although Galtung obviously did not think that the presence of Sámi—or indeed any other ethnic minorities in Norway—was worth mentioning in his discussion of the country's "unusual homogeneity" in 1968, awareness of ethnic diversity was growing in the late 1960s. In fact, the same book where Galtung set forth his views did mention that there were indeed also minorities in Norway—first and foremost the Sámi, but also Kvens, Jews, "Gypsies", European post-war refugees, and immigrant workers from Southern Europe, particularly Italy, Spain, and Yugoslavia. Albeit few in absolute numbers, Finnish workers also made themselves noticed in northernmost Norway (cf. Aubert 1968; Tjelmeland 2003, pp. 89–104). Surprisingly, it seems that neither Galtung in 1968, nor the social scientists citing him in 2013, had noticed this.

Simultaneously with Galtung's description of Norway as an "unusually" homogeneous country, new ways of conceptualising ethnic minorities began to surface in Norwegian research. From the end of the 1960s, young, radical social scientists and historians began to see the Sámi not primarily as a social problem, but as a colonised indigenous population (cf. e.g. Homme 1969). In the 1970s, this new perception of the Sámi was spurred on not least by the momentum of the Sámi political movement, and its struggle against governmental plans to build a hydroelectric power plant threatening the livelihood of Sámi reindeer herders in Finnmark. The Kvens also resurfaced in the research agenda in the 1970s, first among linguists, thereafter also among historians; during subsequent decades, research into many "old" ethnic minorities has steadily grown (cf. historiographical overviews in e.g. Brandal et al. 2017; Lund and Moen 2010; Niemi 1995). Compared to the older pre-

Second World War research, this research has in particular investigated state minority policy and its consequences; rather than seeking solutions to a "minority problem", it sought to strengthen minority positions in different ways (cf. Ryymin and Nyyssönen 2013).

Together with international developments regarding indigenous and minority rights, such research—and more crucially the ethno-political mobilisation among the Sámi, the Kvens, and other ethnic minorities in Norway—led to the growing political acknowledgement of the presence of such minorities in Norway from the 1980s onwards. I might add that these factors also led to the widespread acknowledgement of the long-standing reality of ethnic and cultural *diversity* in Norwegian society. Thus, the *new* ethnic, cultural, and religious heterogeneity in Norwegian society, growing after the onset of overseas labour migration from the early 1970s, took place in a society long accustomed to dealing with cultural and ethnic diversity—even though for a long period, this had taken the form of assimilation, and was seemingly "forgotten" precisely at the historical moment when the "new" migration started.

Concluding remarks

Even though there is thus an abundance of social science and historical research illustrating that a description of Norway as a "markedly homogeneous" country before the onset of overseas migration in the early 1970s is hardly accurate, and despite the fact that such notions are not to be found in recent relevant policy documents,[11] the *image* of such homogeneity still keeps popping up in various domains of research. A historian working not with the history of minorities, but with nationalism, paraphrased Anders Nicolai Kiær's declaration from 1882—albeit with some modifications—as late as 1994: "As to ethnic minorities (…) Lapps and Finns are the most significant exceptions to the comparative ethnic homogeneity of Norway"; note also the use of the, in 1994, *very* outdated nineteenth-century ethnic labels of the Sámi and the Kvens (Sørensen 1994, p. 35). And, as we have seen, both historians and social scientists writing about more recent migration still make similar statements, even omitting the Kvens from the picture. How can this be understood?

One reason may be that research on "old" minorities and the indigenous Sámi on one hand, and research on "new" minorities and migrants as well as "mainstream" historical research on the other, have had rather little to do with each other, existing more or less in isolation. The notable exception to this—a big historical and social scientific study on Norwegian immigration history from 2003 (Kjeldstadli 2003), funded in part by the Norwegian Research Council under the International Migration and Ethnic Relations umbrella—seems to have not made a permanent impact. This gap between the research on historical minorities and the research on post-1970s migration *could* be among the reasons for the persistence of the discursive tradition established by Kiær in 1882, emphasising the alleged homogeneity of Norway in social scientific studies. Historical research on "old" minorities is—possibly—not seen as relevant to social scientific research on "new" minorities, and thus remains underutilised. A reason for such perceived irrelevance may possibly be found in the tendency of a lot of minority historical research to concentrate on the history of *one* ethnic category at a time, and/or the more or less explicitly stated emancipatory goals orienting some such research (cf. Ryymin 2015).

Another possible way of understanding the tendency for descriptions of Norway as "markedly homogeneous" popping up in recent research, and more general societal debate, is to not interpret such statements as genuine attempts at accurate historical description, but rather see them as *rhetorical commonplaces* (loci communes) serving quite different functions than accurate description. In some cases, the main function of repeating this commonplace might be to signal the importance of one's own field of research—for example in the 2013 case where the assessment of "homogeneity" highlighted the societal impact of "new" migration, and thus emphasised the importance and desirability of the subsequent study. In other cases, its function might be to question prevailing migration policies by implicating the allegedly destructive consequences of migration within a presupposed "homogeneous" Norwegian society (see e.g. Tvedt 2017). In such cases, original "homogeneity" (reminiscent of "purity") is implicitly valued over prevailing or future "heterogeneity" (reminiscent of "impurity"). Neither of these functions—here discussed as possible ways of understanding why such misleading notions are still put forth in scholarly writing—are primarily to do with factual historical description.

Notes

1 For a more nuanced view, see Brochmann, G. and Hagelund A. (eds). (2010). *Velferdens grenser. Innvandringspolitikk og velferdsstat i Skandinavia 1945–2010.* Oslo: Universitetsforlaget; cf. also *NOU 2011:7 Velferd og migrasjon*, pp. 11–12.
2 The Norwegian state distinguishes between the Roma (traditionally and somewhat pejoratively named 'Gypsies') and the Romani (Tater, Travellers) as separate ethnic groups (cf. *St.meld. nr. 15 (2000–2001) Nasjonale minoritetar i Noreg—om statlig politikk overfor jødar, kvener, rom, romanifolket og skogfinnar* p. 4.) In current European usage, "Roma" subsumes both groups as well as other "travelling" groups (Minken 2009 p. 20).
3 *St.meld. nr. 15 (2000–2001) Nasjonale minoritetar i Noreg—om statlig politikk overfor jødar, kvener, rom, romanifolket og skogfinnar*: 12, pp. 29–30.
4 Cf. e.g. Census 1920, IV, s. 3, Table "Den norske befolkning fordelt efter fødesteder 1865–1920". In 1920, 4.5 per cent of the population in towns were born abroad, 2.8 per cent for the country as a whole—but they were included in the category "The Norwegian Population".
5 "Norges befolkning er i en sjelden Grad homogen". NOS II C 1 (1882) p. 144.
6 "Ved Siden af Nordmændene og de i samme indforlivede spredte Elementer af fremmed Oprindelse findes det kun to særligt udprægede Stammer, nemlig den lappiske og den finske (…)." NOS II C 1 (1882) p. 144.
7 NOS II C 1 (1882): 146. Kiærs' notion of "race" in 1882 was rather ambivalent and unclear, as noted by Einar Lie and Hege Roll-Hansen (2001 pp. 135–150).

8 NOS II C 1 (1882) p. 156. The Sámi and the Kvens were not counted among the "foreign-born".
9 *Folkräkningen den 31 december 1920. II.* Kungliga Statistiska centralbyrån, Sveriges officiella statistik, Stockholm 1925 p. 23: "Sverige [åtnjuter] förmånen av att inom sina gränser hysa en med avseende på nationalitet [stam] mycket homogen befolkning. De enda väsentliga undantagen från denna homogenitet äro dels de båda stammar av främmande ursprung, som jämte den svenska leva i de nordligaste delarna av vårt land, nämligen finnar och lappar, dels de huvudsakligen i några städer boende judarne. Därjämte finnas spridda i riket ett fåtal zigenare eller tattare." [Sweden enjoys the benefit of having within its borders a very homogeneous population, regarding nationality [tribe]. The only noticeable exceptions to this homogeneity are, in part, the two tribes of foreign origin, that live in the northernmost parts of our country besides the Swedes, namely the Finns and the Lapps, and in part the Jews who mainly live in some towns. In addition, there are a few Gypsies or Taters scattered around the realm.]
10 "etniske kjennetegn har noen betydning, idet det fins et samisk innslag i mange bygder i Nord-Norge (...) Dette er med på å bestemme individets sosiale identitet, skjønt det sjelden fører til noe virkelig minoritetsproblem. De etniske kriterier er for uklare til det."
11 Cf. e.g. NOU 2011:7; Meld.St. 6 (2012–2013); Innst. 248 S (2012–2013), SAK 1 21 March, 2013.

References

Aarseth, B. (2006). *Norsk samepolitikk 1945–1990. Målsetting, virkemidler og resultat.* Oslo: Forlaget Vett og Viten.
Alesina, A. and Glaeser, E. (2004). *Fighting Poverty in the US and Europe. A World of Difference.* Oxford: Oxford University Press.
Andresen, A. (2016). 'Vitenskapene og den nye samepolitikken (1945–1963)'. *Historisk Tidsskrift*, 95, pp. 405–435.
Aubert, V. (1964). *Sosiologi*. Oslo: Universitetsforlaget.
Aubert, V. (1968). 'IV. Lagdeling', in N. R. Ramsøy (ed.) *Det norske samfunn*. Oslo: Gyldendal norsk forlag, pp. 177–181.
Aubert, V. (1973). 'Fattigdom i Norge', in L. G. Lingås (ed.) *Myten om velferdsstaten. Søkelys på norsk sosialpolitikk.* Oslo: Pax, pp. 24–30.
Banik, V. K. (2017). 'Avvisning, pragmatisk aksept og inkludering. Aspekter av statlig politikk overfor den jødiske minoriteten 1814–2016', in N. Brandal, C. A. Døving, and I. T. Plesner (eds.) *Nasjonale minoriteter og urfolk i norsk politikk fra 1900 til 2016.* Oslo: Cappelen Damm Akademisk, pp. 113–130.
Bjørklund, T. and Bergh, J. (2013). *Minoritetsbefolkningens møte med det politiske Norge. Partivalg, valgdeltagelse, representasjon.* Oslo: Cappelen Damm Akademisk.
Brandal, N., Døving, C. A., and Plesner, I. T. (eds.) (2017). *Nasjonale minoriteter og urfolk i norsk politikk fra 1900 til 2016.* Oslo: Cappelen Damm Akademisk.
Bruland, B. (2010). 'Norske jøder—historie og kultur', in A. B. Lund and B. B. Moe (eds.) *Nasjonale minoriteter i det flerkulturelle Norge*. Trondheim: Tapir, pp. 71–86.
Evang, K. (1947). *Gjenreising av folkehelsa i Norge*. Oslo: Fabritius.
Galtung, J. (1968). 'XII. Norge i verdenssamfunnet', in N. R. Ramsøy (ed.) *Det norske samfunn*. Oslo: Gyldendal norsk forlag, pp. 445–491.
Haave, P. (2017). 'Hovedtrekk i norsk romani-/taterpolitikk: Assimilering', in N. Brandal, C. A. Døving and I. T. Plesner (eds.) *Nasjonale minoriteter og urfolk i norsk politikk fra 1900 til 2016.* Oslo: Cappelen Damm Akademisk, pp. 95–112.

Hagerman, M. (2006). *Det rena landet. Om konsten att uppfinna sina förfäder*. Stockholm: Prisma.
Hatland, A. (2011). 'Velferdspolitikk og innvandring', in A. Hatland, S. Kuhnle and T. I. Romøren (eds). *Den norske velferdsstaten*. 4th edition. Oslo: Gyldendal Akademisk, pp. 251–270.
Holme, G. (2015). *Politiske forteljingar om nasjonale minoritetar*. MA thesis in history, University of Bergen.
Homme, L. R. (ed.) (1969). *Nordisk nykolonialisme. Samiske problem i dag*. Oslo: Det Norske Samlaget.
Kjeldstadli, K. (ed.) (2003). *Norsk innvandringshistorie*, vol. 1–3. Oslo: Pax forlag.
Kjeldstadli, K. (2008). *Sammensatte samfunn. Innvandring og inkludering*. Oslo: Pax forlag.
Kjeldstadli, K. (2010). 'Fra innvandrere til minoriteter', in A. B. Lund and B. B. Moen (eds.) *Nasjonale minoriteter i det flerkulturelle Norge*. Trondheim: Tapir akademisk forlag, pp. 15–32.
Lie, E. and Roll-Hansen, H. (2001). *Faktisk talt. Statistikkens historie i Norge*. Oslo: Universitetsforlaget.
Lund, A. B. and Moen, B. B. (eds.) (2010). *Nasjonale minoriteter i det flerkulturelle Norge*. Trondheim: Tapir akademisk forlag.
Midbøe, Ø. (1968). *Eilert Sundt og fantesaken*. Oslo: Universitetsforlaget.
Minken, A. (2009). *Tatere i Norden før 1850. Sosio-økonomiske og etniske fortolkningsmodeller*. Tromsø: Universitetet i Tromsø.
Niemi, E. (1995). 'History of minorities: The Sámi and the Kvens', in W. Hubbard et al. (eds.) *Making a Historical Culture. Historiography in Norway*. Oslo: Scandinavian University Press, pp. 325–346.
Niemi, E. (2003). 'Del I. 1814–1860', in K. Kjeldstadli (ed.) *Norsk innvandringshistorie*, vol 2: *I nasjonalstatens tid 1814–194*. Oslo: Pax forlag, pp. 11–174.
Niemi, E. (2010). 'Kvenene—Nord-Norges finner. En historisk oversikt', in A. B. Lund and B. B. Moen (eds.). *Nasjonale minoriteter i det flerkulturelle Norge*. Trondheim: Tapir, pp. 33–52.
Niemi, E. (2017). 'Fornorskingspolitikken overfor samene og kvenene', in N. Brandal, C. A. Døving, and I. T. Plesner (eds.) *Nasjonale minoriteter og urfolk i norsk politikk fra 1900 til 2016*. Oslo: Cappelen Damm Akademisk, pp. 131–152.
Nordby, T. (1989). *Karl Evang. En biografi*. Oslo: Aschehoug.
Putnam, R. D. (2007). 'E Pluribus Unum: Diversity and Community in the Twenty-first Century. The 2006 Johan Skytte Prize Lecture'. *Scandinavian Political Studies*, 30(2), pp. 137–174.
Russett, B. M., Alker, H. R., Deutsch, K. W. and H. D. Lasswell (eds.) (1964). *World Handbook of Political and Social Indicators*. New Haven and London: Yale University Press.
Ryymin, T. (2007). 'Civilizing the "Uncivilized": The Fight against Tuberculosis in Northern Norway at the Beginning of the Twentieth Century'. *Acta Borealia*, 24(2), pp. 143–161.
Ryymin, T. (2015). 'Integration and incorporation: Challenges and perspectives in minority history writing', in E. Heikkilä et al. (eds.) *Participation, Integration, and Recognition: Changing Pathways to Immigrant Incorporation*. Turku: Institute of Migration, pp. 32–42.
Ryymin, T. and Andresen, A. (2009). 'Effecting Equality: Norwegian Health Policy in Finnmark, 1945–1970s'. *Acta Borealia*, 26(1), pp. 96–114.

Ryymin, T. and Nyyssönen, J. (2013). 'Synliggjøring, assimilering, agens. Fortellinger i samisk og kvensk historie', in J. Heiret, T. Ryymin, and S. A. Skålevåg (eds.) (2013). *Fortalt fortid. Norsk historieskriving etter 1970.* Oslo: Pax forlag, pp. 207–239.

Sejersted, F. (2005). *Sosialdemokratiets tidsalder. Norge og Sverige i det 20. Århundre.* Oslo: Pax.

Selle, P., Semb, A. J., Strømsnes, K., and Dyrnes Nordø, Å. (2015). *Den samiske medborgeren.* Oslo: Cappelen Damm Akademisk.

Sørensen, Ø. (1994). 'The development of a Norwegian national identity during the nineteenth century', in Ø. Sørensen (ed). *Nordic Paths to National Identity in the Nineteenth Century.* Oslo: The Research Council of Norway, pp. 17–36.

Tervonen, M. (2014). 'Historiankirjoitus ja myytti yhden kulttuurin Suomesta', in P. Markkola, H. Snellman, and A. C. Östman (eds.) *Kotiseutu ja kansakunta—Miten suomalaista historiaa on rakennettu.* Helsinki: SKS, pp. 137–162.

Tjelmeland, H. (2003). 'Del I. 1940–1975', in K. Kjeldstadli (ed.) *Norsk innvandringshistorie, vol. 3: I globaliseringens tid 1940–2000.* Oslo: Pax forlag, pp. 11–134.

Tvedt, T. (2017). *Det internasjonale gjennombruddet. Fra "ettpartistat" til flerkulturell stat.* Oslo: Dreyers forlag.

3 Myths of ethnic homogeneity
The Danish case

Garbi Schmidt

Introduction

In Denmark, as in many other national contexts, there are widespread understandings of building nationhood based on an ethnically homogeneous past. This chapter's starting point is one of curiosity towards this understanding: Where does it stem from? What anchors, stories, and symbols solidify this understanding? How does this understanding relate to empirical evidence? And how are perceptions of ethnic homogeneity practised in everyday life? While the overall focus of this chapter is on Denmark, the exploration of understandings of ethnic homogeneity in everyday life will focus on two neighbourhoods in Copenhagen. In that regard, a particular question is whether perceptions of ethnic homogeneity or heterogeneity in particular places are linked to the dominant narratives about these places as either 'white' or 'ethnically diverse', and how these perceptions are enacted. Following Steven Vertovec's call for an academic focus on superdiversity (Vertovec 2007), we may ask if such superdiversity is recognised or neglected, and celebrated or ignored, by the people living in these areas and the surrounding nation-state.

To answer the aforementioned four questions, I will use a triangulation of methods and data that are both qualitative as well as quantitative. To illuminate the first two questions, I will—based on historian and sociologist Gerard Bouchard's typology of national myths—go through a number of historical and contemporary examples from Denmark. I will analyse the relevance of this typology for understanding hegemonic discourses around Danish ethnic homogeneity and national identity. To dig deeper into empirical evidence about ethnic homogeneity and heterogeneity in Denmark (question 3), I will use statistical data (mainly from Statistics Denmark), both historical and current. Further, quantitative data—which encompasses both national and particular local developments—will point to the final element of my analysis (question 4): how perceptions of ethnic homogeneity are practised in everyday life. The contexts of this analysis are two neighbourhoods in Copenhagen, where I have conducted two iterations of extensive fieldwork: 57 ethnographic interviews were conducted in Nørrebro between 2008 and 2013, while 23 interviews were conducted in Østerbro between 2016 and 2017. In my ongoing work, I have focused on ethnic diversity in these two neighbourhoods from 1885 until the present day (see e.g. Schmidt 2015; Schmidt 2017; Schmidt forthcoming).

Before moving to my analysis, it's important to briefly point to the relevance of research in understandings, practices, and histories of ethnic homogeneity (or, eventually, heterogeneities). The perspective presented in this chapter critically engages with and deconstructs the world view of nationalism, including its central moments of remembering and forgetting (Connerton 2009). Deconstruction is important for showing the power of such world views, not least in a globally urgent moment of nationalist politics that does not solely build walls between states, but also between groups of citizens within states. In Denmark, the concept of "Danishness" has conquered a central role in public debate, as underlined by the following two examples.

First, in December 2016, The Danish Language Council—a research institution focusing on the use and development of the Danish language—issued their decision regarding "the word of the year". Whereas the 2014 word of the year had been "mobilepay", and 2015's was "refugee waves" [*flygtningestrømme*], the choice in 2016 was the word "Danishness" [*danskhed*]. One of the judges, the director of The Danish Language Council, Sabine Kirchmeier, told the media that "the word encapsulated the public debate of the previous year. This year, we have—more than ever before—discussed what Danishness is" (Midtjyllands Avis 2016). Second, in the same year, the Liberal Party Minister of Culture, Bertel Haarder, called for a *Danmarkskanon*, a code of Danish conduct that enshrined particularly Danish cultural habits and values. The project was launched as a democratic endeavour where everybody could submit their understanding of 'Danish values'. A total of 2,425 suggestions were ranked by a group of 'experts' who decided on ten canonical values. Included in the canon (together with issues that, as critical voices pointed out, were more difficult to classify as "values"), were terms such as "Christian cultural heritage, the Danish language, freedom, liberalism, and hygge".[1] The project emphasised a contemporary ambition to define the characteristics of Danish national identity, while inadvertently bringing to light how inconsistent and blurry its borders can be.

A starting point for this chapter's discussion of ethnic homogeneity is to also ponder what ethnic homogeneity is all about. Ethnicity is an aspect of the human practice of categorisation that builds on perceptions of (self) identity and identification of a (perceived) other (see e.g. Jenkins 1997; Barth 1969). The aforementioned debates around Danishness are examples of negotiations of who is perceived to be on the inside and the outside, and who has the right to define these boundaries. Other examples that I will refer to indicate how nation-state building in the Danish context has become remarkably tied into a particular story of ethnic homogeneity. While we must definitely investigate how current aspects of globalisation have turned cultural identities into consciously political projects (see e.g. Hall 1996), we must also look to the past to investigate the historical background hereof: why did, in this case, the Danish nation-state building project develop as it did?

Anchors, stories and symbols

Classical theoretical thinkers such as Ernest Gellner, Eric Hobsbawm, Benedict Anderson, and Anthony Smith all stress the elusiveness, changeability, blurriness, and historicity of the concept (e.g. Gellner 1983) of the nation. Quoting Walter Bagehot and Ernest Renan in his book on *Nations and Nationalism since 1780*, Eric Hobsbawm describes the difficulty of defining what nationalism and the nation actually is: "We know what it is, when you do not ask us, but we cannot very quickly explain or define it ... getting its history wrong is part of being a nation" (Hobsbawm 1990, p. 12).

An important and useful way to understand nationalism and national identity is to approach such constructs as building upon a myth. Bouchard has offered a useful description of *national myths* as a product of a dynamic configuration composed of seven elements (Bouchard 2014 pp. 4–5): 1) a structuring event or episode ("the anchor"); 2) an imprint, that is, a deep emotion left by "the anchor"; 3) a translation of the imprint into an ethos; 4) the construction of a narrative; 5) the sacralisation of the ethos; 6) the enactment of discursive and communicative strategies to disseminate the message; and 7) the intervention of social actors who construct and promote the myth.

All these elements can be found in the dominant constitutive stories about Danish identity and the Danish nation. Keeping the quote by Hobsbawm in mind, the framing of a Danish national identity is not univocal and clear *per se*, but certain elements and stories frequently appear as elements of myth making. Three anchors seem to appear, each striking a note in the complex construction of what Danishness is about. The first is the largest of the two Jelling Stones, a large carved rune stone from the late tenth century standing in the small Jutlandic town of Jelling. The stone was erected by King Harald Bluetooth in commemoration of his mother Tyra, and his father Gorm, who is said to be the first king of Denmark. The stone is frequently called the "birth certificate" of Denmark—it mentions both Denmark and Norway as parts of the kingdom, and further states that Harald "made the Danes Christian". Apart from this inscription, the stone is decorated with Jesus hanging on the cross. The second anchor is the tale about the origin of the national flag of Denmark, *Dannebrog*. History scholars from the Middle Ages have written about the battle at Lyndanisse (today Tallinn in Estonia) in 1208 (or 1219, depending on the source), where the Danish army—led by their king, Valdemar—prayed for divine interference when they were close to being defeated by the local army.[2] As a divine response, a red woollen banner bearing a white cross fell from the sky. As a consequence, according to the story, the Danish army won the battle. A third anchor is the Danish–Prussian war, in which battles took place in Southern Jutland in 1864. In the nineteenth century, Denmark included both its present-day territory and the duchies of Schleswig, Holstein, and Lauenburg. When the Danish government and king decided that Schleswig should become more closely attached to Denmark, war with Prussia broke out. The Danish army was defeated, and at the peace treaty in the summer of 1864, Denmark was forced to entrust the three duchies to Prussia. It was not until 1920 that parts of these were returned to Denmark.

Other national anchors can undoubtedly be found, but these three are important for several reasons. The Jelling Stone is a symbol of the birth of the nation, although what could then be considered "Danish" and a part of "the Danish nation", was far different from today. It symbolises the Viking past of the nation (a period of superiority and expansion), and furthermore the birth of Denmark as a *Christian* nation. This is exemplified by how in 2008, the Danish government and the Danish People's Party (DPP)[3] earmarked 20.1 million euros for securing Danish cultural heritage, from which 870,000 euros went to the restoration of the Jelling Stone. When the restoration was completed in 2011, the DPP issued a press release presenting their motivation for allocating these funds: "When the stones are called the cradle of the Danish history, it is because the word 'Denmark' is used for the first time on the Jelling Stones". The press release further referred to the large stone's reference to Christianity (Danish People's Party 2011).

While the story of the origin of the Dannebrog is generally described as nothing more than a story, the flag still plays a role in Danish everyday life that is strikingly prominent, and even paradoxical (see also Jenkins 2011). For example, the Dannebrog can be used within local supermarket advertising, and at one point, it was even used by the municipality of Greve as a means of preventing dog excrement (small flag pins were placed in dog excrement left by owners in recreation areas; see e.g. TV 2 2015). Thus, the flag is used in ways that are banal and profane but claims of sanctions regarding the use of the flag are just as frequently voiced. One example are reactions to the singer Basim's use of the flag upon winning the Danish qualifier for the Eurovision Song Contest 2014. After the event, Basim—a young man of Moroccan descent—was criticised for allowing a large Danish flag to backdrop him at the end of his act. One of the largest tabloid papers in Denmark, *BT*, quoted his competitor Bryan Rice as saying that Basim's use of the flag was "repulsive" [*usmageligt*] (*BT* 2014). In Danish media, there was an overwhelming focus on Basim's ethnic background, and in the newspaper *Information*, he was asked about whether he as "an immigrant had experienced discrimination in Denmark?" (*Information* 2014), to which he answered, "I am not an immigrant. I did not migrate from any country". About the use of the Dannebrog, Basim noted that "it was an idea I had. There was to be a party and the flag is a sign of the party" (ibid.). This example illustrates how public perceptions of immigrant identity stick to individuals who are both born and raised in Denmark, and how such identifications create certain expectations as to how such individuals may or may not wield the insignia of nationalism.

Whereas both the Jelling Stones and the Dannebrog point to periods of pride and victory, the defeat in 1864 became understood as a national trauma with long-term effects on Danish national identity. As noted by political scientist Eirikur Bergmann, the Schleswig Wars were a starting point for romantic nationalism "now centred on a parochial urge towards insularity" (Bergmann 2016, p. 42). Of the three aforementioned anchor events, the defeat of the Schleswig Wars has had the strongest and most long-lasting effect on Danish national self-perception. To return to Bouchard's typology, the event resulted in deep emotions, was translated into a (sacralised) ethos, and became a constitutive national narrative.

One of the most important ideological fathers of Danish nationalism was N.F. S Grundtvig (1783–1872), a priest, theologian, poet, politician, and writer. Grundtvig actively participated in the national assembly that authored the national constitution in 1849. Grundtvig's romantic nationalism (inspired by Herder) focused on "the people" [*folket*], which became a keystone of the Danish national ethos. Grundtvig can even be seen as the author of the concept of *folkelighed* [being the people/the nature of the people] (Andersen 2003, p. 69). According to Grundtvig, Danishness was something to be found among the people, not the elites. A telling illustration of Grundtvig's understanding of the people was his attack on the Jewish author Meir Aron Goldschmidt. In 1849, Grundtvig wrote in the magazine *Danskeren* [*The Dane*] that Goldschmidt "has for too long provoked *Folkeligheden* [the sense of being a people] in the country where he has been privy to so much hospitality and behaves as if he is at home" (Grundtvig 1848, see also Thing 2001). Although Goldschmidt was born in Denmark (in Vordingborg), Grundtvig could not accept him as Danish. By being a Jew, Goldschmidt belonged to the Jewish people, not the Danish people. According to Grundtvig, human beings were born into one people—and only one (also Thing 2004).

The idea of "the people" as an unbreakable entity has proven remarkably strong since Grundtvig's time and is an important backdrop for understanding the persistent idea about a Denmark built on ethnic homogeneity. The influence of romantic nationalism, based on the notion of one people with one language and one history, certainly grew out of the crisis of 1864, but also points to the stress on language purity that dawned in the late 1700s, not least as a means to exclude the German minority from the social position they held in that era (Winge 1992, p. 310). Danishness and the ethos of national resistance was a force in the years from 1940 to 1945 when Denmark was occupied by Nazi Germany. The idea that the Danish language included its own maze of meanings that only natives could understand was a tool for non-violent—yet effective—resistance, as, for example, the frequently quoted cabaret song "Man binder os på mund og hånd" ["One ties both our mouth and hands"] shows. To outsiders—including Nazi censors—the song appears to be about free spirits, but to insiders (the Danes) it became an expression of the desire to once again become a free nation. The ethos of *folket* is noticeable in everyday life, political and religious institutions—the Danish

Protestant Church is called *Folke*kirken, and the term is used in the names of several political parties (e.g. Dansk *Folke*parti and Socialistisk *Folkeparti*) (Bergmann 2016, p. 42). However—and very much in line with Grundtvig—there are limits today as to who counts as the people, and who does not, reflected in the infamous 2001 statement in which the Liberal Party minister of integration, Bertel Haarder, presented the government's new integration politics: "This country in many ways has a tribal culture, where a dominant form of control is social control. In many ways we do not need the police." (Politiken 2002. My translation). Crucially, Haarder's understanding of social control is not negative; social control is a prerequisite for law and order. However, more importantly in this context, Haarder's framing of Danes as a "tribe" definitely underlined notions of shared lineage that goes back in time.

Other more recent examples of a historically-rooted notion of ethnic homogeneity amongst Danish people is illustrated by the verbal clash between Martin Henriksen (a Danish People's Party MP, and frequently quoted party spokesperson for immigration, integration of immigrants, and religious diversity) and Jens Philip Yazdani (the president of the Danish Highschool Students' Union) in the TV programme *Debatten* [*The Debate*]:

YAZDANI: We are many, our parents came here. We are born here and raised here, and we are just as Danish ... We have attended Danish public school and gymnasium, and we are just as Danish as everyone else, including the girls in my class who have chosen to wear a scarf.

HENRIKSEN: They have distanced themselves from Danish society.

YAZDANI: They are democratic citizens.

TV HOST: Now, take it easy. Yazdani is born in Denmark. He is raised in Denmark, has attended Danish public school and Danish high school—is he not Danish?

HENRIKSEN: I do not know him, so it is difficult for me to tell. I can only conclude that you cannot bring the entire world to Denmark and that their children automatically become Danish. That is simply a vulgarisation of the debate that is directly offensive towards those generations who built this country.

The dispute of different understandings of Danishness between Henriksen and Yazdani is a telling illustration of current struggles around Danishness. Some actors in this debate allow themselves (and are allowed) to take a privileged position based on their claim to ancestry and race—a term that is almost never used in the Danish context, just as recognising Denmark's colonial past as integral to the country's nation-building processes is whitewashed from popular discourse (see Andreassen 2014; Jensen 2012, 2016). The "Danishness" of Yazdani, a young man who was born and raised in Denmark, was questioned because one of his parents was not born in the country.

Ethnic homogeneity? Concurrent and historical aspects

But is the idea of ethnic homogeneity actually trustworthy? Here, historical findings and DNA research has (particularly throughout the last decades) helped to modify the picture. For example, in 2015, DNA analysis was conducted to learn more about one of the most famous archaeological finds in Denmark, a mummified corpse from the Bronze Age referred to as the *Egtved Woman*. The analysis revealed that the woman was not born within Danish territory: she most probably came from Schwartzwald in what is now Germany. One headline in the newspaper *Politiken* stated that "The Egtved Woman was an immigrant" (*Politiken* 2015); this statement highlighted an ongoing internal conflict between those who advocated for open borders, and those who wanted to close borders towards (Syrian) refugees who applied for asylum in Denmark that year.

During the Viking Age, religious and ethnic diversity was a result of geographical expansion—a result of both trade and war. Subsequently, Denmark deliberately sent for and incorporated groups of immigrants into societies, even offering refuge for groups of religious minorities (particularly if they could bring skills, professional networks, and trade to Denmark). A well-known advocate of this position is King Christian II, who in 1521 signed a letter of privilege that enabled 184 Dutch farmers to settle on the island of Amager, just outside Copenhagen. The Dutch farmers were given rights and privileges (for example, in terms of inheritance) that far exceeded the rights Danish farmers had at the time (Thavlov 1994). Another immigrant group that arrived as a result of royal decree were the French Huguenots who settled in Fredericia from 1720 onwards, assisting in strengthening the position of the city. They too were offered special privileges, including farming fields within the city, and gardens outside its borders (fredericiashistorie.dk, n.d.).

Denmark fosters an international reputation for its exceptional archive data, which demarcates various population nuances, such as immigrant background. The first national census was carried out in 1787, and from 1845 onwards it included information about the birthplace of each registered individual. Census data and statistics extracted from such data can serve as a backdrop for understanding the historical prevalence of ethnic diversity in relation to nation-state, neighbourhood, street, and even individual houses. This section provides empirical details about the prevalence of 120 years of both national and local diversity.

The first Danish national statistics yearbook appeared in 1896, and included data about the birthplace of citizens, including those foreign born. Table 3.1 describes the total number of inhabitants as well as immigrants in Denmark and the capital of Copenhagen from 1890 until 1921. Throughout this period of 30 years, the percentage of immigrants both in the country and the capital was quite stable: in the country 3 percent of the inhabitants were immigrants, while in the capital, the percentage was a little higher—between 6 to 8 percent. The dominant immigrant groups were Swedes, Norwegians, and Germans.

Table 3.1

Year	1890		1901		1911		1921	
	Denmark	Copenhagen	Denmark	Copenhagen	Denmark	Copenhagen	Denmark	Copenhagen
Total population	2,172,330	312,859	2,449,540	400,575	2,449,540	462,161	2,757,076	700,610
Immigrant population	70,900	23,470	80,018	27,693	80,018	29,708	84,879	44,400
% immigrants	3	8	3	7	3	6	3	6

Sources: Statistics Denmark 1904, 1911, 1925.

However, I argue that Denmark's past ethnic homogeneity cannot be confirmed simply on the basis of foreign residency. The table does not, for example, include information about sojourners and foreign workers who stayed temporarily in the country. Neither does it take into account the number of foreign seamen, traders, artists, criminals, and intellectuals who visited Denmark and Copenhagen throughout that period. In my own work with the history of migration in Copenhagen, I have come across groups of foreigners that, for example, were registered by the police as living in a specific house in Copenhagen but were not registered in the national census. One credible reason could be that these foreigners only stayed in Copenhagen for a few days, weeks, or months, and then moved out of the country. Other sources underline that large groups of seasonal workers—in particular those from Poland and Sweden—worked in the Danish countryside (Østergaard 2007). In sum: while some immigrants were registered, there is evidence that many (and it is impossible to say how many) were not. If anything, Table 3.1 underlines that census data is narrow and does not capture a comprehensive understanding of migrants who move from one national context and settle in another (at least for so long that they can be registered by the authorities). Here, studies of the disrupted routes of current migration can usefully refine this perspective (Collyer and de Haas 2012). One question to be asked, is how long (or how little) a person should stay in a country to actually be perceived as contributing to its ethnic diversity?

Also—and drawing on perspectives from transnational migration studies, studies of globalisation, and cultural geography (Wimmer and Schiller 2002; Faist, Fauser, and Reisenauer 2013; Massey 2004)—simply perceiving a country as a container where some people arrive and some people leave is far from sufficiently nuanced. Such a view is blind to transnational ties, the complexities of globalisation, and the social fields transcending the nation-state, of which both individuals, families, companies, finance and political parties, and communities are—and have been—a part (also historically). To provide an example from the Danish Statistical Yearbook from 1911:

> From 1910 to 1911, a total of 139,717,350 letters were sent inside Denmark, and 16,616,782 were received while 16,960,918 were sent abroad.
> From 1910 to 1911, 1,212,529 letters containing money were sent inside Denmark and 55,758 letters containing money arrived from abroad. 21,111 letters with money were sent abroad.
> From 1910 to 1911, 141,123,455 magazines and journals were sent inside Denmark and 2,450,010 magazines and journals were received from abroad. 2,660,333 magazines and journals were sent abroad.
> Between 1 April, 1910 and 31 March, 1911, 749,733 telegrams were sent to or from Denmark.

These numbers show that Denmark and citizens in Denmark were engaged in networks of communication that exceeded the space of the nation-state. Denmark was—perhaps not surprisingly—a part of a larger world. In that

44 *Schmidt*

sense, I will argue that the question, "was Denmark historically an ethnic homogeneous or heterogeneous country?" cannot solely be answered by focusing on the immigrants who settled there. Not only because available statistics are flawed, but because a narrow focus on sedentary patterns is inept at grasping migration as a fragmented process, and its impact upon the transnational social, financial, cultural, and political fields of which Denmark has historically been a part.

Present implications of diversity in Nørrebro and Østerbro

Continuing to my final question—how perceptions of ethnic homogeneity are practised in everyday life—I will now focus on ethnographic interview data from two neighbourhoods in Copenhagen: Nørrebro and Østerbro.

Both Nørrebro and Østerbro were established onwards of the 1850s, when the city of Copenhagen expanded in space and demography. Today, Nørrebro is Copenhagen's most densely populated neighbourhood, housing the highest concentration of immigrants and their descendants[4] in the city. In 2017, 21,105 (26 percent) of Nørrebro's 79,951[5] residents were immigrants or the children of immigrants (of whom 9,022 came or originated from other countries in Europe).

While Nørrebro has for more than a century been known and portrayed as Copenhagen's rebellious, unruly, working-class neighbourhood, the story of how Østerbro has been enshrined is quite different. The two neighbourhoods are actually located next to each other—Nørrebro is north of the city centre, while Østerbro is located between Nørrebro (to its east) and the Oresund strait (to its west). The central street of Nørrebro (Nørrebrogade) is packed with shawarma take-outs, pizzerias, a few shops selling Islamic attire for women, and budget fashion stores and cafes—the latter an indication of the ongoing gentrification of the neighbourhood. In contrast, the central street of Østerbro (Østerbrogade) is characterised by expensive fashion boutiques and an almost Parisian boulevard ambience. Here you will also find shawarma take-outs and pizzerias, albeit without Nørrebro's density. A chic and bourgeois aura (or "boredom", as some of my respondents noted) seems to innately characterise Østerbro. The neighbourhood is also known as "2100 spelt", a combination of the neighbourhood's postal code and the Danish word for "spelt wheat"; an element constructing Østerbro's bourgeoisie narrative is that its residents overtly focus on healthy and organic food.

Walking through Østerbro easily provides the impression of an all-white, all middle-class neighbourhood. However, if you have a cup of coffee in one of the neighbourhood's many cafes, you will hear many languages besides Danish being spoken: English, Italian, Spanish, Norwegian, and several more. Statistical descriptions of the ethnic composition of Østerbro add to the picture. In 2007, a total of 67,330 people lived in Østerbro, of which 9,485 (14 percent) were immigrants or so-called descendants (5,401 originated in another European country). In 2017, a total of 77,975[6] people lived in

Østerbro, of which 14,845 (19 percent) were immigrants and descendants (8,206 were born elsewhere in Europe).

In 2017, one in four of Nørrebro's residents was an immigrant or descendant of an immigrant, while one in five in Østerbro was an immigrant or descendant. However, although statistics reveal that both neighbourhoods have large segments of immigrants (the number of immigrants actually increasing in Østerbro in the described period and decreasing in Nørrebro), the immigrant/descendant segments in Østerbro and Nørrebro are characterised by one important distinction: in Østerbro, more than half of the immigrants/descendants originate from other countries within Europe, while the residents in Nørrebro with immigrant/descendant background originate from outside Europe.

Interestingly, qualitative interviews with residents in Østerbro underlined that most residents did not understand their neighbourhood as characterised by immigrant populations, while respondents in Nørrebro did. When I compared data from the two neighbourhoods[7] it was obvious that the term immigrant itself had fuzzy connotations for my respondents, *not* referring to groups of *invisible* migrants (people who count as "white"[8] from Europe or North America), but definitely referring to groups of *visible* migrants (people who count as "non-whites", from the Middle East, Asia, and Africa). How the belonging of race was linked to specific understandings of particular neighborhoods in the city was, for example, underlined by Smiljana, a young woman of Bosnian descent who lived in Nørrebro:

> I arrived here by accident, and I really did not think I was going to like it [Nørebro]. I was told that there were many foreigners and that the neighborhood was trashed. But I arrived and just thought that it was fantastic—much better than other places. I belong here. I am very neutral here—not too light-skinned, not too dark. I fit [into the fabric]. I think, that if I lived in Østerbro or Frederiksberg, other people would look at me more.

To Smiljana (and others), Nørrebro was an ethnically diverse neighbourhood *per se*. Being neutral—an expression of fitting in so well that one became invisible—was linked to skin colour. Nørrebro was not all white—but it was not all dark either.

When I asked Østerbro respondents whether they knew of immigrants living either in their apartment building or close by, they responded "no" or "very few". As Allan, who had lived in Østerbro for more than ten years, stated:

> I do not see many immigrants. There are of course some. I do not expect the people working in the pizzerias to actually be Italians, even when they pretend to be so. In reality, they are perhaps [inaudible] or Turks or Pakistanis … [Pizzeria owners] are typically Turks.

In this part of the interview, Allan provided a noteworthy description of "the immigrant". To him, immigrants included the owners of pizzerias and mostly came from countries such as Pakistan or Turkey. When I asked him to broaden the definition of "the immigrant" to include people from Europe, Allan—like many other respondents—pointed to Russian immigrants or groups of immigrants from Eastern Europe. Allan's reflections provided a clear indication of the implications of at least one aspect of racialisation—processes that "differentiate people, stabilise these differences and legitimate power differences based on them" (Keskinen and Andreassen 2017, p. 65). Allan's statement reflects how being perceived as an immigrant is not only a question of having crossed a national border to settle in Denmark, but also a question of skin colour, and the meanings and structures of power connected hereto.

The implications of visible and invisible groups of immigrants, and how they signify and reinforce the narrative of a "white" Østerbro, was also a topic I discussed with Rashita, a woman in her late forties who had migrated to Denmark from India and had lived in Østerbro for approximately 12 years. One aspect that she found peculiar—not least as an academic—was the expectation that she, with her brown skin colour and black hair, could not live in Østerbro:

> I think people expect me to live in Nørrebro, because I am who I am. And my skin colour is the way it is. And then I think, I actually like it. That I defy that stereotype too … But I think, I fundamentally feel that people's understanding of, you know, ethnicity and social class, immigration, sits in very narrow boxes … And this is something I have said right from the beginning, when I came to Denmark. Why is it that ethnicity, religion takes predominance? And no one speaks about social class? It's extremely amazing that it all boils down to this, that if you're a good migrant, then you live in Nørrebro, right? So fine, I live in this very boring place, apparently.

Rashita's statement is interesting for several reasons. First, because it points to the importance of race and processes of racialisation in the Danish context. Second, because she points to the spaces where the racial other is seen as a natural component, and where it is not. Rashita lived in Østerbro, but since the neighbourhood is understood as "white", she is often met with surprise when she tells others she lives there. Due to her skin colour and black hair, she does not fit into the conventional Østerbro narrative. Besides, she pointed to the often-neglected implication of social class in the Danish context, and *also* how class intersects with racialisation. While Østerbro is framed as posh, wealthy, and white, Nørrebro is framed as downmarket working class, and brown. Rashita's statement reflects some of the *spatial and racial* positionality within which neighbourhoods such as Nørrebro are entrenched—these are understandings that Smiljana also proffered.

Conclusion

This chapter started out with four questions: 1) Where did the idea of ethnic homogeneity in Denmark stem from? 2) What were the anchors, stories, and symbols that solidify this understanding? 3) How does the understanding relate to empirical evidence? 4) And how are perceptions of ethnic homogeneity and the (in)visible other practised in everyday life?

In my analysis of the first two questions I used, for instance, Gerard Bouchard's typology of national myths to present some of the anchors, symbols, and stories that reinforce the idea of ethnic homogeneity and "Danishness", and perceptions of a tribal understanding of "the people". My description showed how these ideas festered and grew strong after the Danish defeat of Prussia in 1864, which coincided with the dawn of national romanticism. I also showed how the idea of ethnic homogeneity is strongly invoked in current political debates and is used as an argument to exclude racialised others from the national community.

My discussion of question three was mainly based on quantitative data. I showed that if we focused on sedentary patterns of migrants in the period where data is available (1890 onwards), the number of immigrants in Denmark was low (although higher in the capital Copenhagen). However, I also showed that it was necessary to move *beyond* the focus of sedentary patterns to understand the implications of migration in a given context. Migrants did not always stay in Denmark, but also included temporary workers, seamen, traders, irregular migrants, travelling people, and others, who—as a consequence of their mobility—were and could not be registered. If we want to understand both the contemporary and historical implications of migration on the nation-state, we must establish better methods to do so.

In my discussion of question four, the perspective shifted from the overall national context, to two neighbourhoods in Copenhagen—Nørrebro and Østerbro. My descriptions underline how perceptions of ethnic diversity in these two contexts were a) a result of how the neighbourhood—including its past—was framed and narrated; b) built on understandings of "whiteness" and "brownness" that made some bodies visible (and thus possible to categorise as migrants), while others were not; and c) how class and processes of racialisation clearly intersected when perceiving the other.

In summary, this chapter underlined the strength of national mythmaking on the narrating of historical pasts and presents, and how such storytelling is far from innocent in including and excluding some groups as a part of the story. The continuing racialisation of "the migrant" is linked to this storytelling, building on one version of the national past to present the diversity of the present as an abnormality.

Notes

1 See danmarkskanon.dk (accessed August 18, 2017).
2 Aarhus University's site for Danish history describes the event: http://danmarkshistorien.dk/leksikon-og-kilder/vis/materiale/dannebrog/ (accessed 29 August, 2017).

3 Established 1995, The Danish People's Party is a national conservative populist party with a clear anti-immigration and social welfare profile. At the national election in 2015, the party became Denmark's second largest party in parliament. The party has had a significant influence on Danish politics in the first decades of the twenty-first century.
4 In Denmark, migration statistics not only include immigrants (born outside Denmark) but also often so-called "descendants". Statistics Denmark defines a descendant as a person that is born in Denmark, but neither of its parents have Danish citizenship. If one or both parents obtain Danish citizenship, their children are no longer registered as "descendants" (Statistics Denmark, n.d.).
5 As of 31 December, 2016 (Municipality of Copenhagen, n.d.).
6 As of 31 December, 2016 (Municipality of Copenhagen, n.d.)
7 Both projects were made possible via funding from the Danish Research Council.
8 Suvi Keskinen and Rikke Andreassen emphasise the importance of including a perspective on whiteness when investigating race and processes of racialisation: "whiteness often acts as the unspoken norm against which 'others' are measured and defined, creating hierarchies not only among groups of people but also ways of life, embodied characteristics, residential areas and so on." (Keskinen and Andreassen 2017, p. 66).

References

Andersen, Balder Mørk (2003). 'Grundtvig og folkelighedsbegrebet'. *Grundtvigstudier*, 51(1), pp. 65–87.
Andreassen, R. (2014). 'Danish Perceptions of Race and Anthropological Science at the Turn of the Twentieth Century', in N. Bancel, ed., *The Intervention of Race: Scientific and Popular Representations*. New York: Routledge.
Barth, F. (1969). *Ethnic Groups and Boundaries: The Social Organization of Cultural Difference*. Long Grove: Waveland Press.
Bergmann, E. (2016). *Nordic Nationalism and Right-Wing Populist Politics*. London: Palgrave Macmillan.
Bouchard, G. (2014). 'The Small Nation with a Big Dream: Quebec National Myths (Eighteen-Twentieth Century)', in G. Bouchard, ed., *National Myths: Constructed Pasts, Contested Presents*. New York: Routledge.
BT (2014). 'Basim afviser kritik af Dannebrog: Stolt af mit land'. March 9.
Collyer, M. and de Haas, H. (2012). 'Developing dynamic categorisations of transit migration'. *Population, Space and Place*, 18(4), pp. 468–481.
Connerton, P. (2009). *How Modernity Forgets*. Cambridge: Cambridge University Press.
Danish Peoples' Party (2011). Press release: The Jellinge Stones have been secured. http://www.danskfolkeparti.dk/Jellingstenene_er_sikret [accessed August 29, 2017].
Faist, T., Fauser, M., Reisenauer, E. (2013). *Transnational Migration*. London: Polity.
Fredericiashistorie.dk (n.d.). Den reformerte menighed. fredericiashistorie.dk/side/den-reformerte-menighed (downloaded September 20, 2017).
Gellner, E. (1983). *Nations and Nationalism*. Ithaca: Cornell University Press.
Grundtvig, N. F. S. (1848). 'Svar på Hr. Goldschmidts Udfordring til Danskheden', *Danskeren, et Ugeblad*. November 10.
Hall, S. (1996). 'Introduction: Who Needs Identity?' In S. Hall and P. de Gay, eds., *Questions of Cultural Identity*. London: Sage.
Hobsbawm, E. (1990). *Nations and Nationalism since 1780: Programme, Myth, Reality*. Cambridge: Cambridge University Press.

Information (2014). 'Basim'. March 22.
Jenkins, R. (1997). *Rethinking Ethnicity: Arguments and Explorations.* London: Sage.
Jenkins, R. (2011). *Being Danish: Paradoxes of Identity in Everyday Life.* Copenhagen: Museum Tusculanum Press.
Jensen, L. (2012). *Danmark: Rigsfællesskab, tropekoloni og den postkoloniale arv.* Copenhagen: Hans Reitzels Forlag.
Jensen, Lars (2016). 'Beyond the Rot of Colonialism?' *Postcolonial Studies*, 18(4), pp. 440–452.
Keskinen, S. and Andreassen, R. (2017). 'Developing Theoretical Perspectives on Racialisation and Migration'. *Nordic Journal of Migration Research*, 7(2), pp. 64–69.
Massey, D. (2004). 'Geographies of Responsibility'. *Geografiska Annaler* 86(1), pp. 5–18.
Midtjyllands Avis (2016). 'Sprognævn kalder danskhed årets ord'. December 17.
Municipality of Copenhagen (n.d.). Statistikbanken. http://sgv2.kk.dk:9704/analytics/saw.dll?PortalPagesandPortalPath=%2fshared%2fStatistik%20Rapporter%2f_portal%2fStatistikbankenandDone=PortalPages%26PortalPath%3d%252fshared%252fStatistik%2520Rapporter%252f_portal%252fStatistikbanken%26Page%3dForside%26ViewState%3ddpo8sg5kkgg5s0de3clof4t3qq [accessed September 26, 2017].
Østergaard, Bent (2007). *Indvandrerne i Danmarks historie.* Odense: Syddansk Universitetsforlag.
Politiken (2002). 'Danmark er en stamme'. January 21.
Politiken (2015). 'Egtvedpigen var indvandrer'. May 21.
Schmidt, G. (2015). *Nørrebros indvandringshistorie 1885–2010.* Copenhagen: Museum Tusculanum Press.
Schmidt, G. (2017). 'Going Beyond Methodological Presentism: Examples from a Copenhagen Neighborhood 1885–2010'. *Immigrants and Minorities*, 35(1), pp. 40–58.
Schmidt, Garbi (forthcoming). 'Sammenhængskraft – at være hjemme mellem stenkast og fodbold'. In K. Vitus, T. G. Jensen and G. Schmidt, eds., *Sammenhængskraft – en antologi.* Copenhagen: Samfundslitteratur.
Statistics Denmark (1904). *Statistisk Aarbog 1911.* Copenhagen: Statistics Denmark.
Statistics Denmark (1911). *Statistisk Aarbog 1911.* Copenhagen: Statistics Denmark.
Statistics Denmark (1925). *Statistisk Aarbog 1925.* Copenhagen: Statistics Denmark.
Statistics Denmark (n.d.). *Indvandrere og efterkommere.* http://www.dst.dk/da/Statistik/emner/befolkning-og-valg/indvandrere-og-efterkommere/indvandrere-og-efterkommere [accessed September 28, 2017].
Thavlov, L. (1994). Den hollandske indvandring til Store Magleby. *Nyt fra lokalhistorien* 4.
Thing, M. (2001). *Den historiske jøde – essays og ordbog.* Copenhagen: Forum.
Thing, M. (2004). 'Grundtvig, Goldschmidt – og Langballe'. *Information.* February 6.
TV 2 (2015). 'Nyt kommmunalt tiltag i Greve: Dannebrog i hundelorte.' March 25. http://nyheder.tv2.dk/samfund/2015-03-25-nyt-kommunalt-tiltag-i-greve-dannebrog-i-hundelorte [accessed August 29, 2017].
Vertovec, S. (2007). 'Super-Diversity and its implications'. *Ethnic and Racial Studies*, 30(6), pp. 1024–1054.
Wimmer, A. and N. G. Schiller (2002). 'Methodological Nationalism and Beyond: Nation-State Building, Migration and the Social Sciences'. *Global Networks* 2(4), pp. 301–334.
Winge, V. (1992). *Dänische Deutche – deutche Dänen.* Heidelberg: Carl Winther – Universitätsverlag.

4 Finnish media representations of the Sámi in the 1960s and 1970s

Niina Siivikko

Introduction

Being 'Finnish' can be interpreted through both citizenship and nationality: as being ethnically Finnish, or as having Finnish nationality—although the term 'ethnic' was rarely used during the Sámi Renaissance, the period this chapter discusses. These were often intertwined in written (media) discourses about Finnishness, as in Finnish *kansa* can refer to both people and nation. In these discourses, the Sámi are both referred to as having Finnish citizenship, and of possessing the ethnic nationality of Sámi[1]—being *kansalainen* of both Finland and Sámi. This created an in-between state for Sámi living in Finland—the feeling of belonging nowhere and having no fatherland—as being Sámi granted them the ethnic nationality of Sámi, but citizenship of Finland (not Sámi). At the same time, it can be seen as contradictory to be a good Finnish citizen, while critically demanding equal rights as a Sámi national.

Identifying as part of something also means drawing borders around one's own identity, self-identifying in the process, too. At the same time, 'us' is perceived as the normal, neutral state, whereas 'them' is something different and exotic, possibly dangerous, beyond the norm. This dynamic both includes and excludes 'us' and 'them' from positions of power (e.g. Pietikäinen 2002, pp. 28–31). This becomes further emphasised when considering ethnic identity. Whereas being a Sámi is considered an ethnic identity, it is not as common for Finns to consider themselves part of a Finnish ethnic identity, but a nationality instead.[2] Ethnicity is once again a tool to separate 'us' from 'them', where *we* are the norm and *they* are something different, something exotic—something ethnic. The Sámi end up at the crossroads of ethnic and national identities, being both included and excluded in media discourses. This is also a problem when analysing media texts: often the assumption of 'Otherness' or the Finnishness of the Sámi is not written out. They struggle to act in-between identities that are not explicitly articulated or agreed upon. Examining Sámi representations in the media is vital in analysing their position in Finnish society.

The representations and self-representations of Finnish Sámi as political actors in Finland have been studied by Jukka Nyyssönen (2007), who notes the different developing identity strategies used by the Sámi during the twentieth century; one of the most important of this time was the "natural people" imagery from the Indigenous Peoples Movement. How were the Sámi defined and categorised in Finnish media both inside the notion of Finnishness—as 'our minority'—and also outside it, as the racialised, exotic 'Other', a strange remnant of a primitive past? And in which ways were these conflicting views presented and constructed? This chapter argues that this duality is also evident in the ways the Sámi's pursuit for equal rights and possibilities is seen as both the responsibility of the Finnish nation, but also something out of Finnish hands. This resulted in the Sámi adopting strategic essentialism: presenting themselves as one people and emphasising their similarities, instead of reiterating that there are a variety of Sámi languages, livelihoods, and aims that both differ inside these groups, and on an individual level.

The Sámi people in Finland are a familiar image to both Finns and many foreigners: the image of a Sámi person in the mountains, colourfully dressed, herding reindeer, is used time and again in Finnish travel marketing. As the only indigenous peoples of the EU, the Sámi have struggled through times of varying amounts of forced assimilation in the countries they live in: Sweden, Norway, Russia, and Finland. Despite this apparent visibility, the Sámi people are still unfamiliar in Finland, and among Finns there is little to no general knowledge about Sámi culture. Within the current heated debates about migration and the homogeneity of Finnishness, the Sámi are almost constantly forgotten, together with other 'old' minorities like the Roma and the Tatars, as are the political issues these groups wish to amend. Still, the Finns and the Sámi people have lived together in the current area of Finland for thousands of years. How is it possible for the Sámi to continue to remain strangers, feeling voiceless and powerless in Finnish society? How are they still seen both as 'our minority'—as almost something to be owned by the Finns—and simultaneously an exotic stranger, the 'Other'? Why have they not been able to disturb the perceived homogeneity of Finnish society? I argue that the role of the Sámi within the nation was very ambiguous, and they were constantly seen as both belonging and not belonging; they were in a state of becoming, already being, or not even wanting to be Finnish.

In this chapter, I address these questions by examining cases of Sámi representations in the Finnish media during the 1960s and 1970s. This is the time of the so-called "Sámi Renaissance", the revival of Sámi culture that had been on the brink of extinction. This happened concurrently with the efforts of different indigenous peoples and other minorities around the world, separately and spurring each other on (Smith 2012, pp. 112–116). This time period is interesting to examine because of the way the new Sámi generation—referred to in the news as the so-called "Young Radicals"—tried to take their representations into their own hands and be heard on their own terms. How did newspapers situate the Sámi in relation to the Finnish nation-state in their news articles, as the Sámi became increasingly active and critical of the government and Finnish attitudes towards them?

The media has a key role in describing, altering, and constructing ethnic and political hegemonies (e.g. van Dijk 2000, pp. 33–49). Representations become increasingly emphasised when dealing with minorities, who are rarely represented on their own terms, if at all. Representations can be seen as a form of control (Fiske 2003, p. 152).

My main sources are the leading Finnish newspaper *Helsingin Sanomat* (Helsinki), and the local northern newspaper *Lapin Kansa* (Rovaniemi), in which the Sámi are clearly more visible. While the latter was easier to obtain for the Sámi as readers and writers, the former was the main reflector and constructor of their representations in Finnish media.

In this cultural–historical study, my aim is to critically examine how Sámi representations were constructed, challenged, and/or confirmed within language practices, especially those used in newspaper articles concerning the position of the Sámi within the Finnish nation-state. I approach my data qualitatively through critical discourse analysis, where my starting point is to critically examine the discursive representations of the Sámi within the historical context of the existing power imbalance in Finnish society.

First, I introduce the Nuorgam family, who were sent to represent Finland—and more particularly, Finnish Lapland—to Spain in 1965, a few years before young Sámi radicals took a stand to fight against the assimilation of their culture. Then, I present conversations between young Sámi activists and government officials concerning Sámi rights in Finland in 1971. In both cases, my attention is on the way the Sámi were simultaneously situated inside the idea of Finnishness and outside of it, perhaps ending up stuck in-between—not a separate people of their own, but not seen as Finns, either. How are the Sámi considered to be Finnish, representative of Finland, and belonging to Finland? Their ever-shifting positions can be discerned from the ways they and their rights and representations are described—what is taken as a given, and what is contested?

Historical context: The Sámi in twentieth-century Finland

The Sámi people are spread across four countries—Finland, Sweden, Norway, and Russia—and have traditionally made their livelihood through reindeer herding, fishing, and other natural sources. As Irja Seurujärvi-Kari et al. describe (2011, pp. 27–28), researchers disagree on whether the Sámi can be seen as victims of colonisation (in support of this position, see, for example, Eidheim 1997; Kuokkanen 2007; Niemi 1997; for against, see Enbuske 2003; Lähteenmäki 2004), but as Lehtola (2012) states, terms like colonialism and subjugation are also useful starting points to examine the dynamic between the Sámi and the majority—not merely as victims of the colonising West, but not equal participants, either. He underlines the multiplicity of situations that can be seen in these interactions. He sees both the colonising majority, and the colonised Sámi, as a varied group of people with various motives and positions from which to act (Lehtola 2012, pp. 15–17). This is where I position my research, too: I see the Sámi as objects of colonisation, but not solely as helpless objects; instead, I see them as actors capable of bettering their own situations, no matter the result.

Within the contexts of these four countries, the Sámi had somewhat different lived experiences, but they all—more or less—faced forced assimilation strategies. Sweden took the route of preserving the Sámi: they had special nomad schools, and their livelihood was relatively well protected, but at the same time, those giving up on reindeer herding were seen as giving up on being Sámi. In Norway, the state was extremely involved in 'transforming' the Sámi to Norwegian through strong assimilation policies. This was implemented, for example, by tying the right to own land to passing a difficult Norwegian language test. Before and after Finnish independence from Russia in 1917, the rise in a Finnish sense of nationalism meant that the Sámi were seen as inferior. Also, seeing the Sámi and their livelihoods as inferior was common for many Western countries (Lantto 2010 pp. 549–550). Finnish scientists interested in eugenics measured Sámi skulls and tried to categorise them amongst the then considered inferior 'Asian' races, while at the same time trying to enshrine that there was a long history of 'civilisation' among Finns. After all, Finns themselves had been seen as having 'Asian' roots in the nineteenth and early twentieth century, and this was something from which the newly independent nation wanted to distance itself (Lehtola 2012, pp. 179). To actively reposition themselves in the modern Western world through science, the Finns framed the Sámi as a people without history, a primitive remnant of what had been—something opposite to Finns. This racialisation of the Sámi provided the young nation-state's project with the means to become part of the 'civilised', modern West. Discourses around the Sámi revolved mainly around whether it was already too late to preserve them, or if it was better for the Sámi themselves to become modern: to become Finns.

For Finland, the Second World War ended with the Lapland War in 1944. After a treaty with the Soviet Union, the last German soldiers retreated from Lapland in 1945. To prepare for the upcoming acts of war, most of Lapland's population was evacuated south to Ostrobothnia, while others went to Eastern Sweden. The Sámi spent the half-year long war in Ostrobothnia, in the middle of Finnish farming society; many arrived without possessions or money. They also had limited means to do well this far away from their familiar environments, as their livelihoods were so closely tied to Lappish nature. For many Sámi, this was also the first time their livelihoods, traditions, and habits were viscerally compared to Finnish agricultural society, and met with prejudices (e.g. Lehtola 2012, pp. 371–380). Combined with the devastating circumstances they faced, this created a strong feeling of inferiority when comparing themselves to the surrounding Finns. These feelings were additionally reinforced after they were able to return home—during the war, the retreating German troops had demolished most of Lapland's infrastructure. Everything had to be rebuilt, and so houses built by Finnish standards replaced the old traditional Sámi buildings. Along with the rebuilding came Finnish builders and more Finnish customs, compounded by expanding road networks, and an increasing number of Finnish settlers. All this caused rapid assimilation of the Sámi into Finnish society; the Skolt Sámi also resettled in Finland, having previously been based in Soviet Russia.

Another major factor that contributed to assimilation was the school system. Before the changes that came as a result of the 1947 law of compulsory education, children living in remote districts were not participating in state-run education. In Sámi areas, this meant that education was provided by Sámi-speaking catechist teachers, who travelled from village to village, teaching children a programme of reading and writing, combined with Christian lessons. In 1947, the state decreed that children in remote areas were also required to attend school. There were good intentions behind the changes —now all children would receive an adequate and 'equal' education. However, this was implemented by creating the new residential school system, which resulted in severe ramifications for Sámi children and their parents. As northern Finland still lacked roads, Sámi children often had no means to visit home during their schooling years. In many schools, it was more or less forbidden to use Sámi languages, including outside of school hours. Because of this, many children were able to visit their home only during longer holidays, and many of them became alienated from their native language, and traditional Sámi handicrafts and livelihoods. Many reports also recount stories of strong hierarchies that involved abuse or intense bullying (Rasmus 2008; Lehtola 2014). On top of these hierarchies were Finnish children, and the Sámi often had to endure racist name-calling, mocking, and harassment (Puuronen 2014, pp. 328–331). For many Sámi children, the experience of their school years convinced them that their own culture was a dying, primitive one, and that it was best to try and become Finnish. This was also something Sámi parents often firmly believed in—despite identifying that their children were drifting away from their traditions and language, many felt that it was the only way for the children to survive. The school system ingrained in children a strong sense of Finnish cultural homogeneity. Many Sámi children started to try and hide their heritage, "to become more Finnish than the Finns themselves", as Iisko Sara recounts in a 2010 documentary *Suomi tuli Saamenmaahan* [Finland came to Sámiland], that described the effects of Sámi residential school experiences (*Suomi tuli Saamenmaahan*, 2010).

In her pamphlet *Saamelaiset* [The Sámi], Sámi author Kirsti Paltto described her feelings of going through the Finnish educational system, and becoming aware of the fact that her own Sámi heritage was considered inferior:

> All this raised a strong suspicion in me, if I had the right to belong to [something] other than the Finnish race. I started to be afraid and ashamed of being a Lapp[3], because I naturally didn't want to be an uncivilised fool. I wanted to be a human, equal to other Finnish citizens. I started to hide my being a Lapp. (Paltto 1973)

The residential school system played a major part in crafting Sámi identity in the latter half of the twentieth century, causing feelings of inferiority and shame. At the same time, it also created new kinds of networks and possibilities for young Sámi to operate in Finnish society, which contributed to the launching of the Sámi Renaissance from the late 1960s. A new, educated, more radical Sámi generation started to rise and debate Sámi rights. These so-called "Young Radicals" were products and witnesses of the assimilating Finnish residential school system; they were educated according to Finnish standards, and capable of working within Finnish society and its rules. They started to both actively revitalise Sámi culture, and act in different political spheres, seeking to gain equal rights in Finnish society, and to ensure the continuity and vitality of the stigmatised Sámi culture.

One of the young generation's undeniably brightest stars was Nils-Aslak Valkeapää (in Sámi: Áillohaš), a musician, painter, and writer who understood the evolution of Sámi culture as something essential to keep alive. He felt that a living culture needed to be adaptive—not something to be preserved in its most traditional forms, but something in which traditions and the present met. He wanted to "be genuine, but not in a preserving way—my will is to create something new, live in the culture I happened to be born into, and also breathe along with influences from new cultures" (Valkeapää 1971, p. 61). His thoughts were met with both praise and resistance inside the Sámi community. Sámi yoik artist Ivvár Niillas (in Finnish: Nils Porsanger) stated in a 2008 interview that Áillohaš was "otherwise a great man, but completely destroyed the traditional yoik" (Hirvasvuopio 2008, p. 62). Valkeapää's work on reviving Sámi culture through adaptation not preservation was met with praise and criticism throughout his career.

These 'young radicals' were also taking a new, more critical look into politics and the position of the Sámi in Finnish society. They identified differential treatment between the Sámi people and the Finns, and demanded that they should be allowed and supported to live as Sámi, use Sámi languages, and practise Sámi livelihoods. As *Lapin Kansa* wrote in 1965: "The young ones are not anymore settling for images of themselves constructed by others, but are observing their situation critically, demanding remedies for ongoing issues" (Lukkari 1965). The new generation was not approached as heroes by the older generations, but quite the opposite: by criticising the Finnish government, they were seen as endangering the sympathetic relations the Sámi previously had with Finns—they were not seen as good citizens anymore, but ungrateful instead. Residential schools created 'native' intellectuals who had the means to function in Western society on its terms, but who were simultaneously educated away from their indigenous cultures, both geographically and ideologically. This widened the gap between them and the older, uneducated generations (Smith 2012, pp. 71–75). In Finland this gap was specifically manifested in the struggles around the representational body for the Sámi. *Samii Litto* was founded in 1945 as the first Sámi-run association in Finland, with the aim of empowering the Sámi to act on their own behalf with the authorities (Lehtola 2012, p. 452) rather than being represented by Finnish-led organisations. However, by the end of the 1960s, the younger generation strongly felt that *Samii Litto* was too old-fashioned to represent all Sámi in Finland; additionally, it was inaccessible to new members. They suggested that the Sámi needed a new, genuinely common Sámi association to act as their representative body. In the end, the matter was settled by the Finnish government, which appointed a Sámi committee in 1971. Based on the committee's work, the Saami Delegation was elected first by trial election in 1972 and confirmed in a second election in 1974 (Lehtola 2005).

New, more conscious Sámi identity politics were also being built in the Nordic Sámi cooperation. The Sámi took a step towards strategic essentialism, representing themselves more tightly as one entity, instead of several minority Sámi groups speaking different languages and sharing different cultures (Valkonen 2009, pp. 79–84). As declared in the Sámi Cultural Policy and decided upon in the 7th Sámi Conference in 1971: "We are Sámi and we want to be Sámi. [...] We are one people, we have our own language and our own culture and social structure" (Nordic Saami Council 1974). This more well-organised approach gave the Sámi more visibility and built a stronger spirit of solidarity within the whole Sámi community. It was also connected to the rising global indigenous movement, with which the Sámi people associated themselves. There were still several different strategies in use, and as Nyyssönen notes (2007), some of them underlined the role of the Sámi as objects to save, while others described them as capable actors. This fluctuation was also seen in news reporting—for example, *Helsingin Sanomat* seems to have changed their viewpoint during the 1970s, transitioning from writing about "the last years of the Sámi" (e.g. Saari 1970) to presenting more active descriptions, such as a people fighting for their rights and survival (e.g. Korhonen 1971b).

This process of creating a more unified Nordic[4] Sámi community also resulted in internal disharmony within the community. The diversity of Sámi cultures again became less visible to the general public. Many Sámi people also felt that their voices were not being heard, as differing aims and opinions were stifled in order to cater for the demand for unanimity. From an outsider's perspective, these internal negotiations were seen as signs of petty infighting; the media frequently stated that the Sámi needed to be unanimous and clear about their aims, otherwise these uncertainties could be interpreted as indecision and a lack of conviction.

This demand for unanimity was often voiced in the media. During the 1971 "Sami Culture Week", the governor of Lapland, Martti Miettunen "hoped in his speech that the Sámi would be unanimous among themselves" (Helsingin Sanomat 1971a). The demand was not wholly unreasonable: to reach one's goals, one must first set them. Though upon closer examination, it becomes problematic, especially when constantly repeated. What was considered unanimous enough? How is it possible for any large group of people to strive for exactly the same goals, and to prioritise them unanimously? Even the founding of the democratic Sámi Parliament in the early 1970s did not resolve this dilemma. In theory, the Sámi had elected certain persons to speak on their behalf, but the discussions about unanimity persisted. For example, in 1980, Otto Timonen from the province-based federation of Lapland (*Lapin Maakuntaliitto*) remarked in his *Lapin Kansa* writing series about Sámi politics: "Articulating Sámi politics within party politics is an extremely difficult and delicate task, since many decisions concerning the Sámi require such comprehensive unanimity" (Timonen 1980). Without unanimity, there seemed to be no progress, despite the role of the elected Sámi Delegation as the only official Sámi representative. Striving for unanimity also delayed many debates and created more discordance inside the Sámi community

In the last decades, the Sámi have managed to take many steps forward. For example, Sámi languages are more available in Sámi area schools, and they are represented in a daily news report *Ođđasat*, produced by the national broadcasting services in Finland, Sweden, and Norway. At the same time, the Sámi still feel that their voice is not heard. Finland has rejected many essential laws to secure and enshrine Sámi culture, and has made several decisions concerning Sámi areas and livelihoods without consulting the Sámi people, or the Sámi parliament.

Representing our nation

In 1965, a Sámi family was chosen by the Finnish airline company Finnair to act as travel ambassadors for Finnish Lapland. The Nuorgam family—consisting of father Hans, mother Ida, and two of their eight children, Hilma and Eino—was sent to Spain in May 1965. The family spent a few weeks touring the country and giving a vast number of interviews to the Spanish media. Hans Nuorgam was appointed an honorary consul general of Benidorm, and the family even met General Franco. Despite the distance between Finland and Spain, the 'operation' was widely covered by the Finnish media, with almost daily reports, especially by *Lapin Kansa* (e.g. 1965a, b, c). The family's journey provides an interesting case through which to examine Sámi representations in Finland—after all, they were handpicked to represent Finland.

The journey was proudly reported in the Finnish media to have been a success. It was also announced that although General Franco had received several guests in addition to the Nuorgam family during the same day, only the Nuorgam family was used to illustrate the reception event in every Spanish newspaper; some newspapers were even said to have featured them in front page pictures and interviews (Lapin Kansa 1965d). The family was further noted to have been a perfect choice as "the delegation", as they "represented their own tribe and our nation" in a trustworthy and pleasant manner throughout the journey. In this description, both the inclusion and the exclusion of the Sámi is apparent, as they are represented as both 'us' and 'them'.

Hans Nuorgam was particularly praised for not slipping out of his gentlemanly manner, despite enjoying the vast and readily available free alcohol.

The 18-year-old son Eino was reported as abstaining from alcohol completely. It was possible this was noted because Sámi stereotypes of the time often involved alcohol. The family was applauded at the end of the journey for "making Finland known" in such an effective way (Lapin Kansa 1965d). The family itself was reported as responding to all the "hubbub" around them with quiet, amused calmness (L.P. 1965).

Irja Seurujärvi-Kari notes how indigenous people around the world are often instrumentalised as exotic tourist attractions, but are otherwise ignored when, for example, making claims to rights and demanding changes (Seurujärvi-Kari et al. 2011). In Finland, the Sámi were repeatedly used to illustrate and represent the genuine, exotic Finland (or more specifically, Lapland). However, authentic Sámi culture was not valued as important; many newspaper articles from the 60s and 70s depict visiting heads of states, international sports competitions, or tourist groups adorned in fake Sámi costumes. Invoking the idea of the Sámi was more important than accurate representations of Sámi people. This was also rarely problematised within media discourses. On some occasions, the use of Sámi costumes—or more specifically, the use of Sámi-like costumes—was criticised by Sámi representatives, but their complaints seem to have mainly been dismissed by the media (e.g. Lapin Kansa 1971; Pelleilyyn kyllästynyt 1966). Notably, there was also internal dissent among the Sámi, especially from the older generation: some felt the fake costumes should be understood as a sign of admiration—imitation as a form of flattery—towards their colourful culture, and so should not be criticised. The Nuorgam family was also expected to constantly wear their colourful, traditional, woollen costumes throughout their trip (Saijets, 2018).

According to Sari Pietikäinen (2000), who studied the representations of ethnic minorities in *Helsingin Sanomat* in 1985 to 1993, the Sámi are rarely written about in the Finnish media. They are seldom provided with a chance to provide a statement or reflect upon issues that concern them. Instead, this authority is given to non-Sámi Finnish authorities. The news related to Sámi people also often concentrates on contexts of crisis, problems, or searches for the value of a certain exoticness, and in many cases, those finally permitted to speak are ostracised within their own communities for being singled out for this privilege. It becomes more galling that these are the conditions which seem to naturally dominate those few instances in which the Sámi *are* talked about, considering these are situations when they should have the possibility to speak for themselves. This 'speaking about' can also be identified earlier in the twentieth century, during the Sámi Renaissance (Siivikko 2015).

Sending the Nuorgam family to Spain in 1965's 'Operation Lapland' resulted in the media literally concentrating on the exotic value of the Sámi in relation to travel marketing, especially (but not only) in Lapland. This trope has become more evident in recent years, as stereotypically Sámi imagery is still carelessly used as markers of 'genuine Finland'. In 2015, the Finnish government's tourist bureau, *Visit Finland*, promoted travelling to Finland with their video series *100 Days of Polar Night Magic*. In one video, a

'Western' couple was depicted travelling in Lapland, among the snow and mountains. Occasionally, the video cut to a Sámi hut, where actors, faces dirtied, were dressed in fake Sámi costumes, dancing in an animal-like trance. Sámi representatives contacted the bureau and the offending parts were subsequently removed, but the marketing director of *Visit Finland* replied in a statement to the Sámi: "I'm very sorry if this person has felt this is disrespectful, it has not been our intention, but we wanted to highlight certain folk traditions" (Yle Uutiset 2015). As is made clear by this incident, the conversation around cultural appropriation of Sámi culture in Finland has not even properly started. Notably different from Operation Lapland in the 1960s is of course the fact that during that time, it was still considered important to send actual Sámi people to Spain, instead of actors wearing fake Sámi clothing.

"Also a Finn"—Belonging to the Finnish nation-state with rights and responsibilities

> Today a Lapp is also a Finn. He would like to improve his conditions, become a Finn in all areas of his life, too.[5] (Kalervo, 1969)

The above quote from *Lapin Kansa*, seems to suggest two things: "a Lapp"—a Sámi in Finland—is already a Finn, but also that becoming a Finn *completely* is about changing and enhancing one's living conditions. It embodies the differing opinions on how 'the Sámi situation' should be solved, implying that how Sámi people live(d) is inherently defective, and they need to change and improve these 'conditions'. Overall, the situation was framed so as to very much be dependant on the actions of the Sámi themselves.

Together with equal rights came equal responsibilities, as another editorial in *Lapin Kansa* stated in 1970:

> The situation is such that our Lapps are considered a part of the whole Finnish people and feel like it, too, whenever their rights and responsibilities are concerned. ... All [development of Sámi rights] is, in the end, the sole responsibility of the Lapps themselves. Unless they don't see it necessary to solve it by themselves, the Finns have no way of doing so. The sole responsibility of Finnish society will be to take care that the legislation will not hinder but instead support the aspirations of maintaining their distinctive culture. (Lapin Kansa, 1970)

Assurances were often made that once the Sámi made their aims clear, then legislation would not stand in their way.

From the Finnish point of view, Sámi rights were understood from two perspectives. On the one hand, the significance and value of Sámi culture were seen as notable: Sámi livelihoods, handicrafts—and most importantly Sámi languages—were all seen as worth preserving if possible, as evidenced by their importance to Finnish travel marketing. The achievement of these goals was reported with pride and joy, even though some commentators were at the same time certain that all hope was already lost, no matter how many books were to be published in Sámi languages. It was often acknowledged that the Sámi needed governmental help in supporting their culture, but at the same time, it was repeatedly mentioned that they were not discriminated against in any way, or if they were, it was not intentional. As Justice of the Supreme Court, Voitto Saario, said in 1971: "In Finland—as far as the government is concerned—no group of people has intentionally been driven into a worse position than the rest of the population" (Helsingin Sanomat 1971b). This sentiment was often repeated in the media. The Sámi were seen as Finnish citizens with equal rights to live in Finnish society, and if there were any defects in the system, they were not there intentionally and would be repaired as soon as the Sámi voiced their clear opinion on what should be done. Unfortunately, this did not seem to happen.[6] A current research project on the development of indigenous issues considers this ever-renewed hope for change as another tool to exercise power, without ever needing to actually facilitate change (Yle Areena 2017). Perhaps the deep gap between the older, more moderate generation, and the young Sámi radicals came from this hope, too. The former wanted to hang onto that hope, thinking it was necessary to remain as "good citizens" in the eyes of the Finns, while the latter were more doubtful, and openly critical of the state.

Some authors saw the decision of becoming a Finn as also a question of language, arguing that Sámi languages could not be sustained for practical reasons alone. As someone wrote under the acronym A.Y-S in *Lapin Kansa*:

> They have to choose whether they want to be a member of Finnish society, in which case they need to use Finnish, or if they want to be part of a Fennoscandic Lappish group, as sort of "Northern Kurds" [...] As Finnish citizens the Lapps have the same rights and possibilities as everyone else in this country. (1975)

Not everyone agreed with the author that Sámi people should give up their language in order to become part of Finnish society, but the notion of the solution being a choice made by the Sámi became enshrined. With Skolt Sámi, the importance of responsibility and progress was especially noted, as a columnist called Huki wrote in *Lapin Kansa*: "Finnish society is not discriminating against anyone looking for or doing honest work. When it comes to the vanishing of the Skolt culture, it's the expected progress and the natural fate of the people" (1970). This notion was also repeated in an article in *Helsingin Sanomat*, where the "fragile Skolt culture" was constructed as extremely endangered, and the author pondered whether "the Skolt children had the ability to transition into the Finnish lifestyle" (Korhonen 1971a). The Skolts were perhaps seen as less able to make the choice to 'assimilate' than the rest of the Sámi. The headline for the article was 'The Skolt on the first steps of "the ladder to better living standards"'. A better life was seen to be more out of reach for the Skolts than other Sámi communities. It was also framed as somewhat questionable as to whether they were actually able to make it, the implication being they had only managed "the first step" of the ladder so far.

The Skolts were treated as an exotic minority within an already exotic minority. Evacuated from the Soviet Union after the Second World War, they differed from the rest of the Sámi due to their orthodox religion and the demanding situations they faced as settlers. They were often referred to as separate from the other Sámi, as a headline describes in 1968: 'The problems of the Sámi and the Skolts' (Aikio 1968). The main difference in the media's treatment seems to have been pity: the Skolts were often presented as pitiful and in dire need of help (e.g. Tanhua 2014). In the end, they were still seen as responsible for their own fate, as a columnist in *Lapin Kansa* wrote in 1970: "As long as the Skolts—and the Lapps, too—are able to present reasonable and realisable plans and hopes, then Finnish legislation is on their side every step of the way" (*LK* 10 January, 1970). So again, it was argued that it was wholly the responsibility of the Skolts and other Sámi people to enhance their situations; despite wielding the majority of societal power, the Finns could only play a 'supporting' role, following their lead to address changes in legislation and policy.

van Dijk (2000) refers to Barker's (1981) concept of a "new racism" that aims to present racism as "democratic and respectable". Its forms are dominant, ethnically hegemonic, and seemingly legitimate, which renders minorities' resistance almost futile (van Dijk 2000, pp. 33–34). The ideal of democracy embedded in the racialisation of the Sámi was also clearly visible in Finnish discourse on the Sámi, as hints or direct accusations of racist or undemocratic actions were seen as dangerous insults against Finnish society (e.g. Kansalainen 1971). The older Sámi generation seems to have agreed with this view. They believed in the possibility of Sámi participation in the Finnish political sphere and were not against it; they strongly believed that they had equal opportunities, given they were often active participants in municipal administration (Nyyssönen 2007).

The Sámi were seen as the responsibility of Finnish society, but at the same time it was highlighted that they had the same responsibilities and rights of any other Finnish citizen. Because of this, did the responsibilities of enhancing Sámi rights fall solely on Sámi shoulders? The Sámi were struggling to decide the best strategy to survive, and many disagreed on the details of possible suitable solutions. It was heavily debated whether it was possible to remain Sámi while still exercising equal rights in Finnish society, or whether this meant that one had to assimilate to a Finnish way of life; this led to debates about whether this shift in identity could be seen as an inevitable, positive, or undesirable development.

The exotic 'Other': Accepted even as 'faulty'?

> Being a Sámi has been seen as a fault, which has tried to be repaired. [...] As a general feature, there seem to be two possibilities in curing the Sámi. One, where they become part of the majority population and are accepted by them, and the other, where there seems to be no real recovery, as these Sámi don't understand that their condition is faulty. As the representative of the Sámi, I present as the optimal solution that the majority accepts us as 'faulty', as different, as Sámi. The other option is that being Sámi is not seen as a fault anymore. (Lapin Kansa 1975)

In the above quote, Iisko Sara exhaustively sums up the views of the young Sámi radicals of the time. They felt strongly that "becoming a Finn" was not their aim, but it was something that was repeatedly demanded of them. Instead, they wished to be equal as Sámi people, a separate, independent group, clearly different from the Finns. For the younger generation, this view was perhaps formed in the residential schools, where ethnic borders were often more distinctively drawn. Ethnic groups often become more tight-knit in residential school environments (Eriksen 2003 pp. 90–91). For the young Sámi radicals, the shared 'Sámi spirit' acted as a source of motivation.

However, this view was not only something shared among the young, residential school-trained Sámi community. Professor Erkki Asp, a Finnish sociologist who had studied the Sámi, recognised the Sámi as both Finnish and a separate group from Finns:

> It is important to remember that the Sámi living in Finland are Finnish, and so under the same treatment as any fellow countryman. But it's also important to underline that the Sámi, with their cultural background and livelihoods, form a group for which we have to be extra attentive. (Asp 1971)

For the Sámi, the Sámi Cultural Policy of 1971 was a clear illustration of this. By declaring that they wanted to be seen as one people with their own distinctive and valuable culture, they took a decisive step away from assimilation, stating that it was not a way of improving Sámi life (Nordic Saami Council 1974).

Many Sámi people also felt that Western scientists had treated the Sámi as an inferior group—as objects to research, measure, and examine. Nils-Aslak Valkeapää said during the Sámi Culture Week in 1971: "[The Sámi] have been researched scientifically, so that they'd feel inferior to the other Finnish people" (Paakkolanvaara 1971). He positioned the Sámi within other people in Finland but argued that they were (made to feel) inferior. Scientific research, especially earlier eugenic practices, had racialised the Sámi, and created profound shame and feelings of inferiority regarding their own culture, of being a Sámi. These experiences of being racialised through examinations, measurements, and observations are common among indigenous peoples. As Linda Tuhiwai Smith writes: research is seen as one of the dirtiest words within indigenous communities (Smith 2012, p. 1).

Conclusion

After being on the verge of assimilation, the young educated Sámi generation rose to demand equal rights from the Finnish government. Their claims were received with conflicting views in the Finnish media, both within Sámi and Finnish communities. The development in Finnish Sámi discourse is already visible in the Nuorgam family trip in 1965 and continues through to Sámi Culture Week in 1971. Whereas in 1965, the Sámi were seen from inside the community as in need of more active politics, in the early 1970s, that discussion had already shifted, and the younger generation were considered to be *too* active. At the same time, they had taken steps to actively wield the Sámi image instead of being silent and smiling representatives of the Finnish nation-state. Valkeapää, for example, hosted *Juoigamat*, a yoik television programme where he presented differing Sámi narratives to viewers, and performed in the fells with other yoik artists (1971). It was a much more active role, and this form of speaking underlined the possibility to separate Sámi identity from the Finnish projection of "our minority". For the older generations, the assimilation of Sámi culture was prevented by preservation, and staying on good terms with the state—acting as 'good citizens'. For the younger generations, assimilation was rejected by constantly renewing their cultures, and demanding to be treated as citizens, even when identifying as Sámi nationals, not Finns.

The language used in the studied news articles defined both Sámi and Finnish national identities as diverse, and the Sámi were situated in various positions, depending on the context or the writer. The Sámi presented themselves, and were represented, both as dying and revitalised; helpless victims and capable actors; and as an 'Other' outside Finnish society that is also included within it. This created a difficult position for them: as Finnish citizens, they seemingly had access to all the possibilities within Finnish society, but just not as non-Finnish nationals—as Sámi. Even though they were seen as citizens, they were not Finnish nationals, but instead racialised as non-equal 'Others'. A more in-depth analysis of the linguistic choices within this period of news discourse still remains to be done, and will no doubt support a fruitful summation into these dualling attitudes and the prevailing assumptions embedded in them. The Finnish/Sámi situation is after all, still largely conflicted and unresolved, and so this historical context can hopefully provide new perspectives that will help to break the cycle of delays and reassessments that have plagued efforts to enshrine Sámi autonomy and agency within Finnish politics and legislation thus far.

Notes

1 In this chapter I use the term 'Sámi' to refer to many different Sámi groups living in Finland. It is important to note that there are actually three different Sámi languages spoken: Northern Sámi, Skolt Sámi, and Inari Sámi. Of these, the latter two are most in danger of disappearing today.
2 I identify as a Sámi researcher of Finnish nationality.
3 "Lapp" (in Finnish: Lappalainen) is nowadays seen as a pejorative term by many. In my own writing, I use the term Sámi.
4 The Russian Sámi joined the Nordic Saami Council in 1992, at which time the name was changed to Saami Council.
5 All translations from the Finnish media are by me.
6 For example, land ownership rights still remain largely unsolved. A recent study conducted by the Finnish government found several challenges in different aspects of Sámi rights in Finland. For more, see: Heinämäki, Leena et al.: *Saamelaisten oikeuksien toteutuminen: kansainvälinen oikeusvertaileva tutkimus.* Valtioneuvoston selvitys- ja tutkimustoiminnan julkaisusarja 4/2017. Helsinki, 2017.

References

Aikio, O. (1968). 'Saamelaisten ja kolttien ongelmat'. *Lapin Kansa*, 4 September.
Asp, E. (1971). 'Saamelaisuuden tulevaisuudennäkymiä'. *Lapin Kansa*, 2 March.
Eidheim, H. (1997). 'Ethno-political development among the Sami after World War II. The invention of selfhood', in H. Gaski (ed.), *Sami Culture in a New Era*. Kárášjohka: Davvi Girji OS, pp. 29–61.
Enbuske, M. (2003). 'Lapin asuttamisen historia', in I. Massa and H. Snellman (eds.), *Lappi: maa, kansat, kulttuurit*. Helsinki: SKS.
Eriksen, T. H. (1993/2003). *Ethnicity and Nationalism*. London: Pluto Press.
Fiske, J. (1993/2003). 'Toimi maailmanlaajuisesti, ajattele paikallisesti'. Transl. Juha Herkman. Original title: 'Act globally, think locally'. Original book: *Power Plays, Power Works* (1993), in *Erilaisuus*. Ed. Mikko Lehtonen and Olli Löytty. Tampere: Vastapaino, 2003, pp. 131–153.
Helsingin Sanomat (1971a). 'Viiden teesin ohjelma saamelaispolitiikalle', 1 March.
Helsingin Sanomat (1971b). 'YK:n rotusyrjintäsopimus edellyttää toimia Suomelta', 26 May.
Hirvasvuopio, A. (2008). *Gárddi luhtte lávddi ala—Poroaidalta esiintymislavalle. Saamelaiset elementit tenonsaamelaisessa musiikissa kolmen sukupolven aikana.* MA thesis, University of Tampere, Tampere.
Huki (1970). 'Tätäkö on olla koltta Suomessa'. *Lapin Kansa*, 10 January.
Juoigamat (1971). [TV programme] TV2: Yle.
Kalervo (1969). 'Taka-Lapin maisemat houkuttelevat kulkijaa'. *Lapin Kansa*, 25 September.
Kansalainen, L. (1971). 'Myötä ja vastavirtaan'. *Lapin Kansa*, 25 February.
Korhonen, J. (1971a). 'Koltat elintasotikkaiden ensimmäisillä askelmilla'. *Helsingin Sanomat*, 24 January.
Korhonen, J. (1971b). 'Saamelaiset taisteluun oikeuksiensa puolesta'. *Helsingin Sanomat*, 27 February.
Kuokkanen, R. (2007). 'Saamelaiset ja kolonialismin vaikutukset nykypäivänä', in J. Kuortti, M. Lehtonen and O. Löytty (eds.), *Kolonialismin jäljet. Keskustat, periferiat ja Suomi*. Helsinki: Gaudeamus, pp. 142–155.

Lähteenmäki, M. (2004). Kalotin kansaa. Rajankäynnit ja vuorovaikutus Pohjoiskalotilla 1808–1889. *Historiallisia Tutkimuksia*, 220. Helsinki: SKS.
Lantto, P. (2010). 'Borders, citizenship and change: the case of the Sami people, 1751–2008', *Citizenship Studies*, 14(5), pp. 543–556.
Lapin Kansa (1965a). 'Nuorgamit matadorien seurassa Madridissa', 1 June.
Lapin Kansa (1965b). 'Franco otti eilen vastaan poromies Nuorgamin perheen', 3 June.
Lapin Kansa (1965c). 'Hans Nuorgamista kunniapääkonsuli', 6 June.
Lapin Kansa (1965d). 'Operaatio Lappi' komeili Espanjan lehtien etusivuilla', 9 June.
Lapin Kansa (1970). 'Saamelaisten asia oikeille raiteille', 17 July.
Lapin Kansa (1971). 'Saamelaispuvun käyttö jälleen pohdittavana', 5 February.
Lapin Kansa (1975). 'Vähemmistöt haluavat yhteistyötä', 19 April.
Lehtola, V. (2005). *Saamelaisten parlamentti*. Inari: Saamelaiskäräjät.
Lehtola, V. (2012). *Saamelaiset suomalaiset*. Helsinki: Suomalaisen Kirjallisuuden Seura.
Lehtola, V. (2014). 'Katekeettakouluista kansakouluihin—saamelaisten kouluhistoriaa 1900-luvun alkupuoliskolla', in P. Keskitalo, V. Lehtola and M. Paksuniemi, (eds.) *Saamelaisten kansanopetuksen ja koulunkäynnin historia Suomessa*. [online] Turku: Migration Institute of Finland, pp. 44–62. Available at: http://www.migrationin stitute.fi/files/pdf/A50.pdf [Accessed 14 August 2018].
Lukkari, H. (1965). 'Saamelaisuus—illuusioko?' *Lapin Kansa*, 24 January.
Niemi, E. (1997). 'Sami history and the frontier myth. A perspective on Northern Sami spatial and rights history', in H. Gaski (ed.), *Sami Culture in a New Era*. Kárášjohka: Davvi Girji OS, pp. 62–85.
Nordic Saami Council (1974). Saamelaisten kulttuuripoliittinen ohjelma. Hyväksytty VII pohjoismaisessa saamelaiskonferenssissa Jällivaarassa 11.–14.8.1971.
Nyyssönen, J. (2007). *"Everybody recognized that we were not white". Sami Identity Politics in Finland, 1945–1990*. Tromsø: University of Tromsø.
Paakkolanvaara, H. (1971). 'Saamelaiskulttuurin viikko. Tietoja vähemmistöille enemmistön ehdoin'. *Helsingin Sanomat*, 26 February.
Paltto, K. (1973). *Saamelaiset*. Helsinki: Tammi.
"Pelleilyyn kyllästynyt" (1966). 'Miksi saamelaisten kansallispuku'. *Lapin Kansa*. 18 February.
Pietikäinen, S. (2000). *Discourses of Differentiation*. Jyväskylä: University of Jyväskylä, pp. 21.
Pietikäinen, S. (2002). 'Etniset vähemmistöt uutisissa—käsitteitä ja aikaisempien tutkimusten kertomaa', in P. Raittila (ed.) *Etnisyys ja rasismi journalismissa*. Tampere: Tampere University Press, pp. 14–30.
Puuronen, V. (2014). 'Saamelaiset, koulu ja rasismi', in P. Keskitalo, V. Lehtola and M. Paksuniemi (eds.) *Saamelaisten kansanopetuksen ja koulunkäynnin historia Suomessa*. [online] Turku: Migration Institute of Finland, pp. 320–337. Available at: http://www.migrationinstitute.fi/files/pdf/A50.pdf [Accessed 8 October 2018].
Rasmus, M. (2008). *Bággu vuolgit, bággu birget. Sámemánáid ceavzinstrategiijat Suoma álbmotskuvlla ásodagain 1950–1960-logus*. Oulu: Giellagas.
Saari, M. (1970). 'Elääkö saamen heimo viimeisiä vuosiaan'. *Helsingin Sanomat*, 19 April.
Said, E. (1978/2003). *Orientalism*. London: Penguin Books.
Saijets, M. (2018). Saamelaisperheen erikoinen matka diktaattorin vieraaksi—Nuorgamin perhe piipahti Francon hovissa yli 50 vuotta sitten. [online] Yle Uutiset. Available at: https://yle.fi/uutiset/3-10215303 [Accessed 8 October 2018].

Seurujärvi-Kari, I., Halinen, P. and Pulkkinen, R. (eds.) (2011). *Saamentutkimus tänään*. Helsinki: SKS.

Siivikko, N. (2015). *Kaikuja Saamenmaalta. Saamelaiskysymys suomalaismediassa vuonna 1971*. MA thesis, University of Turku, Turku.

Smith, L. (2012). *Decolonizing methodologies*. 2nd ed. Dunedin: Otago University Press.

Suomi tuli Saamenmaahan. (2010). [film] Directed by A. Ahola. Finland: Ima filbma- ja sátneduodji.

Tanhua, S. (2014). *Kurjat koltat, siirtomaaherrojen uhrit?: kolttasaamelainen yhteisö lehdistön kuvaamana vuosina 1964–1972*. MA thesis, University of Oulu, Oulu.

Timonen, O. (1980). 'Suomen saamelaispolitiikasta III'. *Lapin Kansa*, 15 March.

Valkeapää, N. (1971). *Terveisiä Lapista*. Helsinki: Otava.

Valkonen, S. (2009). *Poliittinen saamelaisuus*. Tampere: Vastapaino.

van Dijk, T. (2000). 'Media research and ethnic minorities: Mapping the field', in S. Cottle (ed.), *Ethnic Minorities and the Media*. Maidenhead: Open University Press, pp. 33–49.

Y-S, A. (1975). 'Lapin asiat rakentuvat'. *Lapin Kansa*, 3 May.

Yle Areena (2017). Alkuperäiskansat ja toivon valta. [podcast] Alkuperäiskansat ja toivo. Available at: https://areena.yle.fi/1-4174764 [Accessed 8 October 2018].

Yle Uutiset (2015). "Likaiset lappalaiset, sekö myy maailmalla?"—Visit Finlandin mainosvideo suututtaa. [online] Available at: https://yle.fi/uutiset/3-8312073 [Accessed 8 October 2018].

Part 2
Governing and negotiating differences

5 Knowledge about Roma and Travellers in Nordic schools

Paradoxes, constraints, and possibilities[1]

Jenni Helakorpi

Introduction

Roma and Travellers (*resande/romanifolk/tatere*)[2] are national minorities in Finland, Sweden, and Norway. Although education systems purport to treat everybody equally, surveys indicate that students who identify as Roma or Travellers have distinctive educational experiences, paths, and outcomes. According to national surveys, Roma and Traveller pupils are at greater risk than their peers of dropping out of basic education (i.e. comprehensive school), and of not continuing to upper secondary education (AoI 2009; MSAH 2009; NOU 2015; SOU 2010). Furthermore, Roma and Traveller pupils are subjected to prejudice, racism, and bullying in schools (Junkala and Tawah 2009; NOU 2015; Rajala et al. 2011; Rajala and Blomerus 2015; SOU 2010). Finland, Sweden, and Norway have acknowledged the inequities in the educational outcomes of Roma and Traveller pupils and have introduced policies and practices to improve the educational situation. As one key measure, policies, and practices that promote the provision of knowledge about Roma and Travellers for the school communities have been recommended by different agencies (Helakorpi, Lappalainen, and Mietola 2018).

Providing knowledge about minoritised groups is a widespread measure in educational policies and practices aimed at promoting equality (Gorski 2006, 2016; Kumashiro 2002). In my view, the measure can be characterised as a "traveling discourse" in education (Lahelma 2005; Lindblad and Popkewitz 2003), which can be found in various contexts globally. The provision of knowledge about minoritised groups usually aims to diversify school curricula and lessons by including knowledge about different groups, and to counter stereotypes and false information. These measures are based on the assumptions that information about minoritised groups evokes feelings of empathy within pupils who occupy privileged positions, and that this empathy leads to changes in schools and societies (Kumashiro 2002). Kevin Kumashiro (2002), however, warns that although well intended, such practices may enhance the processes of Othering. Like Kumashiro, Paul C. Gorski (2006, p. 165) claims that rather than simply providing knowledge about minoritised groups, the promotion of justice in education would call for institutional transformation with "a continual analysis of institutional power and privilege" (see also hooks 1994). Nevertheless, current policies promote increased knowledge about Roma and Travellers in schools in Finland, Sweden, and Norway, and the individuals working to promote the education of these groups are expected to provide it (see also Helakorpi, Lappalainen, and Sahlström 2019; Helakorpi et al. 2018).

Drawing from feminist post-structural theories in education (e.g. Davies 2004; St. Pierre and Pillow 2000; St. Pierre 2000), this chapter sets out to investigate the ways in which 18 interviewees—who identify as Roma or Travellers, and who work to promote the basic education of these groups—make sense of the practice of "provision of knowledge about Roma and Travellers"; giving lectures about Roma and Travellers was one of the practices the research participants were developing and establishing to improve the basic education of the groups. In the interviews, the research participants describe why and how they provide knowledge about the groups, and what they understand the tenets of that knowledge to be. Drawing from Bronwyn Davies (2004, pp. 4–5) I understand the descriptions of the practice from a post-structural (Foucauldian) viewpoint as indicating "the ways sense is being made", and the ways in which this making sense becomes possible within available discourses (Davies 2004, pp. 4–5; St. Pierre 2000).

This data does not provide possibilities to make systematic comparisons between nation-states. However, in this chapter, the practices aimed at promoting the basic education of Roma and Travellers are understood as "analogical incidents" which are analysed "in various cultural contexts" (Lappalainen, Lahelma, and Mietola 2015, pp. 845–846). The practices are perceived as analogical because they are emerging in the intersections of similar kinds of national policy processes, which are entangled in supranational policy processes: the internationalisation of Roma and Traveller policies, minority policies, and education policies (Brubaker 1996; Kymlicka 2007; Vermeersch 2006; see also Helakorpi, Lappalainen, and Mietola 2018). Furthermore, the three countries have historically co-operated and are currently co-operating in Roma and Traveller policies, and the policies are intertwined historically and currently (Pulma 2006; AoI 2009; MSAH 2016; SOU 2009). The ways the interviewees make sense of their practices are constituted in relation to "networks and supranational authorities and organisations [...] who mobilise particular ways of reasoning about and engaging in educational matters" (Lindbald and Popkewitz 2003 p. 11). Although the contexts differ, the interest of the analysis lies in cross-cultural patterns.

Diverse groups categorised and controlled

The umbrella term 'Roma and Travellers', or often just 'Roma', covers multiple Roma and Traveller groups; Roma and Travellers, however, have varying perceptions of the use of the transnational identity of 'Roma and Travellers' (Bunescu 2014; CoE 2012). The groups have been persecuted and racism[3] against them is still commonplace and systematic (Brearley 2001; Hancock 1989; Izsák 2015; FRA 2018). Today, international governmental organisations pay special attention to Roma and Travellers as a distinctive transnational group, and Roma and Traveller groups have been defined as national minorities in many European countries (see e.g. Vermeersch 2006; van Baar 2012).

This chapter discusses policies and practices targeted at those Roma and Traveller groups who have national minority status in Finland, Sweden, and Norway. In Finland, the national Roma minority includes one Roma group: Finnish Roma/Kale. It is estimated that today there are approximately 9,000 to 10,000 Finnish Roma in Finland (Rajala and Blomerus 2015)[4]. In Sweden, the national Roma minority includes several Roma groups, which are usually described by the period of their arrival in Sweden: Travellers (*resande*), Swedish Roma, Finnish Roma/Kale, Non-Nordic Roma, and recently-arrived Roma. These groups contain multiple subgroups. It has been estimated that there are around 50,000 people who identify as Roma (or Traveller) in Sweden (SOU 2010). In Norway, two different national minority Roma groups have been defined: Roma (*rom*) and Travellers (*romanifolk/tatere*). It is estimated that there are around 700 Norwegian Roma, and around 4,000 to 10,000 Norwegian Travellers in Norway (Engebrigtsen 2015; Muižnieks 2015).

Current policy categories have diverse and somewhat messy and disputed trajectories. The early history of the emergence of the policy categories is interconnected in all three countries: the first literary notes about Roma in the Nordic countries are from the early sixteenth century. Terms *tattare/tatere* were adopted from the German language to refer to a group of people in the Nordic region, who the officials believed to share the same origin (Pulma 2006; Montesino Parra 2002; Rekola 2012). However, the use of these categories was ambiguous, and varied between regions (Rekola 2012). Especially in territories which are today (parts of) Norway and Sweden, the category was also used to refer to various local and foreign itinerant groups, who the states wanted to control (Pulma 2006). The current Norwegian national minority category Travellers (*romanifolk/tatere*) originates from here. When Norway defined its national minorities, some Norwegian Travellers contested the idea of becoming a national minority and considered the categorisation to be yet another stigmatising practice, and a way to introduce targeted disciplinary measures (St. Meld 2000, p. 46). The national minority Norwegian Roma (*rom*) refers to Roma who migrated to Norway during the 1800s.

In Sweden, the term *tattare* became interchangeable with the term *zigenare*. However, in the late nineteenth century (when Finland was already part of the Russian empire), these ambiguous terms became separated to refer to different groups. The distinction served to make a difference between the nation-state's "own" *tattare* and the later migrated "foreign" *zigenare* (Montesino Parra 2002, 96). In the 1950s, the category of *zigenare* was also divided into categories of "Swedish" and "foreign", when new groups of Roma migrated to Sweden and were categorised as "foreign". Later, the Roma category splintered even further when new Roma migrated to Sweden (Montesino

Parra 2002). Although the diversity of Roma and Traveller groups in Sweden is apparent, the Swedish national minority politics treats Swedish Roma and Travellers as one diverse group called Roma (*romer*), and they are targeted by the same policy processes (SOU 2010). The process of defining the Swedish national minorities was not straightforward, and for instance, some Swedish Travellers have contested being grouped together with Roma (Wiklander 2015).

After Finland became the Finnish Grand Duchy of the Russian empire in the early nineteenth century, the policy category Roma (*mustalainen/zigenare*), which originates from the time Finland was part of Sweden, became quite clear-cut: current research indicates that there were no other itinerant groups in Finland other than Finnish Roma, who now hold a national minority position (Pulma 2006, 48).

The diverse ethnic groupings and identities of Roma and Travellers in the Nordic countries have emerged as a result of complex historical movements and interactions between different people throughout the centuries. Furthermore, these groupings—and the living conditions of people who identify or have identified as part of these groups—have been shaped by nation-state building, scientific racism, different periods of Roma and Traveller politics, and legislation concerning, for example, poverty, vagrancy, and migration (see e.g. Tervonen 2012; Pulma 2006; Montesino Parra 2002). These groups have been marginalised: each group has been subjected to either or both assimilation and/or exclusion in Finland, Sweden, and Norway, based on (racialising) representations maintained in public discourses.

The turn in political discourses from exclusion and assimilation, towards human and cultural rights, is recent. Even after the Second World War, policy programmes for Finnish Roma in Finland included practices such as children's homes which aimed to "normalise" the Roma and assimilate them (Friman-Korpela 2014; Pulma 2006). Furthermore, during the period from 1950 to 1970 (the second phase of Finnish sterilisation politics), the Finnish state's social welfare policies enabled doctors and social workers, amongst others, to subject Roma to sterilisations (Mattila 2005). Sterilisations also took place in Sweden until the mid-1970s, and were directed to some extent towards Roma and Travellers (SOU 2000; Vitbok 2014). Furthermore, many Roma in Sweden were without residence until the 1960s and did not have access to general welfare services (Vitbok 2014). In Norway, sterilisation policies which remained until 1977 likewise included Travellers (NOU 2015). Moreover, as in Finland, Traveller children were removed from their families and placed in children's homes, while adults were made to work in Traveller labour colonies. The aims of these practices were to teach Travellers "the Norwegian" lifestyle, to get them to settle down, and to erode Traveller culture and language. The last of the labour colonies was closed in 1989 (NOU 2015). Most of the Norwegian Roma were caught and sent to Nazi extermination camps during the Second World War, since Norway forbade their return to Norway in 1934 (Pulma 2006; Rosvoll and Bielenberg 2012). The surviving Norwegian Roma were not allowed to re-enter Norway until 1956.

Until the early 1970s, the authorities tried to prevent Roma from coming and settling in Norway (Pulma 2006).

Although the current political discourse today stresses the human and cultural rights of Roma and Travellers, multiple forms of racism and discrimination against Roma and Travellers are widely spread in these societies (e.g. Keskinen et al. 2018; Non-discrimination Ombudsman 2014; NOU 2015; Rosvoll and Bielenberg 2012; SOU 2016).

Data and analysis

Today, Finland, Sweden, and Norway have policy processes which promote the basic education of national Roma and/or Traveller minorities (see Helakorpi, Lappalainen and Mietola 2018), and for this research, I wanted to reach persons who implement these policies locally. I approached interviewees through networks, organisations, and municipalities, and the data for this chapter includes interviews with 18 individuals who identify as Roma or Traveller, and work to promote the basic education of national Roma and/or Traveller minorities.

Seven of the interviewees are from Finland. They worked or had worked as Roma mediators in schools. The Finnish interviews were conducted in Finnish in multiple municipalities. Eight of the interviews were conducted in Sweden, in several municipalities, in Swedish or English. Four of the Swedish interviewees worked as Roma mediators in schools, and four worked in administration, where developing basic education of Roma children was one part of their work. Also included in the data are three interviews from Norway from one municipality: two of the interviewees identify as Norwegian Travellers (interviewed together), and one identifies as Norwegian Roma. The Norwegian interviewees were activists or working for NGOs, and they were developing practices for schools and other institutions. The Norwegian interviews were conducted mainly in Swedish, but partly in Norwegian and English. The interviews were semi-structured, and all the interviews, except for one,[5] were recorded and transcribed. Since the interviewees could be easy to identify, the work of the interviewees is not described in detail, and personal information, such as age and gender, is concealed.

The interviewees hold varying employment positions. The Norwegian interviews in particular differ from their Finnish and Swedish counterparts, since the interviewees were not working for municipalities or governments. This was due to the different Roma/Traveller policy landscape in Norway: municipal and government employees were not Roma or Travellers, and the Roma and Traveller representatives in the field are, for example, activists or representatives of NGOs. In Sweden and Finland, a significant number of employees working with Roma issues identified as Roma. As described earlier, the chapter does not aim to develop systematic comparisons between the nation-states, but to proffer a cross-cultural analysis of "analogical incidents" (Lappalainen, Lahelma, and Mietola 2015, pp. 845–846). From a cross-cultural analysis perspective, the interviewees share positions as individuals implementing national policies.

I initially analysed the interviews by identifying how the provision of knowledge about Roma and Travellers was discussed. I organised the data into two categories: what type of content the interviewees describe (what is this knowledge?), and what they aim to achieve by providing this type of knowledge (what does the knowledge do?). My emphasis was to find possible patterns in their reasoning and choices of topics, and this was done through intensive reading of the data, together with theoretical literature (Koski 2011; Coffey and Atkinson 1996). Finally, I identified that the discussions about the provision of knowledge concentrated on two main topics: the racialisation of Roma and Travellers, and the silence around a Roma and Traveller presence in the nation-states. That these two topics paradoxically contradict each other resulted in inevitable ambivalences and tensions that emerged throughout the process of articulating one's position.

Racialisation

The ways in which the interviewees made sense of their practice of providing knowledge about Roma and Travellers point towards the persistence and frequency of what I name as *the processes of racialisation of Roma and Travellers* in schools. Racialisation refers to the ways race, as a social and political category, is signified and established. Processes of racialisation construct and stabilise categories of Other, connecting certain differences to these categories. Typically, the attributes associated with the Other contain negative signifiers, and the Other is represented as inadequate or threatening. The perceived differences between "us" and the Other begin to seem natural and essential, thus enabling racialised power relations to become legitimised (Mulinari et al. 2009; Lentin 2008). I argue that while my interviewees try to negotiate within these discourses and find ways to use knowledge about Roma and Travellers to disturb the processes of racialisation, the practice of providing knowledge about Roma and Travellers cannot totally avoid contributing to the very same racialising discourses that they aim to tackle.

In all the contexts studied, the interviewees explained that they aim to challenge dominant cultural perceptions concerning Roma and Travellers. One such perception was that Roma would want to remain outside societal or education structures. In the next excerpt, a Swedish interviewee describes how school personnel should know more about the willingness of Roma to educate themselves, gain employment, and be part of society:

I: So when you said that school personnel should know about Roma culture, what kinds of things should they know?
R: It has never been so that one needs to be educated. One needs a job. And that has to do with the fact that one did not have a right to work. And this is what so many Roma have gone through. Education. They have not

had the right to go to school. They have not had the right to a residence, to settle. They have been forced to travel from municipality to municipality. One could live only three weeks in the same place. And Roma culture, this has got into our culture. That we did not have a permission to go to school. And that is what is important. That the school personnel must get to know that. And it is not just that one does not want to go to school. That we don't prioritise education. That we don't want to have a job. That we want to stay out of society. That is not true. We will also be in society and we will also work. And that is what I tell the teachers.

In the above extract, the interviewee reacts to a racialising narrative about Roma: it is widely assumed that Roma culture conflicts with education. The same argumentation was also used when the states' assimilation measures were justified in earlier times (e.g. Pulma 2006). Although this conception has been criticised for not having empirical backing (Brüggemann 2014; Rodell Olgaç 2006, 2013; Matache 2017), the perception is still invoked, repeatedly, in development projects and academic research all over Europe. Through this narrative, Roma are racialised by attaching negative signifiers to them, and they become represented as threats to society. Despite the apparent diversity of groups and histories within the Swedish national minority Roma group, the Swedish interviewee reacts to the racialising narrative by representing a homogenising description of the Swedish Roma and posits themselves as representing all of "us". I understood this as a strategy which draws upon the Swedish discourse around the united group of national minority Roma. Although it is problematic, Elisabeth Eide (2010) has demonstrated how essentialising can be a strategy for individuals positioned as representatives of a minority to get heard; in this case, the interviewee turns our gaze towards the atrocities committed by the Swedish state and challenges the narrative of problematic Roma culture.

In the next excerpt from Norway, a Norwegian Roma interviewee likewise reacts to racialising narratives about Roma:

R: Most important for the Roma today is to highlight their culture. And to show that you are a people in Norway. A minority. Then there are many unique cultural traditions. [indistinct on the tape]. Very important that it is highlighted today in Norway because the Norwegians, I mean the non-Roma [Norwegians], they don't know what we do and what we stand for. And always when they … hear for instance that gypsies (zigenare), which we are often called, so, it is that we are bad people. That we steal, we are criminals. That we are not stable. And that is not true. […] There is [criminality] also among Roma. Those who steal and who are criminals. But they are not many. They are not many. And that is what is regrettable. That does not come up. That in Norway people know more about us just the negative but not the positive. And that is what I feel we should highlight.

The interviewee describes how criminality is associated with Norwegian Roma, and thus Roma are positioned as threats to Norwegian society (see also Rosvoll and Bielenberg 2012). In their account, the Norwegian interviewee does not totally reject the notion of "bad Roma", but emphasises that Roma should actively represent the positive sides of themselves. I have argued elsewhere that similar discursive patterns about representing positive sides of Roma occur in Finnish schools (Helakorpi, Lappalainen, and Sahlström 2019). This notion of making positive representations instead of negative ones demonstrates the underlying assumption in the discourse about the provision of knowledge: that minoritised groups are responsible for the perceptions carried by people in privileged positions. This becomes even more apparent in the next excerpt with a Swedish interviewee, who also responds to racialising narratives about Roma:

R: That we are a heterogeneous group. That is very important. Because people don't have any knowledge about that. But they think that a Rom is a Rom. But it is not accurate. We are very different. And we have very different identities. We have different beliefs. So that is a very big difference in us. Certain girls cannot use trousers for instance. Among some groups. Other Finnish groups just have these [indistinct on the tape] long skirts. So I mean there we don't have that much in common with that group, like we don't speak the same language at all. We don't have the same religion. We don't have the same traditions. They are like behind. They are very … they have not developed their [indistinct on the tape] as much. They keep rock solid this culture and that, while others think … no, it is like medieval, it is Stone Age, like come on. So that is what I try to bring up. That we are very different. So that they often meet the groups which have problems. The good ones are not visible because they merge in. So the image they have about us are these, you know, prejudices. It is this image they have, and that is what I try to eliminate in some way. That you can't just believe that. You need to believe that there are thousands of others who are just like everyone else. Like goes to work. Have hobbies. Go out and do all the other stuff that other people do. Unfortunately you are always unlucky [indistinct on the tape] and see only the bad and worst there are. Peoples can actually have a bad reputation. And that is what we have. We have been labelled. So that is what I try to open, their eyes and ears. So I hope it sticks with them. And often when people go to it [indistinct on the tape] so they say like "I have a neighbour who parties all night". Yeah, well then you are unlucky, and you live in that area just next to that neighbour. I also have a neighbour who parties all night. They go to sleep at ten o'clock. So that, or another "yeah but there was a boy who stole my daughter's bike" or. So those kinds of stories I get to hear.

Yet again, an interviewee responds to racialising narratives of Swedish Roma. In those narratives, Swedish Roma are depicted as behaving badly, stealing, and having problems. The interviewee tackles this by emphasising the heterogeneity of Roma. They list topics such as beliefs, clothing, identity, and traditions that are typically employed to establish the difference of the Other, using these to highlight the heterogeneity of Swedish Roma. However, like the Norwegian interviewee or the Finnish interviewees, this Swedish interviewee does not reject the notion of "bad Roma". On the contrary, the interviewee ambiguously connects negative signifiers such as backwardness and problems to one Roma group. Thus, a paradox can be identified in this interview: while they want to resist racialising descriptions of Roma, they end up making a racialising description of one of the Swedish Roma groups. Although they criticise the way people depend on prejudices, they constitute a narrative of other Roma fitting these prejudiced descriptions.

While most of the interviewees described how they want to counter and change the racialising narratives about Roma, one of the interviewees in Sweden had a different approach: instead of countering the racialisation of Roma, or reinforcing descriptions concerning Roma, their lectures focused on the exclusive mechanisms and normativities of schools in general. Thus, the interviewee turned the gaze from Roma towards the school system. They, however, pointed out that when planning and delivering these types of lectures, one needs to be careful not to make people feel guilty. This indicates the responsibility the interviewees are carrying: it is their responsibility to both change narratives, and do so in a manner that is comfortable for school communities.

I argue that within the sense-making of my interviewees, the limitations and problems of the discursive terrain around "the provision of knowledge about minoritised groups" emerges. I have identified that across all the studied contexts, the interviewees want to react to processes of racialisation of Roma and Travellers in school. However, when aiming to counter the racialising narratives with an opposing narrative, the interviewees often end up employing homogenising descriptions. On the other hand, when trying to disturb racialising narratives by emphasising the heterogeneity of Roma, interviewees do not fully reject the racialising notions, but accept them through reproducing an ambiguous description of "the bad Roma" who are responsible for the racialising notions people possess. The underlying assumption in the provision of knowledge about Roma and Travellers seems to be that Roma and Travellers are responsible for the perceptions people carry: Roma and Travellers need to replace the current narratives with new ones, and/or take the blame by (re)producing an ambiguous category of "the bad Roma" from which the racialising notions originate. Either way, non-Roma/Travellers are not held liable for the persistent reproduction of racialising narratives about Roma and Travellers, or for changing those narratives.

Silence about Roma and Travellers in the nation-states

R: And to learn about us. Because they don't know anything about us. They believe we were people who lived 300 years ago in an adventure book. But we do exist today. So we try to teach them about our culture and history, and have an understanding about the fact that we are here, and who we are.

In the excerpt above, a Norwegian Traveller interviewee describes arriving at the startling conclusion that their very existence is absented from dominant understandings of Norwegian society; there is thus an urgent need for increasing the visibility of Travellers within Norwegian education: "so we try to teach them ... that we are here". In fact, according to the national curricula in all these countries, pupils should learn about national minorities during basic education (i.e. comprehensive school; FNBE 2014; Skolverket 2011; RMERCA). However, Finnish, Swedish, and Norwegian reports have shown that in textbooks—which often drive teaching practices more than national curricula (Pudas 2011)—minoritised groups are hardly visible (Midtbøen, Orupabo, and Røthing 2014; Tainio and Teräs 2010; Institutet för språk och folkminne 2016; SVT nyheter 2016). However yet again, the question arises of how national minorities should be visible. My interviewees described contents such as history, culture, and crafts, and my analysis suggests that the narrative of the relationship between the nation-state and Roma and/or Travellers has a significant role.

Many Swedish interviewees described the relationship between Roma and the Swedish nation-state through historical atrocities and current discrimination, which can be understood as an oppositional and antagonistic positioning. Furthermore, in these descriptions, the Swedish state became represented as unequal and oppressive. Through these types of narratives, the interviewees wanted to build a basis for understanding the present-day position of, and structural discrimination against, Roma in Sweden:

R: Then, when we tell about the history, we go to the Second World War, we go into Josef Mengele, what he, what Hitler did with Roma. How it was in the 1970s. How the change took place. And then we come to the fact that today they are still an oppressed group. Even today, 2015. They don't have their rights. And I mean we live in a Swedish society. It should be different. It is not so today.

The interviewee mentions the persecution of, and medical experiments on, Roma during the Second World War in Europe. Although hundreds of thousands of Roma were murdered in Nazi extermination camps and subjected to inhumane medical experiments (Brearley 2001), the persecution of Roma during the Second World War is still today often ignored (World Roma Organisation 2017; Pulma 2006). The interviewee uses history to draw connections to present-day discrimination in Sweden.

In Finland, the interviewees had a very different perspective when describing the Roma presence, and the relationship between Roma and the Finnish nation-state. The Finnish interviewees seemed to approach history from a lighter and happier perspective than the Swedish interviewees: they marginalised the relationship of Roma and the Finnish state by concentrating on cultural artefacts and micro-histories of individual Roma. However, as the next excerpt with a Finnish interviewee demonstrates, effacing the violent role of the nation-state was strategic, and served a greater purpose:

R: And of course about history. If one does not know history it is difficult to understand the present
I: Mmm
R: So, in the 1600s there were Roma coming to Finland. Of course there are also all these regrettable [issues] and these. I usually don't want to bring these up because it kind of undermines the issue. People stay and chew over the wrong [issue], and they even freeze. The truth is that in history, there are these hard issues, which also many times cause the fears that Roma have
I: Right
R: So it is not, for instance, always futile [to fear]. It has been passed on in a certain way, it has been told [to new Roma generations] what has happened
I: Mmm, right
R: And the fear that children are taken away.

When presenting me with materials concerning Roma, the interviewee introduced a film about a Roma pupil's day at school, descriptions of Roma culture, as well as interviews with Romani elders and youngsters about their educational and employment careers. In the aforementioned excerpt, the interviewee commented on history, noting that some of the fears Roma have are reflective of the historically abusive policies of the state. In fact, the removal of Roma children from their families, and their placement in Roma children's homes, constituted the core of Finnish Roma policies until the turn of the 1970s (Pulma 2006; Friman-Korpela 2014). However, the interviewee decided not to concentrate on "difficult issues", because it was felt that people are unable to handle them. I understand this as my interviewee's strategy: previous studies show that working with diversity in institutions is often better executed in "happier language", because emphasising issues such as racism or historical misconduct may result in the majority's lack of interest in co-operating (Ahmed 2012, p. 175). According to my reading, in Finnish schools, there is little room to present the historical mistreatment of Roma.

The same kind of strategy is visible in the next excerpt, likewise from Finland, where an interviewee describes a Roma history workshop organised for schools. The interviewee had also arranged workshops focusing on music, crafts, and customs:

R: The history [workshop] has been a bit like this time machine thing, where there has been a PowerPoint about how at first, people travelled with sleighs, and now people move with cars.
I: Yeah [*laughs*]
R: [*Laughs*]

The idea of a time machine gives the workshop an entertaining and fun tone. Furthermore, the story of the changing means of transportation positions Roma as part of a common history about changing technology, and the relationship between the nation-state and Roma becomes blurred. Within these narratives of a Roma presence in Finland, the Finnish interviewees may want to resist a narrative of conflict between the Roma and the nation-state. Connecting Roma history to common themes, such as technical developments, ties Roma to the shared history of Finns. Where the Swedish interviewees emphasise the friction between Roma and the nation-state was in part due to the atrocities committed by the state, the Finnish interviewees emphasise the shared nation-space, and the individual stories and resources of Roma.

In the next excerpt from Norway, a Traveller interviewee has yet another kind of approach where, through role play, they bind together both happy practices of multiculturalism, and narratives about the oppressive state:

R: [...] There [in role play] they can live a little bit like in our situation. So that it is a little bit like a play [acting], music and songs, and a little bit like playing and make it kind of lively there.
I: Very interesting
R: [...] so, that they do in schools [...] when they teach the youth. Live our life and get dressed like Travellers. So, they dress like us and live like our life. So then they encounter resistance from society. So, they learn to see it from our [indistinct in the tape] [...] so the people who have been a bit negative, when they begin, they become totally the opposite. Thus, they understand. "Oh, is it like this?" Yes. Then they understand it, when they get to live it a little themselves. Thus, it does something to them. [...].

In the excerpt, cultural celebration via music, songs, and clothing is used to discuss discrimination. The Norwegian state is described as oppressive, and at the same time a representation of Traveller life is displayed through artefacts such as clothes. Celebration and the display of cultural artefacts—as the Finnish Roma and Norwegian Traveller interviewees describe—is a fairly typical and recognised way of including knowledge about minoritised groups in the official education system (e.g. Gorski 2016). Thus, schools may be receptive to this way of including Roma and Travellers within educational content. The emphasis on crafts, music, careers, and travelling by different vehicles may aim to emphasise the "capital" of Roma and Travellers, as well as their agency, and how they can be considered resources within the countries. However, in contrast to the Finnish interviewees, the Norwegian

Traveller interviewees use "happy" multiculturalism to also narrate the oppressiveness of the Norwegian state.

Kumashiro (2002, p. 39) claims that for knowledge about minoritised groups to be transformative, it is important to aim to change the underlying story of the nation-state. According to my interview analysis, the narrative of the relationship between Roma, Travellers, and the nation-state is likewise important—however, the possibilities to narrate this are contextually bound. The Swedish Roma and Norwegian Traveller interviewees emphasise the oppressive nature of the Swedish and Norwegian nation-states, and the distinctiveness of the historical experience of the groups, whereas the Finnish Roma bring forth the shared nation-space and minimise historical atrocities. I connect these differences between the countries to current state-level Roma politics and public discourses. As the only Nordic country to do so, the Norwegian government apologised to Travellers in 1998 and 2000 (NOU 2015; St. Meld. nr. 15, 2000–2001) and Roma in 2015 (government.no, 2015) for historical atrocities. In Sweden, a considerable issue in Roma politics has been the release of a white paper—*The dark and unknown history: White Paper on abuses and the rights violations of Roma during the 1900s* (Vitbok 2014)—which also resulted in the founding of a commission against antiziganism during 2014 to 2016 (SOU 2016). The white paper concentrates on abuses during the twentieth century, which was the time period emphasised by the Swedish interviewees, and the commission published and distributed a version of the white paper for pupils and teachers. Furthermore, in 2013, an illegal register about Roma kept by the police was revealed in Sweden. The register included thousands of Roma, from the already deceased to small children. The register received attention in Swedish society and made visible the current discrimination Roma face. While past and present discrimination against Roma and Travellers has been discussed in Swedish and Norwegian society, the Finnish state has never made an account of the abuse and persecution of Roma (see also Nordberg 2015). These differing public discourses may enable and constrain different narratives about the relationship between Roma, Travellers, and the nation-state in schools.

Conclusions: Paradoxes, constraints, and possibilities in providing knowledge about minoritised groups

In this chapter, I have conducted a cross-cultural analysis of the ways 18 individuals who identify as Roma or Traveller make sense of the practice of providing knowledge about Roma and Travellers in schools. According to my analysis, an underlying assumption in the practice is that Roma and Travellers are responsible for those narratives, perceptions, and practices people in privileged positions hold and reproduce. The analysis suggests the processes of racialisation of Roma and Travellers in schools is persistent and commonplace, which my interviewees aim to disturb with the provision of knowledge about Roma and Travellers. The interviewees moved between two strategies:

1) emphasising the heterogeneity of Roma and Travellers, and 2) producing homogenising and essentialising counter-narratives related to the groups. However, neither of the strategies could totally avoid contributing to the very same racialising discourses the interviewees aimed to tackle: when emphasising the positive features and heterogeneity of the groups, an ambiguous category of "some bad Roma" occurred, and was held responsible for current racialising narratives. On the other hand, when challenging racialising narratives with counter-narratives, the interviewees often relied on homogenising and essentialising the groups, which in itself cannot challenge the logic of racialisation either. The underlying assumption in the practice seemed to be that non-Roma and non-Travellers were not accountable for the racialisation of Roma and Travellers in schools and societies, or for changing current racialising discourses.

Another observation in this chapter is that in providing knowledge about Roma and/or Travellers, the narration of the relationship between Roma/Travellers and the nation-state was significant. However, the analysis suggests that this narration is enabled and constrained by context: the differing ways the past and present are being discussed within nation-states is visible in the interviews. Furthermore, the interviewees not only narrated within the limits and possibilities of the public discourses, but also seemed to be sensitive about the school context, and its multicultural practices. In Sweden and Norway, there was space for describing the nation-states as historically and currently oppressive, whereas in Finland no such space seemed to exist.

As described from the outset, previous critical literature analysing the practice of providing knowledge about minoritised groups has emphasised the importance of analysing power within institutions (Gorski 2006; hooks 1994; Kumashiro 2002). One of my interviewees aimed to carry this out by giving lectures about the exclusive mechanisms and normativities present within school systems. However, when conducting these lectures, the interviewee noted the need to be careful not to make people feel guilty. The point raised brings forward yet again that the interviewees are bound by their contexts when developing their practices. This chapter demonstrates that school communities and policymakers should actively analyse power relations to tackle racialising processes within institutions, rather than merely waiting for minoritised groups to bear this responsibility. In addition, a serious rethinking of the narratives of the nation-states, and their historical and current role in injustice and racism, should be undertaken widely within societies and institutions; people in minoritised positions should not be left solely responsible for disturbing the current narratives. To conclude, the analysis of this chapter suggests that the policy measure of the provision of knowledge about minoritised groups should be expanded so that schools and institutions are held responsible for rethinking and re-narrating the nation and its institutions.

Notes

1 This chapter has gone through an external blind review and was accepted by three reviewers. We thank the reviewers for their work with the chapter.
2 Internationally, the term "Roma" is often used as an umbrella term for all Roma groups, including Swedish Travellers (resande) and Norwegian Travellers (romanifolk/tatere). However, in the Nordic context, the term "Roma" is typically understood as excluding (especially the Norwegian) Travellers.
3 Today, racism against Roma groups is often referred to with the specific term "antigypsyism" (see e.g. antigypsyism.eu).
4 The numbers are estimates, as there are no statistics on ethnic grounds in these countries.
5 From one Swedish interview, there are only handwritten notes, since the interviewee asked me not to record.

References

Ahmed, S. (2012). *On being included: Racism and diversity in institutional life*. Durham, NC: Duke University Press.
Arbeids- og inkluderingsdepartementet (AoI). (2009). Action plan for improvement of the living conditions of Roma in Oslo. Retrieved from https://www.regjeringen.no/globalassets/upload/FAD/Vedlegg/SAMI/Nasjmin/Handlingsplan_rom_EN.pdf
antigypsyism.eu (2017). Reference paper [online]. Available at: http://antigypsyism.eu/?page_id=17 [Accessed 8 October 2018].
Brearley, M. (2001). 'The persecution of Gypsies in Europe'. *American Behavioral Scientist*, 45(4), pp. 588–599.
Brubaker, R. (1996). *Nationalism reframed: Nationhood and the national question in the new Europe*. Cambridge: Cambridge University Press.
Brüggemann, C. (2014). 'Romani culture and academic success: Arguments against the belief in a contradiction'. *Intercultural Education*, 25(6), pp. 439–452.
Bunescu, I. (2014). *Roma in Europe. The politics of collective identity formation*. London: Routledge.
CoE [Council of Europe]. (2012). Council of Europe Descriptive Glossary of terms relating to Roma issues. [pdf] Available at: http://a.cs.coe.int/team20/cahrom/documents/Glossary%20Roma%20EN%20version%2018%20May%202012.pdf [Accessed 8 October 2018].
Coffey, A. and Atkinson, P. (1996). *Making sense of qualitative data: Complementary research strategies*. Thousand Oaks: SAGE Publications.
Davies, B. (2004). 'Introduction: Poststructuralist lines of flight in Australia'. *International Journal of Qualitative Studies in Education*, 17(1), pp. 3–9.
Eide, E. (2010). 'Strategic essentialism and ethnification. Hand in glove?' *Nordicom Review* 31(2), pp. 63–78.
Engebrigtsen, A. I. (2015). 'Educating the Roma: The struggle for cultural autonomy in a seminomadic group in Norway'. *Social Inclusion*, 3(5), pp. 115–125. doi:10.17645/si.v3i5.275
FNBE [Finnish National Board of Education]. (2014). Perusopetuksen opetussuunnitelman perusteet 2014. Opetushallitus. Määräykset ja ohjeet 2014:96. [pdf] Available at: http://www.oph.fi/download/163777_perusopetuksen_opetussuunnitelman_perusteet_2014.pdf [Accessed 8 October 2018].

FRA [European Union Agency for Fundamental Rights]. (2018). A persisting concern: anti-Gypsyism as a barrier to Roma inclusion [pdf] Available at: http://fra.europa.eu/en/publication/2018/roma-inclusion [Accessed 8 October 2018].
Friman-Korpela, S. (2014). *Romanipolitiikasta romanien politiikkaan. Poliittisen asialistan ja toimijakonseption muutos 1900-luvun jälkipuoliskon Suomessa*. PhD. University of Jyväskylä.
Gorski, P. (2006). 'Complicity with conservatism: The de-politicizing of multicultural and intercultural education'. *Intercultural Education*, 17(2), pp. 163–177.
Gorski, P. (2016). 'Rethinking the role of "culture" in educational equity: From cultural competence to equity literacy'. *Multicultural Perspectives*, 18(4), pp. 221–226.
Government.no (2015). International Roma Day, 8 April 2015 [online] Available at: https://www.regjeringen.no/en/aktuelt/den-internasjonale-romdagen/id2404809/ [Accessed 8 October 2018].
Hancock, I. (1989). *The pariah syndrome: An account of Gypsy slavery and persecution*. Ann Arbor: Karoma.
Helakorpi, J., Lappalainen, S. and Mietola, R. (2018). 'Equality in the making? Roma and Traveller minority policies and basic education in three Nordic countries'. *Scandinavian Journal of Educational Research*, DOI: 10.1080/00313831.2018.1485735
Helakorpi, J., Lappalainen, S. and Sahlström, F. (2019). 'Becoming tolerable: Subject constitution of Roma mediators in Finnish schools'. *Intercultural Education*, 30(1), pp. 51–67, DOI: 10.1080/14675986.2018.1537671
hooks, b. (1994). *Teaching to transgress. Education as the practice of freedom*. New York: Routledge.
Insititutet för språk och folkminne (2016). Brister i undervisningen om de nationella minoriteterna och minoritetsspråken [online] Available at: http://www.sprakochfolkminnen.se/om-oss/nyheter-och-press/nyhetsarkiv/nyheter-2017/2017-05-24-brister-i-undervisningen-om-de-nationella-minoriteterna-och-minoritetsspraken.html [Accessed 8 October 2018].
Izsák, R. (2015). Comprehensive study of the human rights situation of Roma worldwide, with a particular focus on the phenomenon of anti-Gypsyism. Report to the Human Rights Council. Available at: https://www.ohchr.org/EN/HRBodies/HRC/RegularSessions/.../A_HRC_29_24_E.doc
Junkala, P. and Tawah, S. (2009). *Enemmän samanlaisia kuin erilaisia: Romanilasten ja nuorten hyvinvointi ja heidän oikeuksiensa toteutuminen Suomessa*. Lapsiasiainvaltuutetun toimiston julkaisuja 2. Jyväskylä: Lapsiasiainvaltuutetun toimisto.
Keskinen, S., Alemanji, A. A., Himanen, M., Kivijärvi, A., Osazee, U., Pöyhölä, N., and Rousku, V. (2018). *The stopped—ethnic profiling in Finland*. Helsinki: Swedish School of Social Science.
Koski, L. (2011). Teksteistä teemoiksi, in Puusa, A., and Juuti, P. (eds.) *Menetelmäviidakon raivaajat. Perusteita laadullisen tutkimuslähestymistavan valintaan*. Vantaa: JTO, pp. 126–149.
Kumashiro, K. (2002). *Troubling education. Queer activism and anti-oppressive pedagogy*. New York & London: Routledge Falmer.
Kymlicka, W. (2007). 'The internationalization of minority rights'. *International Journal of Constitutional Law*, 6(1), pp. 1–32.
Lahelma, E. (2005). 'School grades and other resources: The "failing boys" discourse revisited'. *Nordic Journal of Women's Studies*, 13(2), pp. 78–89.
Lappalainen, S., Lahelma, E., and Mietola, R. (2015). 'Problematizing evaluative categorisations: Collaborative and multisited interpretations of constructions of

normality in Estonia and Finland', in P. Smeyers, D. Bridgges, N. C. Burbules, and M. Griffiths, (eds.) *International handbook of interpretation in educational research.* 1st ed. Dordrecht: Springer Science+Business Media, pp. 843–864.
Lentin, A. (2008). *Racism. A beginner's guide.* Oxford: Oneworld Publications.
Lindblad, S. and Popkewitz, T. S. (2003). 'Comparative ethnography: Fabricating the new millennium and its exclusions'. In Beach, D., Gordon, T., and E. Lahelma (eds.) *Democratic education. Ethnographic challenges.* 1st ed. London: Tufnell Press, pp. 10–14.
Matache, M. (2017). 'Biased elites, unfit policies: Reflections on the lacunae of Roma integration strategies'. *European Review*, 25(4), pp. 588–607.
Mattila, M. (2005). 'Sterilointipolitiikka ja romanit Suomessa vuosina 1950–1970', in Häkkinen, A., Pulma, P., and Tervonen, M. (eds.) *Vieraat kulkijat—tutut talot: Näkökulmia etnisyyden ja köyhyyden historian Suomessa.* 1st ed. Helsinki: SKS, pp. 407–410.
Midtbøen, A. H., Orupabo, J., Røthing, Å. (2014). Etniske og religiøse minoriteter i læremidler Lærer- og elevperspektiver. *Rapport 2014*: 11. Institutt for samfunnsforskning.
Montesino Parra, N. (2002). *Zigenarfrågan: Intervention och romantik.* PhD. Lunds Universitet.
MSAH (Ministry of Social Affairs and Health). (2009). The Proposal of the Working Group for a National Policy on Roma. Working group report. Helsinki: Ministry of Social Affairs and Health. [pdf] Available at: http://urn.fi/URN:ISBN: 978-952-00-2912-8 [Accessed: 8 October 2018].
MSAH (Ministry of Social Affairs and Health). (2016). Enhancing the visibility of the living conditions and status of the Roma in the Nordic countries [news item]. Retrieved from http://stm.fi/artikkeli/-/asset_publisher/romanienelinolot-ja-asema -pohjoismaissa-nakyvaksi?_101_INSTANCE_yr7QpNmlJmSj_languageId=en_US
Muižnieks, N. (2015). Report. Commissioner for Human Rights of the Council of Europe. Retrieved from http://www.humanrightseurope.org/2016/04/nils-muizniek s-human-rights-annual-report-2015/
Mulinari, D., Keskinen, S., Irni, S.ja Tuori, S. (2009). 'Introduction: Postcolonialism and the Nordic models of welfare and gender', in S. Keskinen, S. Tuori, S. Irni and D. Mulinari, (eds.) *Complying with colonialism. Gender, race and ethnicity in the Nordic region.* 1st ed. Farnham: Ashgate, pp. 1–18.
Non-discrimination ombudsman. (2014). *Erilaisena arjessa—selvitys romanien syrjintäkokemuksista.* [online] Helsinki: Vähemmistövaltuutettu. Available at: https:// www.syrjinta.fi/documents/10181/10850/52878_romaniselvitys_verkkoon+(1).pdf/ 584516fc-d3a7-4f88-8ecc-c8b2271ebf41 [Accessed 9 April 2019].
Nordberg, C. (2015). 'Dynamics of recognition: Minority ethnic access to transformative power in the Nordic welfare state', in Kraus, P. A., and Kivisto, P. (eds.), *The challenge of minority integration.* 1st ed. Berlin: De Gruyter Open, pp. 91–107.
NOU [Norges offentlige utredninger]. (2015). Assimilering og motstand Norsk politikk overfor taterne/romanifolket fra 1850 til i dag (NOU 2015:17). [pdf] Available at: https:// www.regjeringen.no/no/dokumenter/nou-2015-7/id2414316/ [Accessed 8 October 2018].
Pudas, A-K. (2011). 'Investigating possibilities to develop textbooks to implement global education in basic education instruction'. *IARTEM e-Journal*, 5(2), pp. 1–22.
Pulma, P. (2006). *Suljetut ovet: Pohjoismaiden romanipolitiikka 1500-luvulta EU-aikaan.* Helsinki: Suomalaisen Kirjallisuuden Seura.
Rajala, S. and Blomerus, S. (2015). Katsaus aikuisten romanien koulutustaustoihin. (*Reports 2015*:8). Helsinki: Finnish National Board of Education.

Rajala, S., Salonen, M., Blomerus, S., and Nissilä, L. (2011). Romanioppilaiden perusopetuksen tilannekatsaus 2010–2011 ja toimenpide-ehdotukset. (*Reports 2011*:26). Helsinki: National Board of Education.

Rekola, T. (2012). 'Romanien varhaisvaiheet Suomessa: 1600-luvulta 1800-luvun puoliväliin', in Pulma, P. (ed.), *Suomen romanien historia*. 1st ed., Helsinki: Suomen Kirjallisuuden Seura, pp. 18–83.

RMERCA [The Royal Ministry of Education, Research and Church Affairs]. Core curriculum for primary, secondary and adult education in Norway. [pdf] Available at: https://www.udir.no/globalassets/filer/lareplan/generell-del/core_curriculum_english.pdf [Accessed 8 October 2018].

Rodell Olgaç, C. (2006). *Den romska minoriteten i majoritetssamhällets skola: Från hot till möjlighet*. PhD. Stockholm: HLS Förlag.

Rodell Olgaç, C. (2013). 'Education of Roma in Sweden: An interplay between policy and practice'. In Horneberg, S., and Brüggemann, C. (eds.), *Die Bildungssituation von Roma in Europa*. 1st ed, Münster: Waxmann Verlag, pp. 197–213.

Rosvoll, M. and Bielenberg, N. 2012. *Antisiganisme, stereotypier og diskriminering av rom*. HL-senterets temahefte nr.14 [pdf] Available at: http://www.hlsenteret.no/publikasjoner/digitale-hefter/pdf/hl_temahefte_14_digital.pdf [Accessed 8 October 2018].

Skolverket. 2011. Curriculum for basic education, pre-school and the leisure-time centre 2011. Sweden [Revised 2016] [pdf] Available at: https://www.skolverket.se/om-skolverket/publikationer/visa-enskild-publikation?_xurl_=http%3A%2F%2Fwww5.skolverket.se%2Fwtpub%2Fws%2Fskolbok%2Fwpubext%2Ftrycksak%2FRecord%3Fk%3D2575 [Accessed 21 May 2018].

SOU. 2000: 20. Steriliseringsfrågan i Sverige 1935–1975 Historisk belysning - Kartläggning – Intervjuer [pdf] Available at: http://www.regeringen.se/49b6c6/contentassets/68b217b7f8e746a799536f3ad851c05e/steriliseringsfragan-i-sverige-1935—1975 [Accessed 8 October 2018].

SOU. 2010: 55. Romers rätt – en strategi för romer i Sverige. [pdf] Available at: http://www.regeringen.se/rattsdokument/statens-offentliga-utredningar/2010/07/sou-201055/ [Accessed 8 October 2018].

SOU. 2016: 44. Slutbetänkande av Kommissionen mot antiziganism, [pdf] Available at: http://www.regeringen.se/49e105/contentassets/b76e2b51299b42eba2c360c58f0754f7/kraftsamling-mot-antiziganism-sou-201644 [Accessed 8 October 2018].

St. Meld. nr. 15, 2000–2001: 7 Det Kongelege kommunal- og regionaldepartement. Nasjonale minoritetar I Noreg – Om statleg politikk overfor jødar, kvener, rom, romanifolket og skogfinnar. [pdf] Available at: https://www.regjeringen.no/no/dokumenter/stmeld-nr-15-2000-2001-/id585195/ [Accessed 8 October 2018].

St. Pierre, E. (2000). 'Poststructural feminism in education: An overview'. *Qualitative Studies in Education*, 13(5), pp. 477–515.

St Pierre, E. and Pillow, W. S. (2000). 'Introduction: inquiry among the ruins', in St. Pierre, E. and Pillow, W. (eds.), *Working the ruins: Feminist poststructural theories and methods of education*. 1st ed., New York: Routledge, pp. 1–25.

SVT nyheter. (2016). Minoriteter saknas i skolans historieböcker [online]. Available at: https://www.svt.se/nyheter/uutiset/svenska/minoriteter-saknas-i-skolans-historiebocker [Accessed 8 October 2018].

Tainio, L. and Teräs, T. (2010). Sukupuolijäsennys perusopetuksen oppikirjoissa. Raportit ja selvitykset 2010:8. Helsinki: Opetushallitus.

Tervonen, M. (2012). *"Gypsies", "travellers" and "peasants": A study on ethnic boundary drawing in Finland and Sweden, c.1860–1925*. PhD. HEC Theses.

van Baar, H. (2012). 'Socio-economic mobility and neo-liberal governmentality in post-socialist Europe: Activation and dehumanisation of the Roma'. *Journal of Ethnic and Minority Studies*, 38(8), pp. 1289–1304.
Vermeersch, P. (2006). *The Romani movement: Minority politics and ethnic mobilization in contemporary Central Europe.* New York: Berghahn Books.
Vitbok. 2014. Den mörka och okända historien. Vitbok om övergrepp och kränkningar av romer under 1900-talet. Ds 2014: 8. [pdf] Available at: http://www.regeringen.se/49baf8/contentassets/eaae9da200174a5faab2c8cd797936f1/den-morka-och-okanda-historien—vitbok-om-overgrepp-och-krankningar-av-romer-under-1900-talet-ds-20148 [Accessed: 8 October 2018].
Wiklander, L. (2015). 'Resandefolket och svensk minoritetspolitik: 1990-talets paradigmskifte'. *Historisk tidskrift (Sweden)*, 135(4), pp. 622–648.
World Roma Organisation. (2017). Press release [online]. Available at: http://www.worldromaorganization.org/index.php/en/component/content/article/35-vazno/190-statement-of-wro-president-regarding-2nd-august-roma-holocaust-remembrance-day [Accessed: 8 October 2018].

6 Problematising the urban periphery
Discourses on social exclusion and suburban youth in Sweden

Magnus Dahlstedt

Introduction

In recent years, there has been increasing attention paid to tensions and conflicts in urban peripheries in Sweden—they are framed as posing a serious threat to the social cohesion of Swedish society. Media reports about burning cars, and stones thrown at police and rescue vehicles, have placed focus on urban peripheries, and particularly on suburban youth as subjects of social disorder and disintegration (Stigendal 2016). In the wake of these debates, calls have been made for enacting a range of specific and targeted security measures against young people, such as mobilising armed forces in urban peripheries.

The aim of the chapter is to further analyse discourses on this situation, with a particular focus on different ways of conceptualising the problem of the social exclusion of suburban youth, and the possible ways to address this problem. Analytically, the chapter draws on Carol Bacchi's (1999) concept of *problematisation*, highlighting the particular ways in which certain phenomena, domains, or subjects in society are described as in one way or another problematic—and thus in need of intervention. Through problematisations, these phenomena, domains, or subjects are made *governable*, that is, the target of certain interventions.

Empirically, the chapter is based on interviews and texts, such as policy reports and debate articles. Forty interviews were conducted with local actors working in three suburban areas in Sweden, including representatives from the police, schools, social services, and locally based projects, as well as youth living in the same areas. The interviews were conducted as part of two research projects that have been carried out between 2014 and 2017, with a focus on measures for youth social inclusion in three Swedish suburban areas. By using snowball sampling, 35 youths aged between 16 and 25 were selected to participate in focus group interviews and can be seen to represent a range of gender positions and ethno-cultural backgrounds. All interviewees worked or lived in three suburban areas where the research projects were carried out (this chapter builds on work presented elsewhere, cf. Dahlstedt and Lozic 2017; Ekholm and Dahlstedt 2017; Dahlstedt 2018). The focus of this analysis is on different ways of problematising the social exclusion of suburban youth, and how different interviewees understand the possible ways of dealing with the problem. Drawing on a discourse analysis method influenced by the work of Foucault (2004), discourses on societal problems are understood not simply as reflections of "reality", but rather as structuring what is thinkable and able to be articulated about certain issues, defining both problems and the proposed solutions. Within these processes of interpretation, the statements analysed were divided into *problematisations* and *solutions*.

As illustrated by the analysis, the problematisations identified by local actors and youth differ. On one hand, the main focus of local actors is to understand the "area of exclusion" and its inhabitants as *causing* the problems of social exclusion. On the other hand, youth identify that they are subject to *mechanisms* of social exclusion, which cause the suburbs and its inhabitants to become problematised and "deserving" of targeted and stringent intervention policies. In turn, these conflicting ways of conceptualising the problem of social exclusion make possible certain ways of thinking about the future, as well as different actors' capacities for social change.

"An alternative social order": A dominant discourse on social exclusion

Debates on tensions and conflicts in the urban peripheries of Sweden are related to transformations in welfare policies that have occurred throughout recent decades. With these transformations, the Swedish welfare model that was developed in the post-war period has gradually been influenced by neo-liberal rationalities (Larsson et al. 2012). Starting in the late 1980s, several principles underpinning the Swedish welfare model were challenged. In all, the centralised welfare state was seen as an obstacle that hindered individual freedom and active responsibility (Boréus 1994). In line with such debates, the Swedish welfare model has undergone a radical transformation. Accordingly, since the early 1990s, Swedish welfare policy has been characterised by a shift from equality to freedom of choice, from redistribution to activation, and from collective rights to individual responsibilities (Dahlstedt 2015).

In turn, these policy shifts have had a range of consequences that have increased social and economic divisions, further intensifying polarisations in the urban landscape (Schierup et al. 2014). For example, in a study of urban polarisation in Stockholm, the following conclusion was drawn:

> Most noteworthy is the strong increase in economic segregation where [the] poor ... are more isolated today than before [...]. Even more isolated from this group are the rich, living more separate than before, and increasingly living their daily lives without meeting or having few meetings with poor individuals. (Statistics Sweden 2014, p. 25)

However, the pattern does not only apply to Stockholm or even the largest cities in Sweden, but also to mid-sized and, in part, smaller cities around the country (Salonen 2011; Fell and Guziana 2016). In this context, public attention has once more been drawn to the suburban areas previously known as part of the Million Programme, a large-scale housing project initiated in the late 1960s as part of broader state-centred Swedish welfare policies, which provided rental apartments for the broader population. From the start, these urban areas were portrayed in terms of deviance and as sites of social problems, tensions, and conflicts—in the 1970s, the focus was on class divisions, and in the 1980s and 1990s, this shifted to ethno-cultural difference (cf. Ristilammi 1994).

In the new millennium, these suburban areas and their residents were primarily characterised in terms of social exclusion [*utanförskap*]—residents were portrayed as excluded and outside the rest of Swedish society, and the suburbs were referred to in public discourse as "areas of exclusion" [*utanförskapsområden*] (Dahlstedt 2015, 2018). The concept of social exclusion was already part of Swedish political discourse in the 1990s, not least informed by equivalent policy discourses in the European Union (cf. Jacobsson 2004; Schierup et al. 2015). But the concept of *utanförskap* became normalised at the beginning of the new millennium, particularly after the 2006 election, when the centre-right government succeeded in defining the main political challenge as a choice between work and exclusion, and active and passive welfare beneficiaries (Davidsson 2010).

Throughout the last decade, the areas defined as "areas of exclusion" have been repeatedly problematised, not least by being characterised by a particular mentality which has been constructed to be based on welfare dependency, alienation, distrust, and political passivity. Although high levels of unemployment are also emphasised as part of the social exclusion problem, once it has taken shape, the specific mentality that is generated by socio-economic conditions is described as having a dynamic of its own (Dahlstedt 2015). Accordingly, the "culture of exclusion" described as characterising suburban life is separated from wider Swedish society. Thus, these suburban areas appear as a standalone container of social problems, that is, they become problems in themselves. In such understandings of social exclusion, the urban periphery becomes a threat to the moral core of Swedish society and its social cohesion (cf. Schierup and Ålund 2018). In relation to this problematisation of the urban periphery, calls have been made for a wide range of interventions to promote greater security and inclusion in the Swedish urban landscape.

Such problematisations may be illustrated by a widely-discussed report published by the Police and the Intelligence unit of its Department of National Operations. The report describes an alarming development in Swedish cities, not least with an increasing number of areas defined as "vulnerable" or "particularly vulnerable".

> In the vulnerable areas, it is estimated that there is a local social order that in various degrees differs from the system of the democratic society, regarding norms, economy and justice. Actors who do not represent the democratic system have had a significant impact on the development of

these areas. These actors are primarily criminal actors, but also religious leaders, spreading messages that are the opposite of Swedish democratic values. (Polisen 2017: 32)

In the report, these areas are problematised as existing outside the law and order of mainstream Swedish society. Furthermore, this position on the outside is described as posing a serious threat to society in the long run and requiring special attention and specific actions to be taken.

The development of an alternative social order has gone further in some areas. There, residents have adapted to the norms developed in the area, finding no greater value in the rest of society to intervene. When the balance is disturbed, this has remarkable consequences for the residents, which means that society's efforts are not always appreciated. These are the characteristic features of a particularly vulnerable area. (p. 33)

Problematising the suburb as a security threat has been further accentuated in recent years, particularly in the aftermath of the 2015 "refugee crisis", in which large numbers of refugees sought refuge in Sweden, mainly from war-torn Syria. Although radical right-wing forces have previously promoted discourses on securitisation which are based on explicitly repressive policy measures targeting migrants—particularly Muslims—such policy measures have gradually been normalised, as can also be seen in more recent political discourses on problems within Swedish suburbs (cf. Dahlstedt and Eliassi 2018). Like several other European countries, more established Swedish political parties have gradually redefined notions of citizenship, placing sharper demands on migrants to adapt to the norms and values of the Swedish majority society (Dahlstedt and Neergaard 2016). Here, the urban periphery has repeatedly been used as a means for legitimising more stringent requirements and introducing repressive measures that target migrants and the areas they inhabit.

"We're en route towards a catastrophe in Sweden": Problematising the suburbs

Shifting attention to local actors, when articulating the challenges facing youth living in suburban areas, the primary reaction is to frame suburban areas and their inhabitants as a problem. Suburban areas in particular are repeatedly described as being characterised by completely different conditions, rules, and norms than those in other parts of the cities, and Swedish society at large. Accordingly, suburban areas are problematised as places where criminality and other forms of antisocial and deviant behaviours are developed among youth, which in turn calls for specific interventions in order to facilitate social change. The main problem of these suburban areas is usually articulated via invoking its population of households with scarce resources, particularly those inhabited by unemployed people and "migrants".

According to the local actors, this in turn makes certain norms appear as more or less "normal", not least among young people, for whom not working and not adapting to the norms of Swedish society becomes the norm. Furthermore, many parents living in suburban areas are described as lacking the skills needed in order to take responsibility for the upbringing of their children (cf. Dahlstedt and Lozic 2017). Instead, other *role models*—such as "criminals"—are anointed as playing an important role in influencing suburban youth. Based on such problematisations, a range of measures have been proposed to address these problems, which are specifically ascribed to these suburban areas and their inhabitants.

The challenges of one city's suburban area are compared with challenges described in similar areas located in Stockholm. According to the initiator of a football project targeting youth in the area, failure to take powerful action will eventually lead to a situation as chaotic as the one described as already existing in the suburban peripheries of Stockholm:

> We're en route towards a catastrophe in Sweden [...] You can see this in Botkyrka, Fittja and Tensta. With a completely different tendency towards violence, with a completely different criminality, with a completely different formation of gangs, Which means—and I mean this in all seriousness—that people look to join gangs. And the gang is more important than surviving. You can murder people who are in opposition, who come from other gangs. This is what we think we must try to avoid.

Even though the situation is described as not yet approaching the chaotic conditions described in the suburbs of Stockholm, there is an explicit risk scenario addressed, which demands certain interventions in order to prevent such developments from happening. As an alternative to such scenarios, providing suburban youth with the possibility of meaningful leisure time activities—particularly in the form of football—is promoted as important.

> And there, the aim is to start right from the first class so that the children will not end up in these criminal gangs, but in the world of sports instead, or preferably within the social world, where people integrate with those who come from other areas. [...] We do not need to assume the worst, but we see that the City has a great deal of ... a strong formation of gangs with very violent activities.

Here, sport and football are promoted as a means of social change, as an alternative to destructive and delinquent behaviours "flourishing" in suburban areas. Such sports-based interventions are based on a pedagogic rationality that focuses on empowerment and activation; teaches youth to take on responsibility and make the "right" decisions in life; promotes discipline and learning to follow the rules; and more broadly promotes assimilation into Swedish norms and behaviours (cf. Ekholm and Dahlstedt 2017).

In another city, the principal of a school in one suburban area described their impression of local parents—and specifically their lack of commitment to engage with the school—as a significant challenge, in contrast to situations described in other parts of the city.

> We rarely manage to get parents to parents' meetings. The ones participating are the parents who have a job and have become included in society, and not all parents have. [...] Among the economically stronger groups, where there are more highly educated parents, [in these areas], schools are more questioned by parents. It is not always the best for the school to be questioned by the parents, but the parents in [the Area] are generally passive.

In this description, parents living in this suburban area are portrayed as different from parents residing in more prosperous areas of the city—they are passive, instead of actively engaging and questioning the principal like parents who live in other areas. The main line of this argument focusing on the passivity of suburban parents also appears in an interview with a teacher working in a suburban school in another city, who describes the situation as follows:

> There is a lot of extreme violence among the students. We are talking about grade one and three ... extensive violence among the younger students ... a huge problem [...] The parents are not at home with the students nowadays, as they used to be. It's different with the parents who are involved. We call a parent meeting and there are three parents showing up.

Once more, suburban parents are framed as an obstacle for the school system to overcome. Recurring problematisations linked to the parents' migrant backgrounds are evident in the responses of local actors. For instance, one police officer speaks of "migrant parents" as having a "completely different mindset about punishment than they have in [the] so-called West", arguing that they think Swedish society "indulges" and "pets people". According to another police officer, there are significant differences between Swedish approaches to authority, and these parents' views on both societal responsibility and upbringing: "if you are talking to a father here, he could hit a child", which according to him would not be possible amongst parents living in other parts of the city.

Such approaches to problematising suburban parents bring about and motivate certain authoritative measures which specifically focus on the parents, who then become the target of a range of interventions that aim to change them as parents and citizens, thus making them *governable*.

One of the interventions proposed and implemented is Home Get-Togethers. This was initiated as a means of establishing meeting places where "migrant mothers" meet representatives from the police, emergency services, and the municipality in the relaxed and familiar environment of the mother's own home. In this particular setting, the aim is to develop content and trusting relationships between mothers and local actors, forging a rapport that is personal and affective rather than juridical, thus blurring the boundaries between the private and the public, and professionalism and friendship. Through such interventions, families are rendered reachable targets for various learning activities, resulting in the possibility to promote change among the mothers as well as their children (cf. Dahlstedt and Lozic 2017).

Among local actors, there is a strong focus on framing suburban areas and their inhabitants both as a problem, and as a site where solutions are to be directed. Here, the main focus is on what could be described as the *effects* or *state* of social exclusion—for instance in the form of distrust, apathy, and criminal behaviour—that is geographically tethered to suburban areas. However, what is left un-problematised are the mechanisms generating the *effects* or *state* of social exclusion, which is the main focus of the discourses that arise within interviews with youths.

"Nobody cares about our rights": Problematising the mechanisms of social exclusion

When turning attention to the youth, quite different understandings of suburban life and the problem of social exclusion emerge. And on the basis of these particular understandings, other scenarios for the future emerge which contradict those emerging out of the problematisations made by local actors. While these suburbs are described as containers of insecurities and social problems within the dominant discourses found in policy debates as well as among local actors, their youth residents contravene these descriptions by framing the suburb as a safe place, as the home of a family-like community, and as a place where they are cared for and feel at home. This particular discourse about the suburb is obviously formed in contrast to counter discourses that circulate in other spheres of Swedish society.

The contradictory relationship between young people's descriptions and dominant discourses can be illustrated by the following conversational excerpt that took place in a focus group interview with youth living within one suburban area.

RESEARCHER: How is life in the Area?
AHMED: It's nice, you feel safe, because you are born and raised here.
EMIR: You know everyone around here.
VEDAT: All those prejudices, I think they're a bit excessive.
RESEARCHER: What makes you feel safe?
AHMED: We are like a family here, everyone knows each other.
RESEARCHER: What do you think about the views of the Area from the outside world?
EMIR: Well, things might happen, but I think it's exaggerated.
SELIM: Things do happen, but the media is always putting a spin on things.

In this dialogue, the youth consistently identify with the suburban area and repeatedly define it as the place where they belong—their "home". They describe the Area as a safe place, contradicting media reports that problematise it as a place of violence, turmoil, and insecurity—a place outside of law and order. The sense of security the young people express is related to the fact that they are born and raised in the Area. In other words, they belong there. This sense of belonging is quite tellingly captured by the usage of the family metaphor. As inhabitants of the Area, the young people "know everyone"—"we are like a family".

As illustrated in an interview with Dimen, one of the young males living in the Area, dominant discourses on "excluded areas" (among them the Area), may have a range of consequences for those portrayed as living in the excluded outside, not least in terms of feelings of alienation and a sense of unfair treatment by dominant Swedish society.

> So, when I watch TV, the media describe the Area as a ghetto ... it's really horrible ... they take pictures and film the shabbiest place. There are shabby places all over the country. If they come and really look at the Area, in the schools, fields, everywhere, they will not see gangs destroying. That's not how it is so. There are gangs everywhere. I cannot deny that gangs do not exist in the Area, because they do. But I think the Area is a wonderful place, like many other places in the city and in Sweden.

As the aforementioned excerpt illustrates, such media and political discourses about the suburb may not seem legitimate to the suburban youth. At the same time, young people need to relate to and develop strategies in order to deal with these discourses, as they confront them in everyday life. They may do so either in terms of identification, or in terms of dis-identification (Andersson 2003; Léon Rosales 2010).

Certainly, there is "stuff happening" in the suburb, as Dimen says, in terms of both violence and criminal acts. But as the young people repeatedly stress, these cases tend to be exaggerated, not least by the media. "In every country, there are excluded suburbs, which are generally referred to as: 'Do not go there, it's dangerous'", Siana says. "But it's just bullshit. There is more murder downtown than here ... I don't think they are aware of it, but they really hurt us".

When young people talk about suburban life, the main challenge they identify for themselves and their suburban peers may be described as *mechanisms* of social exclusion. In their conversation, they illustrate how dominant discourses that problematise the suburb and its inhabitants have a range of effects for those who live in the problematised areas.

For instance, Faduma, one of the young females interviewed, describes how she is treated as a second-class citizen, by not being listened to and constantly being questioned.

> As soon as you ask for help, they will step on you. The police can stop you anywhere and take you to some unknown public space and just leave you there. Nobody cares about our rights. Then when you get upset and the kids do something stupid, you just focus on that. Why don't you see the whole picture? Unemployment, crime, everything is related, but instead you only focus on when someone is throwing the stone.

In the quote, Faduma cries out her desperation: "Nobody cares about our rights". Once more, an unspecified "them" is referred to as causing this particular problem. However, in Faduma's testimony, the police are understood as a symptom of the problem.

Furthermore, Myner, one of the young men interviewed, provides a range of concrete examples of the material consequences that the discourses of a dangerous and unsafe suburb may have for those actually living there:

> It affects us, for example if you are buying a car and you see the cost of the insurance. When you are applying for a job, they very much ask where you live. Everything is getting more expensive because of these prejudices.

By making comparisons and referring to previous experiences, young people describe the suburb as a safe place where they belong and feel at home, in stark contrast to the unsafe outside world in the surrounding society. They describe how they might not feel at home when they travel in other parts of the city. In the following dialogue, some young people discuss their personal experiences of being treated differently in other parts of the city, due to the way they look and dress.

SIANA: You don't feel safe. Here, nobody cares about how you dress. That's how it is.
HAMID: Yeah, it's a matter of what you wear, what clothes you wear. Like Siana says, they always look.
SIANA: They judge you beforehand. They don't even know your surname. But they judge you.
HAMID: When you go to a bar or something downtown … It's always like, ah if you look right, then you are let in. If you're dressed differently, like you're from the hood, then you'll never be let in. That's the way it is.
YOUNES: Just like they're saying. You just feel outside. You really don't want to be part of that.

Some youth become uncomfortable due to experiences of being outside of their suburban area and others looking down upon them, and treating them differently because of the way they dress, their appearance, and their way of speaking and behaving. These experiences, in turn, make the suburb feel even more like a "place of home".

"What doesn't kill you makes you stronger": A will to make a change

The way of problematising the young people's existence today within their safe place of the suburbs also works to shape their imaginations about the future—for themselves, as well as for the suburb at large. Their discussions about the future are dominated by their ambitions to change their current living conditions—that is, they express the will to not give up when trying to overcome the difficulties and challenges they face in their everyday lives.

This desire to make a change is illustrated in the following dialogue between Siana and Hamid:

SIANA: So, it hurts us, but it makes us stronger. It's like, what doesn't kill you makes you stronger, kind of. That's it. We're young, we see and we know.
HAMID: That is, we have a future.
SIANA: Exactly. I don't know how to explain, but we can change it. We will change, we're going to change it and we're about to make a change. It's not that we haven't started. We have started a long time ago. But it's all about really getting down to business and showing that this is how it's like. You know, we have to be strong. You really cannot have an influence on us.

When Siana and Hamid talk about the future, there is a distinction made between "us" and "them", with the major responsibility put on the suburban youth—"us". Siana emphasises that this "we" needs to "get down to business" and "be strong". The excerpt presents a dialogue between Siana and Hamid as spokespeople for suburban youth on one hand, and an unarticulated "them" on the other. Both Siana and Hamid emphasise the need to develop a sense of solidarity and belonging among "us" in relation to the supposed category of "Others". Who these "Others" actually are is not made explicit in the interview. However, what is made explicit is that "You really cannot have an influence on us". Hamid emphasises that it is the youth who *are* the future, as they will be living this future. Siana and Hamid both express a strong belief that suburban youth can and will bring about change—"we can ... we will ... we're going to". As they describe it, the future has already arrived, as changes have already begun: "We have started a long time ago".

In their stories about the future, these young people argue that they can expect to face greater difficulties and challenges, just because they live in a particular suburb. However, the following description of the future and its related expectations is not one-dimensional, but based on harsh descriptions of difficulties, as well as hopes for change and opportunities.

> I'm a woman from Thailand and I don't have a Swedish surname. Few people can pronounce my last name and nobody knows how to spell it [laughter]. I'm also working class. Sure, some people are fighting for equality, that immigrants should have the same opportunities and some

are struggling for the working class, but I am at the bottom in all three categories ... I'm a little afraid of the future. If there are a thousand job applicants and I am one of them, how far will I get? It's a little dark, but I hope it will get better. If you live with that dream, there is still a chance.

Here, Mara illustrates how contemporary life conditions shape her situation, not only today but also in the future, as her future plans are conceived of as restricted and regulated by the fact that she is a young, working-class woman "from Thailand". At the same time, Mara and other youths living in suburban areas have hopes and dreams for the future. What makes the future hopeful is that there is still a chance for change to occur. For this chance to be realised, hope that things can change is needed: "If you live with that dream, there is still a chance". However, it is not only among individual young people living in suburban Sweden that the mechanisms of social exclusion are addressed and negotiated.

"We young ones are no longer grateful": Megaphones of change

Throughout the last decade, a broad repertoire of initiatives have been developed among inhabitants in suburban areas—not least among young people—to address the problematic of social exclusion in other ways so as to propose alternative solutions for the future. There are a number of examples of negotiations and mobilisation taking place today that push back against the existing discourses on social exclusion that accelerate patterns of inequality and welfare changes (cf. Schierup et al. 2014; Sernhede et al. 2016).

The Panthers from Biskopsgården (a suburb outside Gothenburg) are one of many suburban organisations addressing the effects of welfare policies initiated in the last decades, and their impact upon the everyday lives of those living in suburban areas, particularly in terms of the privatisation of the housing market, and the closing down of social services such as libraries, health centres, and youth recreation centres. One of the founding members of the organisation draws parallels between the situation of youth with migrant backgrounds living in today's suburban Sweden, and the situation of youth living in American black ghettos in the 1960s and 1970s, which was the historical context from which the Black Panther Party was born.

The Black Panther Party said they were a result of colonialism. Black people were in the US due to slavery and colonialism, and I can identify with that. We are not in Sweden because we are slaves, but because our parents were forced to escape from dictatorships supported by the US. So, we are also the result of colonialism and imperialism. I live in Sweden, I'm born here, but I'm neither Swedish nor Turkish. Black people are not seen as full citizens in the US, but they are not Africans either. We Kurds are children of the same colonial oppression and we are in exile in France, Germany, England, and so on, without being

Europeans. Our parents were grateful that they got shelter here, but we young ones are no longer grateful, we do not want to be second-class citizens, and that's why we think like the Black Panther Party, and that's why we say change is "by any means necessary". (Sernhede 2018, p. 206)

Even though the specific contexts that birthed these organisations are different, similarities can be found amongst the challenges they face, and the methodologies used to address them. Inspired by the Black Panthers, the Biskopsgården Panthers provide a range of social work activities as a means of dealing with youth-specific challenges. Football tournaments were organised, and new playgrounds and football fields were requested, amongst other initiatives. Summer and winter camps were organised for children whose parents could not afford for them to leave the suburbs during vacations.

The Megaphone, based in Husby, north of Stockholm, is another suburban organisation that strives to speak for suburban youth (Ålund and Léon Rosales 2017). Based on his experience of the work carried out by The Megaphone, as well as his personal contacts with people in Brazil, co-founder Rami Al-khamisi articulates similarities between suburban Sweden and the favelas of Brazil.

> Thankfully, we are not in the situation where Brazil is—where the police systematically kill young, poor and dark bodies. But, constantly, the idea crosses my mind, that we may be on the way there, as the hateful, dehumanised rhetoric and demands for being tough among some political parties will be realised in practice. (Al-khamisi 2017)

As described by Al-khamisi, developments in Sweden are heading in the wrong direction. Rather than focusing on addressing the social and economic conditions that form the basis of growing tensions, distrust, and the spiral of violence that has been highlighted in reports on the situation in Swedish suburban areas, more emphasis is being placed on repressive measures directed specifically at residents of these suburbs.

> The security of the residents is not met when there is no social support, and the media and political stigmatisation of these people continues. The violence takes new forms, and the gangs find new territories to occupy. Mistrust against the institutions can be reversed only by making a change where the residents themselves set the agenda for the efforts made in the area. (ibid.)

According to Al-khamisi, a continued stigmatisation of the suburbs and its inhabitants will help to further deepen the youth's distrust and experiences of having no voice, which he describes as a crucial part of the problem of social exclusion. But as Al-khamisi emphasises, the residents themselves are not the bearers of the problem but are rather part of the solution. Among the residents, these solutions are already acknowledged and addressed by civil society organisations. It is time that those living in the inner city and in other areas of Swedish society listen to the voices of the suburbs.

> Politicians at all levels—in both Brazil and Sweden—have a responsibility to represent the whole country. Even those who are vulnerable. Instead of coming up with new solutions from the safe parts of the inner city, they should turn to the vibrant civil society in the suburbs and favelas. In many suburbs throughout Sweden, there is currently social mobilisation going on. […] The solutions are there waiting for those who are ready to listen. (ibid.)

The main challenge, according to Al-khamisi, is basically the same in the suburbs of Sweden as in the favelas of Brazil, and that is to pave the way for listening to mobilisations that are already taking place in the urban peripheries in Sweden, not least those that involve the youth. As becomes apparent in the youth interviews, the focus once more needs to shift: from problematising the suburb to problematising Swedish society, from problematising the *effects* or *state* of social exclusion to problematising the *mechanisms* of social exclusion. On the basis of such shifts, solutions are also directed *away* from the suburb and outwards—*towards* broader Swedish society. In these struggles for social justice, the local context in the Swedish urban periphery is also related to a transnational context that relates the particular experiences of those in the Swedish urban periphery to similar experiences in Brazilian favelas and American "black ghettos" (cf. Sernhede et al. 2016). Also, in this respect, the ways of problematising and searching for solutions reaches outside of the suburb.

Concluding discussion

This chapter has focused on current discourses about social exclusion and suburban youth in Sweden. In recent years, the challenges facing suburban youth have been a recurring topic in Swedish political debate. In mainstream political debate within the last decade, the urban periphery has been categorised as an "area of exclusion" and has repeatedly been problematised as a threat to social cohesion that requires a range of security measures to be taken. As illustrated, such problematisations are also made by local actors working in suburban areas. When describing the main challenges faced by the suburbs, the responsibility for taking action is placed on the suburb and its inhabitants, and particularly on those with migrant backgrounds. In this problematisation, the "area of exclusion" is decoupled from surrounding Swedish society and its wider structural conditions. Quite tellingly, questions concerning inequality and discrimination are mostly absent in both public debates, and among local actors. Rather, the suburb is described as causing the problem of social exclusion. Accordingly, it is the suburb that emerges as in need of specific measures, such as adapting to the norms and values of broader Swedish society.

In a way, such problematisations are symptomatic of wider changes in Swedish social policy which have taken place in recent decades. Here, political discourses have focussed on placing responsibility for the management of social exclusion on the individual, rather than on demands for structural changes (cf. Davidsson 2010; Larsson et al. 2012). This is illustrated in current discourses on "areas of exclusion" as sites of social problems. In dominant discourses, the main focus is put on social exclusion in terms of static *conditions* located within the excluded "outside", while the manifold *mechanisms* that cause social inequality are left out, and are hence not further addressed in terms of social policy interventions (cf. Stigendal 2016).

However, as illustrated in this chapter, this is not the only way of problematising youth social exclusion. When analysing young people's descriptions of the current challenges faced by suburban areas, it becomes clear that their main focus is directed towards the mechanisms of social exclusion and their consequences, which are both material (in terms of insurance, employment, and education) and immaterial (in terms of their sense of home and sense of belonging). The youth describe how they confront dominant discourses that problematise their home suburb in their everyday lives. However, they also stress that it is necessary and possible to overcome these current obstacles, and in order for things to change, they will have to initiate it themselves—no one else will do it *for* them. Thus, according to the rationale that emerges in such problematisations, the main solution to the problem of social exclusion is—once again—located in the suburbs, with the youth themselves being held responsible for making change happen.

Other strategies to help face the future are provided by suburban organisations such as the Panthers and the Megaphone. Similar to what was articulated through the youth interviews, these organisations address the problem of social exclusion in a way that differs from how social exclusion is problematised in dominant discourses. Here, the main focus shifts from problematising the suburbs to problematising Swedish society, and from the effects and state of social exclusion to the mechanisms of social exclusion. In line with such problematisations, solutions are explicitly redirected away from the suburbs to instead target broader Swedish society.

This chapter has conclusively illustrated that problems such as social exclusion—that are situated in the context of the urban periphery as well as elsewhere—are constantly redefined and renegotiated. There is not *one* problem that summarises the social exclusion of suburban youth, but rather different ways of *problematising* the social exclusion of suburban youth. Here, the urban periphery is a site of ongoing contestation, where it is also possible for suburban youth— today, as well as yesterday and tomorrow—to articulate alternative ways of problematising current societal conditions, to thus create alternative solutions as well as alternative futures. The outcomes of these contestations are yet to be seen.

References

Al-khamisi, R. (2017). 'Sluta föda samma desperation i Järva som i Rios favelor', *OmVärlden*, April 23, http://www.omvarlden.se/Opinion/kronikor1/samma-desperation-i-jarva-som-i-rio. [Accessed 8 October, 2018]

Ålund, A. and Lèon Rosales, R. (2017). 'Renaissance from the margins', in A. Ålund et al., eds., *Reimagineering the nation*. Peter Lang: Frankfurt am Main.

Andersson, Å. (2003). *Inte samma lika*. Eslöv: Symposion.

Bacchi, C. L. (1999). *Women, policy and politics*. London: Sage.

Boréus, K. (1994). *Högervåg*. Stockholm: Tiden.

Dahlstedt, M. (2015). 'Discourses of employment and inclusion in Sweden', in E. Righard et al., eds., *Transformation of Scandinavian cities*. Lund: Nordic Academic Press.

Dahlstedt, M. (2018). *Förortsdrömmar*. Linköping: Linköping University Electronic Press.

Dahlstedt, M. and Eliassi, B. (2018). 'Slaget om hemmet'. *Sociologisk Forskning* [forthcoming].

Dahlstedt, M. and Lozic, V. (2017). 'Managing urban unrest'. *Critical and Radical Social Work*, 5(2), pp. 207–222.

Dahlstedt, M. and Neergaard, A. (2016). 'Crisis of solidarity? Changing welfare and migration regimes in Sweden'. *Critical Sociology*, doi:10.1177/0896920516675204.

Davidsson, T. (2010). 'Utanförskapelsen'. *Socialvetenskaplig tidskrift*, 17(2), pp. 149–169.

Ekholm, D. and Dahlstedt, M. (2017). 'Football for inclusion'. *Social Inclusion*, 5(2), pp. 232–240.

Fell, T. and Guziana, R. (2016). *Stad, rättvisa och boendesegregering*. Västerås: Mälardalens högskola.

Foucault, M. (2004). 'Polemics, politics, and problematizations', in P. Rabinow, ed., *The Foucault Reader*. London: Penguin Books.

Jacobsson, K. (2004). 'A European politics for employability', in C. Garsten and K. Jacobsson, eds., *Learning to be employable*. Houndmills: Macmillan Palgrave.

Larsson, B., Thörn, H. and Letell, M. eds., (2012). *Transformations of the Swedish welfare state*. Basingstoke: Palgrave Macmillan.

León Rosales, R. (2010). *Vid framtidens hitersta gräns*. Botkyrka: Mångkulturellt centrum.

Polisen (2017). *Utsatta områden*. Stockholm: Nationella operativa avdelningen.

Ristilammi, P-M. (1994). *Rosengård och den svarta poesin*. Stehag: Symposion.

Salonen, T., ed. (2011). *Hela staden*. Umeå: Boréa.

Schierup, C-U., and Ålund, A. (2018). 'Re-imagineering the common in precarious times'. *Journal of Intercultural Studies*, 39(2), pp. 207–223.

Schierup, C-U., Ålund, A. and Kings, L. (2014) 'Reading the Stockholm Riots'. *Race & Class*, 55(3), pp. 1–21.

Schierup, C-U., Krifors, K. and Slavnic, Z. (2015). 'Social exclusion', in M. Dahlstedt and A. Neergaard, eds., *International migration and ethnic relations*. London: Routledge.

Sernhede, O. (2018). 'Förorten och det sociala arbetet som försvann', in M. Dahlstedt and P. Lalander, eds., *Manifest—för ett socialt arbete i tiden*. Lund: Studentlitteratur.

Sernhede, O., Thörn, C. and Thörn, H. (2016). 'The Stockholm uprising in context', in M. Mayer, et al., eds., *Urban uprisings*. Basingstoke: Palgrave Macmillan.

Statistics Sweden (2014). *Segregation i Stockholm län*. Stockholm: SCB.

Stigendal, M. (2016). *Samhällsgränser*. Stockholm: Liber.

7 Welfare chauvinism at the margins of whiteness

Young unemployed Russian-speakers' negotiations of worker-citizenship in Finland[1]

Daria Krivonos

Introduction

Within the neoliberal restructuring of the welfare state, a selective logic that distinguishes between 'desired' and 'undesired' migrants, as well as 'deserving' and 'undeserving' social groups in relation to welfare provisions, has become more dominant. In the ideology of economic productivity and competitiveness, unemployment has become a terrain of "failed citizenship"—in particular, in relation to migrants and racialised populations (Anderson 2015). With public concern growing in regard to the burden of migration on the welfare state, it has become more legitimate to argue that welfare benefits should only be reserved for those considered 'natives', who hold a self-evident right to belong to the nation (Keskinen et al. 2016). These notions of deservingness have been shown to be constructed around racialising criteria and othering (Harrell et al. 2014; Keskinen et al. 2016; Lens and Cary 2010).

While the concept of welfare chauvinism has been theorised in relation to ideas around migrants' access to welfare benefits, in this chapter I analyse how Russian-speaking migrants positioned as unemployed draw on a racial grammar to legitimise their place in the Finnish welfare system. The analysis is based on multi-sited ethnographic research into young Russian-speaking migrants' employment in Helsinki, Finland; this is the largest migrant and minority group in Finland, which is disadvantaged in the Finnish labour market, and is strongly affected by unemployment (Statistics Finland 2013). Drawing on ethnographic data and interviews with young unemployed Russian-speaking[2] migrants in Finland, I demonstrate that the use of transnational racialising discourses—which depict non-white groups as essentially having a poor work ethic—allows my research participants to construct themselves as deserving welfare recipients with a strong commitment to work. I show how the boundaries of deservingness and entitlement for welfare benefits are racialised and interconnected with the idea of whiteness. The analysis suggests that through the reproduction of the non-white work-shy Other, young unemployed Russian-speaking migrants not only construct their whiteness, but also their belonging to a form of neoliberal citizenship which has stigmatised unemployment.

The chapter is structured as follows. First, I discuss the position of young unemployed Russian-speaking migrants in the context of welfare chauvinism, the neoliberal restructuring of citizenship, and normative whiteness in Finland. I show how the organisation of labour has been central for how whiteness operates, and how unemployment is constructed as a loss of whiteness, respectability, and worker identity. I start the analysis with a description of how Russian-speakers experience their precarious labour market position in Finland, which acts as a backdrop for the analysis of their racialising discourses against other migrants. Finally, I show how their use of transnational racialised hierarchies helps Russian-speakers reinscribe themselves into whiteness and respectable worker-citizenship. I conclude by discussing how colonial depictions of non-white populations as lazy converge with contemporary neoliberal capitalist ideologies of deservingness and productivity.

Welfare chauvinism, whiteness and Russian-speakers in Finland

This chapter aims to analyse how meanings of whiteness work in a neoliberal capitalist ideology of 'deservingness' unfolding in Finland, in particular, in relation to groups that have lost their white privilege after migration. Russian-speaking migrants' racialised and precarious position in Finland needs to be elaborated upon in a context characterised by normative whiteness, welfare chauvinism, and the recrafting of citizenship and state under neoliberalism. The concept of welfare chauvinism has been adapted to research the views and policies on whether migrants should have rights to receive benefits, and under what conditions (Keskinen et al. 2016). This political agenda has centred around questions of deservingness and entitlement in relation to welfare benefits. Discourses around the welfare state have been used to draw distinctions between 'us' and 'them', and it has become increasingly more legitimate to argue that welfare benefits should be reserved only for 'natives', or for a part of those who live and work in the country, that is, not for all residence permit holders. The notions of deservingness and entitlement have centred around exclusionary ethno-nationalist and racialising criteria, with non-Western Others portrayed as 'undeserving' and abusers of the system (Jørgensen and Thomsen 2016; Keskinen 2016).

This has taken place against the backdrop of the dismantling of the welfare state itself, which has increased income disparities and the stigmatisation of a racialised underclass (Mäkinen 2017). In Finland, neoliberal policies have increasingly targeted the unemployed via the introduction of labour activation policies that also target young migrant and racialised groups presumably having problems with 'employability' (Krivonos 2019). Finland has experienced a slow but steady transition from a welfare state towards a workfare state, which means shifting from universal needs-based entitlement for welfare support, towards contractual relations between the state, market, and citizens

(Kananen 2012). This restructuring has reconfigured discourses around unemployment—it is no longer a structural problem, but predicated on an individual's responsibility, lack of work ethic, and moral failure. This has strengthened the idea that the norm of employment functions as a key 'integration' criterion for migrants (Keskinen 2016, p. 6; Jokinen et al. 2011).

Besides the neoliberalisation present in unemployment and welfare chauvinist discourses, the context of Finland is characterised by normative whiteness, from which Russians have been excluded. Like other Nordic countries (e.g. Habel 2012), Finland has defined itself as innocent of colonialism and racism, while describing itself in racialised terms as a 'white' nation (Keskinen et al. 2009). In Finland, the term 'immigrant' is itself a highly racialised and class-based category (Haikkola 2011; Rastas 2005). The politics of invisibility is an important mechanism for labelling foreigners as 'immigrants' in Finland, and one's belonging to ethnic Finnishness can be contested on the basis of an individual's physical appearance (Leinonen 2012).

Russian-speakers' ostensible whiteness has not protected them from being racialised as the Eastern Other in Finland (see also Helakorpi's Chapter 5 about whiteness and the racialisation of Roma people in Finland, and Siivikko's Chapter 4 about the racialisation of Sámi people in Finland). Clearly, whiteness does not just refer to skin pigmentation, but is also associated with factors such as history, class, clothing, citizenship, gender, and accent, which can be constructed through racialised discourses (McDowell 2008). The politics of whiteness are deeply implicated in the politics of domination, which establish hierarchies of whiteness. Rather than being a white/non-white binary, whiteness is theorised as a geographically contextual phenomenon, a contingent social hierarchy granting differential access to economic and cultural capital, intersecting with, and overlaying, class and ethnicity (Garner 2012; Loftsdóttir 2017). Whiteness has been historically constructed in relation to non-whiteness, which in turn has excluded non-European forms of whiteness (Bonnett 2008). Finnish whiteness has itself been constructed in opposition to, and subjugation of Sámi people (see Siivikko in Chapter 4).

The contexts of work and organised labour have been long constructed to enable the working of whiteness (Leonard 2010). W.E.B. Du Bois' (1935) "wages of whiteness" denotes how white labourers in the US embraced an identity of a dominant white group, rather than unite with recently freed enslaved people through class solidarity. Through organising along racial lines, white workers received a material and psychological "wages of whiteness". The processes through which the meaning of whiteness was established through work is also demonstrated through Irish workers, who distanced and pushed non-white groups from their workplaces, subsequently becoming "white" through this labour (Ignatiev 1995). Nowadays, ordinary whiteness is associated with the respectable, intellectual middle classes, as opposed to physical labourers (Leonard 2010).

While their embodied white capital can sometimes allow them to pass as white Finns in Finland (Krivonos 2015), Russian-speakers do not occupy a structural position of privilege, and their ostensible whiteness does not translate into social mobility in Finland. The legacy of the historical past relationships between the Soviet Union and Finland makes the position of Russian-speakers highly visible in the public discourse of migration in Finland (Leinonen 2012) and is reflected in predominantly negative attitudes towards Russian-speakers (Tanttu 2009). Russian-speaking migrants in Finland are over-represented in low-skilled jobs, with the most common occupations being cleaning, shop sales assistance, construction, and storage labouring (Statistics Finland 2014), which often do not correspond to their educational qualifications (Krivonos 2017). In addition, Russian-speaking migrants in Finland are heavily affected by unemployment (Statistics Finland 2013). Thus, their precarious position in the manual labour market excludes many Russian-speaking migrants from the norm of respectable, intellectual, middle-class whiteness.

However, it is important to pinpoint that Russian-speakers do not only cross national borders through which their whiteness as a structural position becomes misrecognised, but they also move between different sets of classification systems that are tied to local, national, and transnational hierarchies (see also Lundström 2017). Conceptual insights offered by transnationalism have shown how migrants draw upon multiple nations and communities in the construction of their identities (Schiller 2010; Nowicka 2017). Although Russian-speakers are racialised as not 'properly' white in Finland, racial structures in Russia have positioned dominant Russians as white. Russia has constituted itself as an empire through the colonisation and racialisation of its own subaltern Others (Tlostanova 2003). Although Russia is a multinational imperial state comprising more than 185 ethnic groups (Census 2010), Russianness in Russia is constructed through being white and looking Slavic, and colour-based terms are used in everyday language in relation to migrants and Russian citizens alike (Sotkasiira 2016). In addition, the Russian mediascape importantly works as a transnational mediator of racialised hierarchies and knowledge (Davydova-Minguet 2017). Dominant Russian media has been producing moral panics around whiteness and representations of Europe as being flooded by uncontrolled flows of non-white migrants. This has reinforced that dominant Russianness is white and superior.

Against these racial structures in Russia—which equate Russianness with whiteness and privilege—upon arrival in Finland, many Russian migrants lose some of their white privilege and, as a result, take a racialised position as low-skilled workers and unemployed migrants. I suggest that through the use of transnational racial knowledge—which grants them privileged whiteness in Russia vis-à-vis other groups—they symbolically re-inscribe themselves into respectable citizenship in Finland through racialising non-white Others. Through racialising other migrants as non-white and undeserving, they "make their contested whiteness work" (Leonard 2013), which grants access to respectable citizenship.

It is precisely the context of neoliberalised citizenship, unemployment, and transnational whiteness (Lundström 2014) that guides my analysis of young

Russian-speakers' racialisation of Others. In the analysis, I explore how the neoliberal notions of welfare entitlement, deservingness, and the norm of worker-citizenship are intertwined with, and constituted by, the construction of transnational whiteness.

Methodology and ethical concerns

Empirical data was collected as part of a larger research project—'Migrant Youth Employment: Politics of Recognition and Boundaries of Belonging' (2014-2017, funded by the University of Helsinki, Kone Foundation and Emil Aaltonen Foundation). Within the project, I conducted a multi-sited ethnographic study of young Russian-speakers' employment in the Helsinki metropolitan area in 2014 to 2016, during which I interviewed a total of 53 young Russian-speakers (20 to 32 years old). Through my ethnographic fieldwork, I did observations in the contexts of integration, language, and CV courses, as well as youth career counselling services, to better understand their efforts to find work in Finland. My interviewees came from Russia, Estonia, Moldova, Ukraine, Belarus, Kazakhstan, and Armenia, however a majority of participants came from Russia and Estonia, and it is their narratives that I refer to in this chapter. All but one were born outside Finland, and had obtained vocational or higher education in their home countries. Only those born outside Finland are mentioned in the analysis. Despite coming from different countries and ethnic self-identifications, young people were often identified as Russians in Finland due to their mother tongue. It is important to mention that most of the research participants come from majority backgrounds in Russia and ethnic minority backgrounds in Estonia, however as I show, they position themselves as white in Finland, and sometimes more 'European' than Russians from Russia. After migrating to Finland, many experience a status discord, and downward social mobility when their education and work experience from their home countries are not recognised in Finland, which forces them to move to less skilled occupations, or become unemployed.

The interviews were conducted in Russian, lasted on average 80 minutes, and were structured around young people's biographies—their lives before and after moving to Finland, and in particular, their experiences of unemployment and work. The interviews were transcribed. The interview transcripts were analysed using thematic analysis, which means organising interview materials around key themes that emerged from the data. Although whiteness did not inform my research questions in the beginning of my fieldwork, whiteness as a theme emerged through references to other migrants in Finland, and young Russian-speakers' visions of themselves within Finland's racialised hierarchies.

A relative experience of commonality and an atmosphere of informality—which I developed with some of my participants due to my Russian background—created challenging situations from an ethical point of view. As I show below, my research participants sometimes tended to express racist views towards other migrants in Helsinki. Such situations reminded me of

108 *Krivonos*

Catrin Lundström's (2010) "white spaces of privilege" in ethnographic fieldwork, with the only difference being that Russian-speakers themselves are largely disadvantaged against majority Finns. On the one hand, I wanted to hear more about my participants' feelings and experiences, while on the other, I did not want to confirm and reproduce their racist views with silence. The solution was that I tried to intervene in their assumptions about 'race', stating that I disagree with their ideas, and offering different interpretations of other migrants' unemployment.

"You dream of success but then you become unemployed"

The absence of work, and subsequent social downgrading, provoked strong emotional responses, indicating the importance of decent work for young Russian-speakers' perceptions of self-worth in Finland. As one of my participants Alexey[3] summarised, "you dream you will become wealthy and successful, and then you move to Finland, become unemployed, and receive unemployment benefits". Similarly to others, Alexey expressed his frustration with being positioned in a stigmatised category of dependency. Their inability to find decent work, and their resulting lower social status—especially for those who obtained higher education degrees—left my participants feeling frustrated, tired, and disappointed. They not only suffered from the loss or absence of a secure work-based identity, but also from the loss of their white privilege, which those coming from a majority background experienced. My research participants found themselves in long-term periods of unemployment rotating with short-term work contracts and felt trapped in unpaid work trials or labour activation courses. Some, like Maria, mentioned cases of discrimination when applying for jobs in Finland:

MARIA: The woman said straight to my face: "Yes, you would be fit for this job, but how can we employ you if you are an Estonian national?"
DARIA: So you think it matters that you are not a Finn when trying to get a job here?
MARIA: Totally, it does.

Maria has lived in Finland since she was 12 years old and has extensive work experience in the Finnish cleaning and customer service sectors. After finishing school in Finland, Maria obtained short-term work contracts that rotated with periods of unemployment. This struggle to secure a better and more permanent job left her thinking about migrating elsewhere, which I discuss later.

I was also told stories about when Russian-speaking migrants had to quit heavy physical work such as cleaning, due to injuries and health problems. After quitting cleaning work, many had problems finding work in other sectors. Olga, a young woman with higher education living in Finland, told me how she had to take painkillers every day in order to be able to do cleaning work. She told me that when she visited a doctor, he told her: "If you have education in a different field, you would best quit cleaning, it is bad for your health". Olga told me she decided to leave her job knowing that she might have few chances finding work elsewhere.

Egor—a Lithuanian national who moved to Finland from Russia—also told me how he worked in a warehouse for ten hours a day to compete with others for a permanent work contract, in order to provide his wife with a family reunification residence permit. Once his wife moved to Finland, he quit his job and became unemployed, subsequently facing difficulties finding a better job in other sectors. Besides difficulties with employment, my interviewees would also frequently mention how they try to avoid speaking Russian in public places in their everyday lives. For example, Egor mentioned how he was once assaulted in the street once the perpetrators heard him speaking Russian:

> I was walking on the street, and two girls started looking at me. They first looked very friendly and smiled at me. But when I passed by, they heard that I was speaking Russian on the phone, so they threw a chocolate wrapper at me and said: "Yuck, smelly Russian!"

In this case, his audible visibility (Toivanen 2013) as a Russian-speaker in public space made him identifiable as a Russian, resulting in assault. This shows multiple processes of racialisation when language and accents are also at play in the processes of othering.

Even though my interviewees often laughed while presenting these stories as funny and meaningless, these and many other examples from my interview data show that young Russian-speakers do face hostile treatment—what Philomena Essed (1991) has conceptualised as "everyday racism". This means that some Russian-speakers face everyday, mundane, negative attitudes towards them by the Finnish majority. It also shows how they experience their structural position in Finland and the obstacles they face on their ways to employment. Unable to get the jobs they are qualified for, my participants with qualifications have been left without secure work-based identities that challenged their subjectivities as skilled professionals and workers.

It is these power structures—and Russian-speakers' vulnerabilities in Finland—through which I interpret their racialising arguments related to welfare chauvinism against other migrants. Relational identity work and the making of boundaries takes place in the process of defining one group's status against other groups, and is manifested in unequal access to, and unequal distribution of, resources and social opportunities, as Lamont and Molnár (2002, p. 168) have argued. I now move to explain how whiteness produced vis-à-vis other groups allows them to construct respectable worker identities.

Becoming white and deserving welfare claimants

In the interview, Lisa, who grew up in Finland and obtained a Finnish education, told me that she found it difficult to find work in Finland, and how she was conscious of the fact that employers can hear her Russian accent on the phone and read her Russian name in job applications. However, she added that it is not Russians who are discriminated against, but:

> Muslims are discriminated against, and I can totally understand why. It is their own fault that they don't want to understand Finnish culture. Why do Western countries allow them here? So that they would accept Finnish culture. But they are in their own world, they don't want to achieve anything. They just sit at home, they are given all the welfare, as Finland is a wealthy country, while they just do nothing. Have you seen them working anywhere? I saw only one Somali girl working in a shop.
> Daria: What if they just can't find work, just like you?
> Then you need to go somewhere, do something, be active and not stay at home. Just like me, for example, I am going to get a hygiene pass [*hygieniapassi*, a requirement for working in cafes and restaurants in Finland], it is useful anyway.

Although Lisa is concerned that her Russian origin may be an obstacle in Finland, those whose discrimination she justifies and explains are 'them'—"Muslims". Several intertwining discourses are depicted in this narrative. Lisa reproduces racialised discourses of welfare chauvinism, demarcating the boundaries of who is entitled to benefits and who is not. It is constituted through the convergence of racialised and neoliberal discourses of activeness and 'race': deserving, active, white Western 'us', and undeserving, lazy, racialised 'them'. The discourse of welfare chauvinism is mobilised to draw the boundaries between respectable citizens—like her—who are unemployed yet active and get a hygiene pass to prove that they don't simply drain resources, and 'them', who exploit the state at the cost of hard-working citizens. The notions of activeness, merits, and achievement—which are at the heart of neoliberal citizenship—are symbolically loaded with racialised meanings, which grant symbolic access to welfare entitlement to people who belong to the 'West' and 'Western values' of work ethic and achievement—"not sitting at home" and "getting a hygiene pass" even when unemployed. The value of work ethic is further reinscribed through the norm of a full-employment society, which is foundational for the Nordic welfare state project (e.g. Esping-Andersen 1990). In addition, Lisa constructs Finnish culture as part of the 'Western world', which she sees herself as having become part of, as opposed to the racialised 'them', who are essentially unable to integrate, and do not recognise Western values. Although unemployed herself and concerned about being identified as a foreigner, Lisa symbolically aligns herself with Finnish culture and the superior and wealthy 'West' through the exclusion of those who are essentialised as outsiders to the Western project, its work ethic, and entitlements for welfare benefits. By mobilising a Muslim 'them', Lisa tries to make her whiteness derived from Russia's racial hierarchies "work"

(Leonard 2013), claiming a position of belonging through her strong work ethic, and deserving position as a welfare recipient.

The constructions of non-white uncivilised Others, through which Russian-speakers' own whiteness is produced, are highlighted in Lyuba's narrative:

> I am not racist but really, they are so uncultured, they come from some desert with no civilisation. And I am sorry to tell this, they smell of food and spices. And then they can't even behave on the bus stop, always rush and push other people.

Lyuba gave this answer when I asked her if she ever felt any problems in Finland because of being from Russia or being a migrant. Similar to the previous example, she referred to a homogenous racialised non-white 'them'. Lyuba depicts Others through the prism of cultural inferiority, through which her own whiteness is constructed. A couple of instances after, in the interview, Lyuba continued talking in an essentialising way about other migrants as welfare recipients, and how they do not fit in her rather well-off neighbourhood in Helsinki:

> I live in [name of the district in the centre of Helsinki], there used to be no Somalis there, three years ago there were none. Now I see them more and more. This is an expensive district; I would not say that the apartments are cheap there. So the state and the welfare must be helping them. Because after two years there are so many of them.

Lyuba claims that Somalis do not have a place in her wealthy neighbourhood and the only way they could get housing in the district is through welfare. Through reifying Somalis as only being able to achieve things through welfare, she excludes them from belonging to the neighbourhood of "wealthy" and hard-working people. Although Lyuba receives unemployment benefits herself, she does not question her place in her district, which shows she values herself as deserving of living and fitting into the neighbourhood. Beverley Skeggs (2004) has argued how locatedness is a way of speaking about class indirectly. 'Race' and class also constitute each other in the making of who can belong to her district. Such a class-based description of wealth and exclusion—of Somalis "on welfare"—suggests how the meanings of whiteness, wealth, and hard work become conflated in her description of the district. In Lyuba's narration, racialised references to culture and "civilisation" go hand in hand with the construction of the boundaries of deservingness and entitlement for welfare. The bodies of non-white Others become sticky with the lack of culture and work ethic (Ahmed 2004), which is why they essentially are "bodies out of place" (Puwar, 2004) that cannot deserve to live in a "wealthy" neighbourhood, unlike her. Both Lisa and Lyuba embraced norms of activeness, merit, and hard work, which tie into heavily racialised notions of non-white people being ascribed with the traits of laziness and a poor work ethic.

Activeness, work ethic, and entitlement thus become synonyms with whiteness: one cannot be deserving, without being white, according to the logic of my research participants. In her research on Swedish migrant women in the US, Catrin Lundström (2017) has shown how, while white housewives are expected to reproduce the nation through their reproductive labour, non-white women in the same position run the risk of being subject to discourses of welfare abuse. Lisa and Lyuba produce a similar narrative: while constructing themselves as white through transnational racialised hierarchies, they simultaneously create space for becoming deserving and entitled welfare claimants, precisely through reproducing discourses of non-white Others abusing the system. I then suggest that they not only construct their racial whiteness through boundary-making, as previously argued (Fox 2013), but also prove their worker-identities and deservingness as welfare claimants in the context of their precarious labour market position.

After an interview in a café, I walked with Vladimir towards a metro station, and he started sharing his views on migration. Vladimir is a history teacher from one of the former Soviet Union republics, who is unemployed, and whose residence in Finland is based on family reunification. His wife found a job in Helsinki, which allowed him to obtain a residence permit in Finland and become entitled to welfare and integration courses. His inability to find non-manual work made him feel frustrated, and he was currently undergoing an integration course to become a car mechanic. Despite his own difficulties, he expressed his anti-immigrant stance, and became entangled in contradictory constructions of migration and welfare. As we left the café, Vladimir started:

VLADIMIR: You know, I am not a supporter of migration. They are just taking all these lazy asses, asylum seekers, who don't even want to work, and who are not able to work. Do you know the points system in Austria? You can migrate only when you get enough points, when you can work in the country. They should only take those people who can work. Do you know how much unemployment benefits [his home country] pays to its citizens? 20 dollars!

DARIA: But how would you then survive in Finland without work yourself?

VLADIMIR: I wouldn't survive! I have a wife who works, and through her I could get the benefits. This is family or work, through which I could migrate here. And they, instead, just come here with no obstacles, they just come so easily while I have a permit based on family reunification and my wife had to work so that I could move here.

Vladimir gets involved in a thinking which contradicts his own interests—why advocate for the reduction of unemployment benefits and stricter control over migration when being a migrant receiving benefits himself? His narrative reveals the convergence of welfare, migration, and whiteness, as well as his own insecurities about losing his social status. First, by stating that he does not support migration, he does not refer to himself or his wife, but to "lazy asylum seekers". This reference reconstructs an 'immigrant' figure as someone who is not white, does not work, and 'drains' public resources. He then emphasises that although he is without work, his own residence in Finland and welfare benefits were *deserved* through his wife's work, and were not just *granted* to him, unlike asylum seekers. Yet, he feels that these efforts were not fully rewarded, as he moved to Finland only to lose his social status, having to study to become a car mechanic while not being economically active. He then sees "asylum seekers" as having their residence and welfare benefits supposedly granted by the state "with no obstacles", rather than deserving them through hard work. When I asked Vladimir how he would then survive himself in Finland in the system he proposed, he immediately distanced himself from a position of a 'dependent migrant' by stating that he would not, in fact, drain public resources and would rely on his wife's work.

What Vladimir's contradictory narrative reveals is his own insecurity about being positioned as a 'migrant on welfare', similar to those he deems inferior to him through considering himself white. Whiteness then works as a form of distinction, and a resource to disassociate from a 'migrant' figure who is racialised as non-white and on welfare. When failure has become an individual and moral responsibility rather than a result of structural forces, people draw on various resources to prove that they just happened to fail once, and are in fact good workers, rather than those who systematically abuse the system.

A similar construction of belonging and respectability through whiteness and work ethic is demonstrated by Maria's case. Maria—who gave an example of discrimination against her Estonian nationality in the previous section—spoke about her plans to move to Norway, which, according to her, provides a lot more opportunities for workers, and is a destination for people willing to work, rather than receive unemployment benefits:

MARIA: I don't want to stay in Finland. I want to move to Norway. It is not an EU member, it has higher standards of living and better wages. Also, those who want to work move there, and not those who want to receive unemployment benefits, suck money from the state, and wait until it offers something, like asylum seekers do. They are also cutting welfare in Finland, education and health care, nowhere are unemployment benefits so small like in Finland, you can't live on them—even though I have always paid 24 percent of taxes when I worked. Also these asylum seekers coming here …
DARIA: What's wrong with them?
MARIA: Because they just come here to do nothing, they do nothing so they cut from other people in order to maintain all the lazy asylum seekers.

Exactly like in previous cases, Maria is placed in a similar structural position like other migrants who might not have access to desired jobs, and who instead work in precarious low-paid jobs. However, as Maria says herself, neither hard work nor paying taxes guarantee social security once the work contract is over. She resents that resources are distributed 'unfairly', and that as a taxpayer she was not rewarded with liveable welfare benefits. This is why she aspires to move to a place with better opportunities. Yet, Maria constructs herself as a respectable worker-citizen: as a taxpayer in Finland and a potential worker—rather than a benefits claimant—in Norway. She draws the contours of respectable citizenship by claiming that asylum seekers are instead the ones who take without contributing to the system. While the neoliberal citizenship regime promises success and inclusion for hard workers, these promises are not met, as Maria says, due to austerity and rolling back welfare services (see also Mäkinen 2017). Her insecurity about her life precarity is then channelled towards "asylum seekers", who are depicted as not having the capacity for economic productivity, due to their 'cultural background'.

What is common among all these narratives by young Russian-speakers is insecurity about their own social position, and feelings of failure and misrecognition, despite considering themselves to be white hard-working citizens. It feeds their claim that they should be positioned differently in Finnish society and labour markets, and not be considered 'migrants on welfare'. These narratives also show their disillusionment with the promise of success through education, hard work, and a strong work ethic. Their stigmatisation of other migrants should then be read as an attempt to prove that they are not failures, not 'migrants on benefits', but rather are without work temporarily. When unemployment is understood within the domain of "failed citizenship" (Anderson, 2015), then both "racist ideological syntax" (Hall 1997, p. 341) that circulate in public discussions and normative whiteness become mobilised as a resource to create distinctions between 'us' and 'them'. In fact, both would have similar interests in pursuing anti-racist struggles.

Conclusions

In this chapter, I analysed how young unemployed Russian-speaking migrants who receive welfare benefits contour themselves as deserving of respectable citizenship, through re-inscribing themselves into whiteness by racialising Others. Racialising discourses of welfare chauvinism have found a fertile ground among people who themselves carry the stigma of being a racialised Other who has lost a sense of respectable work-based identity. I have argued that their racialisation of Others should be read against the backdrop of neoliberalised citizenship and class relations, as well as the rise of worker-citizenship, from which many Russian-speakers have been excluded through racialisation and unemployment. They have produced the norm of work, activeness, and merit as a grounds for inclusion to the nation—a position from which they have been simultaneously excluded.

Yet, rather than questioning and challenging the neoliberal work-based construction of citizenship that failed them, they have mobilised a racialised logic of deservingness. Racialised non-white Others were perceived as naturally lacking the culture of work, and thus are essentially unable to become the 'deserving' unemployed. Thus, through depicting non-white Others as lazy, they disassociated themselves from people in a similar structural position and constructed themselves as 'deserving' welfare claimants. My participants' racialisation of Others should then be analysed not just as a racial subjugation of Others, but as an attempt to reinscribe themselves into citizenship to resist a stigmatised subject position of a 'dependent migrant' with no access to respectable jobs.

The stories I have discussed are also the narratives of insecurity of being regarded a failure in worker-citizenship. Their stigmatisation of asylum seekers and racialised migrants should be read as an attempt to dis-identify with those in a similar position to their own (see also Krivonos 2017). Their transnational racial knowledge which positions them as white, and above non-white groups, works as a resource to distance themselves from the racialised undeserving poor and to produce respectability. These contradictory narratives thus indicate a powerful convergence around the norm of whiteness, work ethic, and welfare entitlement; how racism breaks class solidarities has long been studied.

In a similar way, in a neoliberal citizenship regime, the struggle is centred around notions of entitlement and deservingness. Unemployment is not only perceived as individual failure and a lack of work ethic, but as a pathological trait of certain racialised groups. Although as old as colonialism itself (Fanon 1961), racial depictions of non-white others as lazy and lacking discipline easily tie into contemporary neoliberal discourses of activeness, hard work, and merit, as well as stigmatisation through passivity and dependency. According to this logic, while the unemployed whites just happen to fall on hard times, the non-white Others are essentialised as indolent and unable to be part of a competitive nation. Centuries-old colonial depictions of non-white people as lazy and lacking work ethic become an opportunity for contested whites, such as Russian-speakers, to mobilise racial hierarchies to show that they are deserving and failed just by chance—precisely because they consider themselves white. Contemporary neoliberal capitalist ideologies formed around the centrality of a strong work ethic, the rolling-back of welfare, and the impetus for individual responsibility thus tie into the norm of whiteness in a particularly felicitous way.

Notes

1. The chapter develops ideas discussed in Krivonos (2017) on young unemployed Russian-speaking migrants' claims to whiteness in Finland. The chapter discusses the argument in relation to the notions of welfare entitlement and deservingness.
2. Russian-speaking migrants are the largest migrant group in Finland, representing one quarter (66,379 people) of all foreign-born nationals in Finland (Statistics Finland 2017). Besides Russian migrants coming from Russia, Russian-speaking migrants also come from former Soviet Union republics such as Ukraine, Moldova, Belarus, Azerbaijan, Armenia, Georgia, Kazakhstan, and the Baltic States. My

participants testified that due to their mother tongue, many of them are actually identified as Russians by Finns; 'mother tongue' is used as a classificatory system to define persons with a foreign background in Finland.
3 All the names are pseudonyms.

References

Ahmed, Sara (2004) 'Collective feelings'. *Theory, Culture and Society*, 21(2): 25–42
Anderson, Bridget (2015) '"Heads I win. Tails you lose". Migration and the worker citizen'. *Current Legal Problems*, 68(1): 1–18
Bonnett, A. (2008) 'White studies revisited'. *Ethnic and Racial Studies*, 31 (1): 185–196
Census (2010) Russian Census 2010. Available from http://www.gks.ru/free_doc/new_site/perepis2010/croc/perepis_itogi1612.htm
Davydova-Minguet, Olga (2017) 'Suomen venäjänkielinen media ja monietninen julkisuus'. *IDÄNTUTKIMUS*, 3: 3–19
DuBois, W.E.B. (1935) *Black Reconstruction in America, 1860–1880*. New York: Harcourt, Brace
Esping-Andersen, G. (1990) *The Three Worlds of Welfare Capitalism*. Cambridge: Polity Press
Essed, P. (1991) Sage series on race and ethnic relations, Vol. 2. *Understanding Everyday Racism: An Interdisciplinary Theory*. Thousand Oaks, CA, US: Sage Publications
Essed, Philomena (2006) *Understanding Everyday Racism: An Interdisciplinary Theory*. Newbury Park, CA: Sage
Fanon, Franz (1961) *The Wretched of the Earth*. New York: Grove Press
Fox, Jon E. (2013) 'The uses of racism: Whitewashing new Europeans in the UK'. *Ethnic and Racial Studies*, 36 (11): 1871–1889. doi:10.1080/01419870.2012.692802
Garner, Steve (2006) 'The uses of whiteness: What sociologists working on Europe can draw from US research on whiteness'. *Sociology*, 40(2): 257–275
Garner, Steve (2012) 'A moral economy of whiteness: Behaviours, belonging and Britishness'. *Ethnicities*, 12(4): 445–464. doi:10.1177/1468796812448022
Habel, Y. (2012) 'Challenging Swedish Exceptionalism? Teaching While Black', in *Education in the Black Diaspora: Perspectives, Challenges, and Prospects*, edited by Freeman, K. and Johnson, E. Routledge: New York and London
Haikkola, Lotta (2011) 'Transnational and local negotiations of identity. Experiences from second generation young people in Finland'. *Nordic Journal of Migration Research*, 1(3): 156–165. doi:10.2478/v10202–10011–0019–0018
Hall, S. (1997) 'Old and New Identities, Old and New Ethnicities', in *Culture, Globalization, and the World-System: Contemporary Conditions for the Representation of Identity*, edited by King, E. (pp. 41–68). Minneapolis: University of Minnesota Press
Harrell, Allison, S. Soroka and K. Ladner. (2014) 'Public opinion, prejudice and the racialization of welfare in Canada' *Ethnic and Racial Studies*, 37(14): 2580–2597. doi:10.1080/01419870.2013.851396
Ignatiev, N. (1995) *How the Irish Became White*. London: Routledge
Jokinen, Eeva, Könönen, J., Venäläinen, J. and Vähämäki, J. (2011) *Yrittäkää edes! Prekarisaatio Pohjois-Karjalassa*. [You'd better try! Precarisation in North-Karelia] Helsinki: Tutkijaliitto
Jørgensen, Martin Bak and Thomsen, Trine Lund (2016) 'Deservingness in the Danish context: Welfare chauvinism in times of crisis'. *Critical Social Policy*, 36(3): 1–22. doi:10.1177/0261018315622012

Kananen, Johannes (2012) 'Nordic paths from welfare to workfare: Danish, Swedish and Finnish labour market reforms in comparison'. *Local Economy: The Journal of the Local Economy Unit*, 27(5–6)

Keskinen, Suvi (2016) 'From welfare nationalism to welfare chauvinism: Economic rhetoric, the welfare state and changing asylum policies in Finland'. *Critical Social Policy*, 36(3): 1–19. doi:10.1177/0261018315624170

Keskinen, Suvi, S. Tuori, S. Irni, and D. Mulinari. eds. (2009) *Complying with Colonialism: Gender, Race and Ethnicity in the Nordic Region*. Farnham, UK: Ashgate

Keskinen, Suvi, C.O. Norocel and M.B. Jorgnesen. (2016) 'The politics and policies of welfare chauvinism under the economic crisis. Introduction to the Special Issue of welfare chauvinism'. *Critical Social Policy*, 36(3), pp. 1–9

Krivonos, D. (2015). '(Im)mobile lives. Young Russian women's narratives of work and citizenship insecurities in Finland'. *Sosiologia*, 52(4), 350–363

Krivonos, Daria (2017) 'Claims to whiteness: Young unemployed Russian-speakers' declassificatory struggles in Finland'. *The Sociological Review*, 66(6), 1145–1160

Krivonos, Daria (2019) 'The making of gendered "migrant workers" in youth activation: the case of young Russian-speakers in Finland'. *Current Sociology*, 67(3): 401–418

Lamont, Michèle and Molnár, V. (2002) 'The study of boundaries in social sciences'. *Annual Review of Sociology*, 28: 167–195

Leinonen, Johanna (2012) 'Invisible immigrants, visible expats? Americans in Finnish discourses on immigration and internationalization'. *Nordic Journal of Migration Research*, 2(3): 213–223. doi:10.2478/v10202–10011–0043–0048

Lens, Vicky and Cary, Collen (2010) 'Negotiating the discourse of race within the United States welfare system'. *Ethnic and Racial Studies*, 33(6): 1032–1048. doi:10.1080/01419870903259538

Leonard, Pauline (2010) *Expatriate Identities in Postcolonial Organisations*. Surrey: Routledge

Leonard, Pauline (2013) 'Making whiteness work in South Africa: A translabour approach'. *Women's Studies International Forum*, 36 (Jan–Feb): 75–83. doi:10.1016/j.wsif.2012.08.003

Loftsdóttir, Kristin (2017) '"Being the damned foreigner": Affective national sentiments and racialisation of Lithuanians in Iceland'. *Nordic Journal of Migration Research*, 7(2): 70–78

Lundström, Catrin (2010) 'White ethnography: (Un)comfortable conveniences and shared privileges in field-work with Swedish migrant women'. *NORA - Nordic Journal of Feminist and Gender Research*, 18(2): 70–87.doi:10.1080/08038741003755467

Lundström, Catrin (2014) *White Migrations*. Basingstoke: Palgrave

Lundström, Catrin (2017) 'The White side of migration: Reflections on race, citizenship and belonging in Sweden'. *Nordic Journal of Migration Research*, 7(2): 79–87

McDowell, Linda (2008) 'On the Significance of Being White: European Migrant Workers in the British Economy in the 1940s and 2000s', Chapter 5 in *New Geographies of Race and Racism*, edited by Dwyer, C. and Bressey, C.Aldershot: Ashgate

McDowell, Linda (2009) 'Old and new European economic migrants: Whiteness and managed migration policies', *Journal of Ethnic and Migration Studies*, 35(1): 19–36.

Mäkinen, Katariina (2017) 'Struggles of citizenship and class: Anti–immigration activism in Finland'. *The Sociological Review*, 65: 218–234

Nowicka, M. (2017) '"I don't mean to sound racist but…" Transforming racism in transnational Europe'. *Ethnic and Racial Studies*. Advance online publication. http://dx.doi.org/10.1080/01419870.2017.1302093

Puwar, Nirmal (2004) *Space Invaders: Gender, Race and Bodies Out of Place*. Oxford and New York: Berg Publishers

Rastas, Anna (2005) 'Racializing categorisation among young people in Finland', *Young*, 13(2): 147–166

Schiller, Nina Glick. (2010) 'A Global Perspective on Transnational Migration: Theorising Migration Without Methodological Nationalism', in *Diaspora and Transnationalism: Concepts, Theories and Methods*, edited by Bauböck, Rainer and Faist, Thomas, 109–131. Amsterdam: Amsterdam University Press

Skeggs, Beverley (2004) *Class, Self, Culture*. Abingdon, UK: Routledge

Sotkasiira, Tiina (2016) *Russian Borderlands in Change: North Caucasian Youth and the Politics of Bordering and Citizenship*. London: Routledge

Statistics Finland (2013) Employment Statistics 2011 (Database). Population by Main Type of Activity, Language, Occupational Status, Sex and Year. Retrieved from http://pxnet2.stat.fi/PXWeb/pxweb/en/StatFin/StatFin__vrm__tyokay/027_tyokay_tau_104.px/?rxid=4a24d8b1-c9fb-484c-99a8-1ba44edf1c22

Statistics Finland (2014) Employment 2011. Occupation and Socio-Economic Status. http://www.stat.fi/til/tyokay/2011/04/tyokay_2011_04_2013-11-06_tie_001_en.html (Accessed March 11, 2018)

Statistics Finland (2017) Population Structure. http://www.tilastokeskus.fi/tup/suoluk/suoluk_vaesto.html (Accessed March 27, 2018)

Tanttu, J. (2009) *Venäjänkielisenä Suomessa 2008: Selvitys Vähemmistövaltuutetulle* [Russian-Speakers in Finland 2008: Minorities Report]. Helsinki: Edita

Tlostanova, Madina (2003) *A Janus-Faced Empire*. Moscow: Blok

Toivanen, Mari (2013) 'Language and negotiations of identities among young Kurds in Finland'. *Nordic Journal of Migration Research*, 3(1): 27–35

8 Starry starry night

Fantasies of homogeneity in documentary films about Kvens and Norwegian-Pakistanis

Priscilla Ringrose and Elisabeth Stubberud

Introduction

This chapter examines and compares two documentary films about old and new minority groups in Norway, in light of the notion of national fantasy (Berlant 1991) as "a narrative support, a story that gives consistency to the nation and its subjects" (Fortier 2008). The documentaries explore issues of national identity and belonging in relation to the Kven and Norwegian-Pakistani communities. The interest in examining these specific documentaries together arose from the fact that they were both produced by members of their respective communities, share "insider" perspectives, were aired on Norway's national public television channel, the Norwegian Broadcasting Corporation (NRK), and targeted broad audiences. NRK's self-proclaimed societal mission is to "strengthen and develop democracy", and to contribute to a "better understanding of society, each other, and ourselves" (NRK 2017). NRK also has an explicit inclusionary goal, which can be understood in relation to its efforts to provide a platform for minority groups. Both films also address the impact of assimilationist policies on minorities, but do so via allying themselves in complex and contrasting ways with majority and minority perspectives. In doing so, they tell stories of families which highlight the consequences of the Norwegian state's interventionist approach to family life. Both documentaries also feature journeys outside Norway, which provide insights into the ways in which cultural difference is imbricated in understandings of the nation. Finally, on a symbolic level, we imagine that old and new minorities can learn from each other. As such, we read the two films as being in dialogue with each other, suggesting that the Kven documentary contains both a symbolic warning, and a promise to its Norwegian-Pakistani counterpart.

Kvens are generally defined as people of Kven/Finnish[1] heritage from Northern Norway and are perceived as a white minority who have been racialised in different ways from that of the Sámi population. They are present in Norwegian historical sources from the ninth century, but mainly migrated from what is today Finland, and in some cases via Sweden,[2] to present-day Norway in the first half of the eighteenth century (Niemi 2010).

While there are no official government statistics based on ethnicity, a 2000 survey estimates that there are approximately 10,000 to 12,000 people in the Northern Norwegian regions of Troms and Finnmark who speak Kven or Finnish (Niemi 2010 p. 158).

Immigration from Pakistan began in the 1970s, and most Norwegian-Pakistani communities are concentrated in Southern Norway in the Oslo area. These amount to what some sources estimate to be more than 30,000 people, spanning several generations (Erdal and Oeppen 2013; Døving 2009). As such, the Norwegian-Pakistani community represents a sizable segment of the overall population of migrants and their descendants, that is to say, 940,000 (or around 17 percent) of the more than five million people that comprise the broader Norwegian population (Statistisk sentralbyrå [SSB] 2018).

The 2011 Kven film, *Under en annen himmel* [*Under another sky*], is a documentary in the poetic genre, directed by Anstein Mikkelsen. The film is based around a family narrative that involves the director and his great grandmother. It is aimed at mainstream audiences (in the sense that it explains Kven culture), but it can also be read as an attempt to recruit Norwegians with Kven heritage to identify as Kven, through narratives that aim to revitalise and revalorise this identity. *Frivillig tvang* [*Willingly coerced*] is an expository documentary from 2014, directed by Ulrik Imtiaz Rolfsen. It explores the complex identity negotiations Norwegian-Pakistanis face around integration, focussing on areas of family life such as marriage and eldercare.[3] *Frivillig tvang* aims to explain the worldviews of Norwegian-Pakistanis to Norwegian audiences, and Rolfsen claims his "insider status" gives him special insight into this task. Documentary film is here understood as a social practice which "constructs narratives and meanings", and which enable us to "locate evidence of the ways in which our culture makes sense of itself" (Turner 2006, p. 3). This chapter addresses how narratives and meanings located in these two films provide evidence of the ways in which Norwegian society has and does make sense of itself and its 'others', in relation to the concept of a national fantasy of homogeneity.

Norway's relation to its others is built on a self-image of being a "markedly homogeneous" country, before the onset of more recent overseas migrations in the early 1970s (Bjørklund and Bergh 2013, p. 12). The myth of initial homogeneity ignores Norway's longstanding immigration history and complex relationship with ethnic and indigenous minorities (including the Kvens), who have been subject to harsh assimilation and exclusionary policies (McIntosh 2015, p. 312). From the early nineteenth century, Kvens were perceived as a threat by the Norwegian state, in light of concerns about a potential Russian expansion in the north, and related fears that Kvens would be loyal to Finland and/or Russia in the event of war (Niemi 2005). An official strategy of Norwegianisation was initiated in the late 1800s and aimed to counter this threat by enforcing "prejudicial linguistic and cultural policies" against both the Kvens and the Sámi people. The main mechanism of state intervention was via the school system, which established Norwegian as the main language, and included the establishment of boarding schools where the Kven and Sámi languages were forbidden (Sollid 2013). This led to situations where children were unable to communicate with members of their own family, and to what is now the endangered status of the Kven language (Eldia 2013). The Norwegianisation policy persisted well into the 1970s.

The 1980s marked a turning point in the status of indigenous people and national minorities. In the 1980s, Norway finally recognised that the Sámi had "historically been present in the area when the Norwegian state was established" (Ryymin, Chapter 2). Following this, in 1990, the Sámi were recognised as an indigenous people, as a result of Norway signing and ratifying Convention No. 169 concerning *Indigenous and Tribal Peoples in Independent Countries* (Lindqvist 2009). As of 1998, Kven/Norwegian-Finns, Roma, Romani/Tater, Jews, and Forest Finns were recognised as national minorities in Norway. Sámi, Kven, Romanes, and Romani are also officially recognised as minority languages that are protected by the European Charter for Regional and Minority Languages, which entered into force in 1998. Following several years of debate, in June 2017 the Norwegian Parliament decided to establish a commission to examine Norway's former assimilation policy towards the Kven and Sámi populations (Norske kveners forbund (NKF) [The Norwegian Kven Association] 2018).

While these measures are testimony to recent political acknowledgements of historic ethnic diversity, *the image* of initial homogeneity persists, both in social science and historical research, as well as in the popular imaginary (see *Ryymin* in this book). Ryymin citing Tvedt (2017, p. 111) notes that as recently as 2017, historical debates around immigration, development aid, and other policy areas have referred to the Norway of the 1960s as a sparsely populated and exceptionally ethnically and culturally homogeneous land, soon to be transformed into a diverse nation by an influx of labour migrants. Ryymin further contends that in the context of welfare states—where the idea of a fully functional welfare system is viewed as being contingent on homogeneity—the presupposition of initial sameness means that increased migration can, by default, be regarded as a potential threat (*Ryymin*).

As elsewhere in Scandinavia, this perceived threat—primarily associated with migration from states with Muslim populations—has led to rising Islamophobia; to media attention and state intervention around issues of forced marriage and the veil; as well as to suspicions about welfare tourism and migrants' "inability" to adjust to 'Western' values (Wikan 2002; Keaton 2006; Bowen 2010; McIntosh 2015). Whereas in the Nordic welfare states, integration used to be discussed in relation to participation in work and education (Keskinen 2017), more recently it has become infused with the idea of moral and cultural values as being intrinsic to proper citizenship (Olwig 2011; Keskinen 2017). Proper citizenship is thus reframed within a largely moral framework which intimates that Norwegian values are essentially imbued with goodness, equality, and democracy (McIntosh 2015, p. 312). As a result, racialised minority families who are regarded as morally inadequate, and as representing a potential threat to social norms, have increasingly become the targets of public policy (Keskinen 2017).

According to Berlant, citizenship is increasingly being privatised with "the intimate public spheres [being] produced by personal acts and values, especially acts originating in or directed towards the family sphere" (1997, p. 5). This focus on the intimate dimensions of citizenship serves to naturalise the opposition between "good citizens" who embody cultural norms of liberal individuality and "proper" heterosexuality, and marginalised minorities who need to be "freed" from the burden of constraints which they are considered unable to liberate themselves from (Keskinen 2017, pp. 157–158). The failure of minorities to fully integrate is then attributed to either indoctrination or unwillingness, which in turn enables migrants to be considered responsible both for their own integration, and for the perceived erosion of the nation's social norms (Lentin and Titley 2011; Goldberg 2011).

Keskinen argues that governance via norms and practices which are based on assumptions of liberal individuality then come to define the symbolic boundaries of the nation and have exclusionary and racialising effects (Keskinen 2017). In Norway, such exclusionary practices conflate with the persistence of lingering fantasies of cultural homogeneity amongst the majority population, who are loathe to recognise "the simple truth", namely the undeniably heterogeneous nature of Norwegian society (McIntosh 2015). These lingering fantasies relate to what Hübinette (in the Swedish context) calls "white melancholia"—nostalgia for an imagined "pure white" past, where migration was the problem of other states (Hübinette and Lundström 2011; Hübinette 2012). It is through this sense that the idea of cultural sameness lives on. It persists via nostalgia for an 'innocent' past, and via continuing fantasies of total assimilation which produce non-assimilated others as outside the boundaries of the nation. As Fortier puts it, a fantasy of the nation is brought into being in the public domain "by repeatedly imagining that it exists and iterating it as something real, out there, that binds the 'national people' together" (Fortier 2008, p. 11). Following Berlant (1991), Fortier explains that fantasy in this sense does not correspond to its popular conceptualisation as a form of escape or fabrication, but can rather be understood as a means of self-protection, "a narrative support, a story that gives consistency to the nation and its subjects" (2008, p. 11). Moreover, the fantasy is not in opposition to social reality, but rather represents the necessary "psychic glue" (Rose 1998, p. 3) that enables the nation to consider itself whole, protecting it from the horrors of the "real" that threaten to disintegrate its unity (Fortier 2008, p. 12).

In this chapter, we look at the ways in which the stories of family and journeys outside the nation in *Under en annen himmel* and *Frivillig tvang* reinforce or resist the image of Norway as a bounded 'whole' nation, in the thrall of a fantasy of cultural sameness. We argue that the stories of family in *Under en annen himmel* challenge the fantasy by reviving the markers of a past Kven identity as potentially still available to Norwegians with Kven heritage, and by imagining this identity beyond the geographic and symbolic boundaries of nation. In contrast, we argue that *Frivillig tvang* upholds the fantasy by symbolically ejecting non-assimilated Norwegian-Pakistanis from the boundaries of the state. Despite it giving a voice to Norwegian-Pakistanis who resist assimilation, this resistance is negatively framed by the film's narrator-director, who constructs Norwegian-Pakistanis as individuals who need to be freed from the burden of constraints they are considered unable to liberate themselves from (Keskinen 2017, pp. 157–158). In conclusion, we discuss why both films only fleetingly engage with the structural dimensions of racism and suggest that *Under en annen himmel*'s strategic silence on the mechanics of assimilation opens up new possibilities for inclusive citizenship, and in doing so shines a glaring light on *Frivillig tvang*'s blind spots.

Under en annen himmel

In *Under en annen himmel,* Mikkelsen revives a past and potentially new Kven identity in a contemporary context in which Kvens have received political acknowledgment from the Norwegian state, but at the same time exist as a largely invisible section of society, melding into the mainstream Norwegian population. While the film addresses the consequences of the Norwegianisation policy—particularly the Kven community's gradual loss of language and culture—it remains silent on the ways the policy was enforced, and on the political and social factors which exacerbated these losses.

The main mechanism for enforcing the assimilation policy was the Norwegian school system (Sollid 2013). As the school system expanded within the second half of 1800, Norwegian was established as the country's main oral and written language. As of 1889, the use of Kven and Sámi was only permitted when "absolutely necessary" (Sollid 2013, p. 84). This meant that pupils acquired a different main language than their parents. They first became bilingual Kven-Norwegian, and subsequently monolingual Norwegians. Teachers also pressured parents to learn Norwegian, both in order to support their children's education, and to navigate other "official Norwegian domains" (Sollid 2005 in Sollid 2013, p. 84). This linguistic policy was reinforced by the establishment of boarding schools where Kven and Sámi languages were forbidden. By 1940, approximately 20 such schools were present in Northern Norway. This led to a situation where children would no longer understand Kven and could not speak to members of their family who did not speak Norwegian.

The Second World War had a dramatic impact on the long-term destinies of the Kvens. In 1944, Hitler ordered the north of Norway to be destroyed via a scorched earth policy. Everything of potential use to the Soviet enemy was destroyed. Harbours, bridges, and towns were dynamited, and every building torched. For the Kven population, this meant that language loss was now followed by the loss of virtually all their material possessions, including boats, tools, and instruments. These losses—coupled with the onset of modernisation, and the internalisation of the social stigma of a century of Norwegianisation—extinguished any remaining resistance to integration, making claims to an explicit Kven identity even harder. It was not until the late 1980s that there was a resurgence of Kvens aligning with this identity, coupled with attempts to revitalise the language; this was spearheaded by the establishment of the Norwegian Kven Association in 1987, and followed by the 1998 recognition of Kvens as a national minority. In 2005, the Kven language as an official minority language was formally recognised through the European Charter for Regional or Minority Languages. Today, the estimated number of active users of the Kven language is approximately 1500 to 2500, and it is described as one of the most endangered languages in Europe (Eldia 2013).

Under en annen himmel is thus produced in a context where Kven identity is politically unproblematic to revive, in the sense that it now represents no threat to the nation. At the same time, because of the extent of its linguistic and cultural erosion, it is an identity that is difficult to retrieve. Mikkelsen thus treads a delicate line between establishing loss, and re-establishing (some) presence. He tackles this challenge with an approach that combines a return to historical roots via tracing his family genealogy; by focussing on a geographical space—Børselv—as a locus for identification; and through childhood memories of his great grandmother. This narrative of family is then expanded to encompass a much larger story about migration and migrating cultures, but also touches on narratives of resistance to and within dominant cultures, which challenges the narrow confines of Norway's fantasy of a culturally monolithic 'whole' nation.

The film begins with images of Børselv, a small picturesque village by the Porsanger fjord in Finnmark, Northern Norway, overlayed with the story of Mikkelsen's ancestral relation to this village. These images can be seen as an attempt at establishing social markers for Kven identities. Yet the images are also framed in a manner that makes it clear that these identity-building images and practices only partly belong in present-day Børselv; they are memories from Mikkelsen's childhood, and practices that belonged primarily to his parents', grandparents' and great grandparents' generations. A voiceover reveals that Mikkelsen's ancestors migrated from the Torne Valley in Sweden to Børselv, and, as he explains, "no one lived in the Børselv valley when my Kven ancestors came. [And now] almost 300 years later, there is still a Kven village at the foot of the Hestnes mountain". As Mikkelsen describes how the first Kven settler, Samuli Kippari, came to Børselv in the mid-1700s, we are shown the area around Børselv, and images of traditional ways of using the land, including foraging activities like cloudberry picking; fence fishing and fly fishing in rivers; the building of river boats; as well as farming techniques. We also see images of the starry night sky, the northern lights, close-ups of berries, and coffee being made over an open fire by the river, as Mikkelsen explains how he understands cultural belonging as a Kven in Børselv.

The social and cultural markers that Mikkelsen refers to—which form the basis of Kven identity in his ancestral village—faded fast in the post-war era, as increasingly fewer people maintained a self-sustaining lifestyle that involved living off the land through farming, fishing, and berry picking. Additionally, the language was disappearing fast, and since almost all of Finnmark was burnt down during the war, Mikkelsen's generation had little material and immaterial culture through which to build attachment. This may also explain why Børselv is so important in the film; Børselv is not only the place where Mikkelsen's ancestors settled, but is also a geographical space that can serve as one of several important ancestral homes for Kven identification. As well as being an important Kven settlement, Børselv is also the location of the Kven Institute, and of the Kippari festival, one of two Kven festivals where Kven culture and language is celebrated.

There is a dual function to the rare Kven artefacts which Mikkelsen shows and discusses. Their rarity points to cultural devastation, while their retrieval allows for the fostering of a sense of cultural belonging. The artefacts consist of the *rocker well* or *shadoof*, which is a construction connected to a well (it is comprised of a pole, a bucket, and a weight), and the musical instrument, the *kantele*. These are exceptional 'survivors', because the instrument has survived the war, and examples of the rocker well still exist, and can also be found in old photographs. The film also shows and describes other markers of cultural identity, such as the making of coffee cheese—hard cheese that is put in a cup of coffee and eaten with a spoon, very similar in texture to Indian paneer.

Starry starry sky

After introducing the village, his ancestors, and their ways of life, Mikkelsen moves onto the central memory-based narrative of family, which leads him on a quest to rediscover his great grandmother's starry sky. He describes a moment in 1960 when his great grandmother was 90 years old and he was 4. He talks about the sky that he believes she must have been telling him about when she pointed to the heavens. He tells us that at the time, she understood little Norwegian, and he even less of her language, as she pointed to the sky and spoke in Kven. The quest to try to imagine the meaning of what she was trying to tell him takes Mikkelsen on a journey beyond Norway, which, as we will see, establishes affinities between Kven and other cultures. Mapping these affinities out across geographical spaces becomes a way for him to learn more about Kven culture, and thus also to imagine what his great grandmother might have been saying to him.

The starry sky takes on the role of an important environmental marker of Kven culture. Mikkelsen talks about the fact that in many places, you cannot see the stars clearly because of light pollution. He explains that this is not the case in Børselv, where there is little pollution from lights, making the stars easy to spot—and even more so when he was a child, and the electricity supply in Børselv was unstable. By saying that there are few places left where you can see the stars, and where pollution has not encroached, the Kven starry sky assumes a sense of resistance towards modernity and the tenets of dominant culture. Moreover, by connecting the Børselv sky to his great grandmother's knowledge, he is also articulating why it is important for Kvens today to learn about the starry sky in the manner of the old Kvens.

Mikkelsen ponders the ways in which his ancestors may have talked about and conceptualised the starry sky. This conceptualisation is of central importance to the film. He connects the cultural markers of identity, and then the starry sky, to other places in the world. The *rocker well* can be found in many countries, including in the Torne Valley in Sweden, in Finland, Estonia, Russia, Hungary, Romania, parts of the Middle East, and Egypt (where it may have originated); his ancestors brought the skill of fence fishing with them from the Torne Valley in Sweden, from which they migrated (this form of fishing is now prohibited); the coffee cheese is similar to Indian paneer, and is also commonplace today in Finland; the *kantele* is played in Finland,[4] and is also similar to an instrument used by Karelians in Russia. He compares the names of the Milky Way in Estonian, Hungarian, Estonian, Finnish, Sámi, and Kven, and notes that they are very similar. He explains that some of the images related to the conceptualisation of the sky are also similar across time and space, spanning Norse mythology to present-day Estonian, Kven, and Sámi, where the Milky Way is described as "the bird's way". The way in which the northern lights are described in the north of Finland is the same as the way they are described in Børselv, Mikkelsen notes, highlighting the Kven people's connections eastwards to Finland and Russia, as well as to the Sámi people.

What Mikkelsen is trying to illustrate is that there are similarities in the way the starry sky is talked about in other cultures and places, and in the linguistic roots of the word "sky" itself; both the word "sky" and its conceptualisation interpellate the tracing of patterns of migration and of historic connections between the Kven and other peoples. Mikkelsen uses linguistic connections to show how present-day Kvens draw on their own history of migration by using their language. This focus on connections through space and time can be read as a pro-migration stance, which subverts dominant fantasies of sameness. At the same time, the connection to the world beyond Norway is more that an act of resistance, it is also an act of cultural survival, since Mikkelsen *needs* to travel to find out about the meaning of the Kven sky and stars, because his language is dying out. The highlighting of this relation to spaces outside of Norway also emphasises that he and his Kven community are part of a greater cultural linguistic whole (the Finnish-Ugric language group) which excludes Norway. These wider cultural affiliations are not framed as an explicit stance against Norway. There is no anger expressed, no mention made of the Norwegianisation policy, only a curiosity to learn more, coupled with a palpable melancholy.

Mikkelsen describes that as children, he and his Kven peers had access to "the old world", where people lived from a combination of fishing, farming, and harvesting from nature. Yet when he was a child, he did not know the value of this access to the old world, and these traditional ways of life.

Implicit in this tale is the fact that he and his contemporaries also had access to the Kven language, which is now on the verge of dying out, and as children did not recognise its value. Mikkelsen then interviews Terje Aronsen, a key figure in the revitalisation of Kven language and culture, who points to a bleak prognosis for Kven identity: "I don't see very bright prospects for the future of Kven culture. An important part of Kven culture and ways of being builds on language, and when that disappears, a big part of identity also disappears". Significantly, Aronson here points to the focal point of the film—the starry sky—and identifies a central irony, namely that if Mikkelsen had learned the Kven language from his parents, he would have known what his great grandmother was talking about when she pointed towards the starry sky. Towards the end of the film, Mikkelsen ponders whether anyone will still live in Børselv in 300 years, who they will be, and what languages they will speak.

Under en annen himmel functions as a retrospective act of resistance to assimilation, past and present. It shines a light on the diverse practices and language of the Kven people in a way which positively embraces the migrations of peoples and cultures, destabilising the notion of a homogenous Norwegian culture that is bound to a single territorial space. *Under en annen himmel*, in James Clifford's parlance, looks for "routes", stressing the changing and hybrid character of culture; in contrast, *Frivillig tvang*, returns to "roots" (1997).

Frivillig tvang

Frivillig tvang is a documentary filmed mostly in Norway, but also in the Punjab state. It is based on interviews with predominantly younger people (teenagers to people in their thirties). Pakistani migrations to Norway started around 1970, and mostly consisted of working-class labourers from rural Punjab (Kristin and Åse 2014, p. 490). While beginning as mostly male labour migration, it expanded to encompass family chain migration (Walseth and Strandbu 2014, p. 490). This resulted in the current well-established community of Norwegian-Pakistanis, which what some sources say amounts to more than 30,000 people, spanning several generations (Erdal and Oeppen 2013; Døving, 2009).

The Pakistani community is commonly regarded as a tight-knit social network, with its own cultural and religious organisations (Walle 2011, p. 18). Only 7 percent of young Norwegian Pakistanis marry a person who is neither born in Pakistan, nor born to Pakistani parents outside Pakistan (Daugstad 2009, in Walle 2011, p. 490). At the same time, a sign of upward mobility is that young Norwegian-Pakistanis aged 19 to 24 are more likely to pursue higher education than the population in general. Norwegian-Pakistani females are more likely to enter into higher education than the general female population (Langset 2010, in Walseth and Strandbu 2014). Most Norwegian-Pakistanis live in the greater Oslo region, which is home to more than half the immigrant minority population (Eriksen 2013).

The film gives a voice to young Norwegian-Pakistanis, but as we suggest, does so in a way that upholds an ideal or fantasy of a culturally homogeneous Norway, where citizenship is conditional upon adopting Norwegian values, and where those who do not are imagined as outside the nation. We argue that an emphasis on the intimate and familial in the film frames Norwegian-Pakistanis as members of a marginalised minority who are incapable or unwilling to adopt Norwegian values and are thus distinct from the 'good citizens' who embody cultural norms of liberal individuality.

From the outset, the film's title—*Willingly coerced*—interpellates Norwegian-Pakistanis as a coerced community, as subjects lacking in agency. This implicitly evokes questions around family dynamics, and places integration within the sphere of the personal. At the same time, both the beginning and the end of the film features two Norwegian-Pakistanis who are literally placed outside the framework of the film's main part, as well as being symbolically framed as outside the territory of coercion, as model middle-class assimilated citizens. While initially promising to give an insider's view of the community, narrator Ulrik Imtiaz Rolfsen effectively takes on a majoritarian position. Although not racialised as white, Rolfsen "embrace(s) important aspects of whiteness" (Garner 2014, p. 409). His role can be interpreted as constructing (most) Norwegian-Pakistanis as coerced and tracing the "origin" or the roots of that coercion to Pakistan. The film's postscript features Tina Shagufta Kornmo as the other ideal immigrant. Kornmo is light-skinned, fluent in Norwegian, and has considerable social capital (she is a consultant doctor). The interview begins with direct references to notions of freedom: "You got married and chose your spouse yourself in 1989. How much freedom do Norwegian-Pakistani girls have today?". Kornmo is associated with views which are implicitly against arranged marriage, and as such, is framed as espousing recognisable "Norwegian" values. She is invited to comment on the "typicality" of the film's main interviewees, thus representing an authoritative position. In doing so, she expressed a progress narrative whereby Norwegian-Pakistanis will ideally become more and more integrated through time. Kornmo's understanding of integration converges with that of the narrator, as implicitly conditional on assimilation, and on the rejection of "Pakistani" values.

Given that the film places integration in the sphere of the familial, the main themes of the film are eldercare and marriage practices. The film's negative portrayal of arranged marriage and its sensationalising of forced marriage mimics tendencies which are also evident in Scandinavian policies— to generalise using individual cases to represent the marriage practices of entire minority groups (Bredal 2013). In *Frivillig tvang*, three of the main interviewees discuss their experiences or understandings of marriage, whether related to "forced marriage" (Fatima), parental coercion (Abu), or expectations of the traditional male breadwinner model of marriage (Hassan). As becomes evident, the sustained focus on the theme of coercion in these interviews reinforces what Bredal (2013, p. 347), drawing on Narayan (2001, p. 418), argues is a common tendency to conflate very different attitudes and practices: "Those who resist or fight their parent's plans are placed in the same category as those who uncritically accept tradition, and those who have thought it through and decide to accept arranged marriage".

Marriage practices

The space the film accords to forced marriage normalises the idea of Norwegian-Pakistanis as victims of extreme familial violence. Fatima is presented as fearful, compliant, and as being forced to operate outside the social sphere of her Norwegian classmates, outside the confines of institutional and social norms:

FATIMA: At the meeting with the teacher, mum and dad said that "she can't sit with boys". Always sit with girls. Sometimes I had to sit by myself. The teacher had to rearrange the whole class because of me.
ULRIK: The school let your parents decide where you should sit?
FATIMA: My teacher didn't think she had a choice. Dad was very firm. I said I wanted what my parents said. I was very scared of the consequences at home. When I tried to resist, lots of things happened. I was left without food, had to sit in the basement a couple of hours until my mother told me I could come up. I was smacked in the face, he took off his shoe and beat me with it. I was very bruised. I ended up at the emergency ward.

Fatima describes being duped into travelling to Pakistan and being forced into a marriage, where she is mistreated by her mother-in-law and raped by her husband. Rolfsen quizzes her on the intimate details of her marriage, which Fatima describes in terms of a "living death":

ULRIK: How was the wedding night?
FATIMA: I didn't know where I was. I … didn't feel alive. I felt like I was dead. I didn't want to remember either. I just know that I was crying and screaming, but no one came.
ULRIK: So you were raped?
FATIMA: It happened numerous times. And … something happened to me. I simply felt like I was dead.

Yuval-Davis notes that gendered bodies and sexuality play critical roles in the "territories, markers and reproducers of the narratives of nations", and in the contours of the boundaries of inclusion and exclusions that these construct (1997, p. 39). In the Scandinavian context, the marriage practices of racialised minorities have been framed in terms of "integration problems, 'cultural differences' and dilemmas about gender equality" (Keskinen 2009, p. 259). Fatima's story interpellates media discussions and debates around the case of

Fadime Sahindal, who was killed in 2002 in Sweden by her father. The case divided opinion—some interpreted her case as an example of universal patriarchal violence, and others viewed it as completely divorced from domestic violence experienced by Swedish women (Keskinen 2009). As we will see, *Frivillig tvang* goes on to locate the roots of violence in Pakistan. Here, as in the case of Fadime Sahindal, violence against women is implicitly represented as being "imported" from outside Norway, and as originating in a 'traditional' culture where violence against women is normalised (Keskinen 2009).

In the context of debates around Norwegian policies that relate to forced marriage, Bredal notes that their articulation has similarly rested on questions of "voluntariness" or "free will" (2006a). As Keskinen (2009, p. 261), following Bredal (2006b) elaborates, notions of agency were central to arguments on both sides of the debate, whether based on the right of minorities to choose their partners, or on the assertion that arranged marriages are also often freely entered into. Such debates illustrate that gender relations are crucial in understanding and analysing the phenomena of nations and nationalism (Keskinen 2009, p. 261). Freedom becomes imbricated in ideas of race, ethnicity, and nation, occupying the dividing line between the unfettered 'Norwegian way of life' on one hand, and the lifestyles of minority populations who are perceived as lacking in freedom and are anchored to traditions on the other (Keskinen 2009, p. 261).

In the film, Abu stands for the figure of the Norwegian-Pakistani who is not so free, who is conflicted about his own arranged marriage. He expresses regret at being coerced into marriage, explaining the fear of loss that underpinned his decision:

ABU: I say so much negative stuff about my family that I don't feel manipulated. But I think they used my conscience. I don't think I was manipulated. They never forced me. They didn't say, "You have to do it". But they said, "You should marry a Pakistani girl, ideally". Ideally, I would have fallen in love before getting married. Then it would have been up to us to make the marriage work. Now we can blame our parents [...] I sacrificed a small part of my life for my family. To keep us together. I thought, I don't want to lose my family. You've got friends and all, but family is important. My family is very close.

While Abu's statements point to a complex set of negotiations that involve respect for his parents, and the wish not to hurt them, the film's sustained and intense focus on *degrees of coercion* produces Abu as a victim whose coercion is implicitly relative to Fatima's. While Abu is framed as envious of the presumed "free choice" of other autonomous Norwegian subjects, Hassan, a conservative teenage boy also interviewed, takes a firm stand against 'Norwegian' values of gender equality, as he explains his expectations of marriage.

HASSAN: It doesn't matter who she is, as long as she is Muslim and Pakistani. And knows what is right and wrong in Islam. When men were in charge, the world was a good place. Now that women are with us, I don't like it. Because now that women have got rights, they talk against men.

Following Sernhede (2001, p. 214 in Bredström 2003, p. 85), Hassan's position can be understood as a type of "counter identity". Sernhede contends that counter identities originate from a sense of alienation, of not belonging to society. Counter identities can express themselves as a form of macho-oriented masculinity, which can be understood as an oppositional reaction to the conflation of gender equality and white Norwegianness (Sernhede 2001, p. 214). For Staunæs, this type of "hyper-masculinity" can also be regarded as a symptom of a troubled subject position, a mechanism by which intensified masculinity "compensates for a feeling of weak ethnicity" in contexts where young minority youth are treated with suspicion or hostility (2003, p. 108). As such, ethnic identities and national boundaries need to be understood as being produced, sustained, and subverted in relation to each other, and the role of racism in this process needs to be recognised (Bredström 2003, p. 85). While *Frivillig tvang* makes fleeting reference to Hassan's feelings of isolation when playing in a Norwegian football team, there is no explicit recognition, or discussion around structural racism—the problem of integration, as we will see, is rather intrinsically associated with Pakistani society.

Roots and racism

Frivillig tvang remains silent on discrimination and racism in Norway. Although the interviewees were born in Norway or had been living there most of their lives, the film constantly refers to their roots or national origin. Rolfsen travels to the Punjab where he "locates the roots of violence", and then travels back to Norway, which is explicitly presented as a bastion of gender equality. Positioning Pakistan in opposition to Norway as the locus of gender inequalities allows violence in Norway to be regarded as "an anomaly", while enabling violence to be considered as a "Pakistani import" (Keskinen 2009, p. 259).

Viewers are transported to the rural villages of Pakistan, where the tight-knit clan systems operates around—as the narrator puts it—"welfare, childcare and eldercare". They are introduced to various aspects of Pakistani family structure, including the honour system, and gender segregation. We are then shown images of and interviews with rural young women who are presented as homebound, uneducated cleaners and carers—victims of patriarchy—followed by interviews with their "oppressors". Both the young teenagers and older men discuss honour killings in a normalised, and even casual way.

> If she goes out alone and we hear rumours, then we would put an end to her there and then. You have to have a reason to kill. But you don't

necessarily have to kill. If it's possible to talk it through, then one should do that.

The film then contrasts the most conservative communities of urban Pakistan with the most egalitarian and sexually liberal dimensions of Norwegian media and society. Norway is presented as an ideal welfare state in line with the "Scandinavian 'success story'" portrayed in normative political theory, as being achieved by the "early modernisation of gender relations through gender-equality reforms" (Melby et al. 2009):

> Norway is one of the world's most equal and peaceful countries. The introduction of women's right to vote in 1913 made everyone equal. The feminist battle continued and was crowned with the right to self-determined abortion in 1978. Norway has the longest parental leave for mothers, and affordable access to kindergarten for all. This means that Norway is the country where most women work [outside the home]. Liberal sexual morals and the right to abortion and contraception has meant that strict sexual mores have been wiped away. Sex and nudity is common in TV, newspapers, and advertisements. Norwegian alcohol consumption is high. The result is that rates of rape and unwanted sex are still a problem. When such different cultures meet, there are substantial challenges.

The end of this commentary is accompanied by images of half-naked TV contestants, producing Norway as a freewheeling space of unchecked sexual morals, the very antithesis of conservative Pakistan. At the same time, while the narrative in *Frivillig tvang* departs from the dominant story of sexual violence as the sole preserve of the 'other' when discussing rape in the Norwegian context, it nevertheless frames it as a result of substance abuse, rather than as intrinsically present within Norwegian society.

Eldercare

The Pakistani system of eldercare is framed as incompatible with the Norwegian approach to family, and as counter to the ideals of the dual worker-carer family which precludes familial care, and as such, is antithetical to the ethos of the welfare state. In the course of the film, Hassan is sent by the *Frivillig tvang* producers to a well-appointed care home to 'learn a lesson' about Norwegian values. The older Norwegian people are presented as embodying norms of individuality, and as having freely chosen to spend their retirement years being cared for by the welfare state. The intended aim appears to be to convince Hassan that the Norwegian welfare system of eldercare is both effective, and preferable to the Pakistani system of familial care. However, Hassan resists this lesson, instead choosing to question the residents in the care home about whether they have chosen to live there themselves, or whether they were coerced by their families. Hassan's first interviewee is a very elderly lady, Marie Nordby, who has a sweet and rather uncertain demeanour. His questions to her are direct and unflinching, cutting to the heart of family, loss, and wellbeing:

HASSAN: What does it feel like to live here?
MARIE: I feel safe here.
HASSAN: Do you miss your children?
MARIE: It's not the same as living at home but I feel like I get the help I need. Medicine when I need it. And good food.
HASSAN: How often do you get visits from your children?
MARIE: I get visits from my children and my grandchildren.
HASSAN: You looked after your children when they were small. Why can they not do that for you now?
MARIE: But it was my own choice. My husband and I got sick round Christmas a year ago. Then I could not manage to be at home any more.
HASSAN: So it was your own choice?
MARIE: Yes, and my husband died here.

Hassan's telling question about how often the lady gets visits goes unanswered, and as each of the interviewed residents assert their "free choice", Hassan's repeated probing about the matter suggests that he is unconvinced. The director leaves this scepticism hanging, and instead follows this lesson about the benefits of welfare state eldercare provision by another on the workings of gender equality. Rolfsen challenges Hassan on how he will work and look after his parents if he is intent on being an estate agent. Hassan replies that he intends to delegate this task to his future wife. The director's question thus implicitly reframes familial care as both unnecessary and unpractical within the egalitarian welfare state framework.

Hassan here (re)establishes a gendered order of care by relating the potential care of his parents to his future wife. While this move may be framed by Rolfsen as running counter to the value of gender equality imbricated in the welfare state, his take on Hassan's position turns a blind eye to the fact that the care of the elderly in Norway is also gendered. In this sense, Hassan's position does not point to a bifurcation between gendered and non-gendered forms of care, but rather between public and informal care. In any case, from Rolfsen's perspective, Hassan's refuses to buy into the values and practices associated with the welfare state, and as such is relegated to a position outside the symbolic borders of the nation, standing for all those who are perceived as unwilling and unable to be "proper" citizens of Norway.

Conclusion

> Starry Starry night, Portraits hung in empty halls,
> Frameless heads on nameless walls,

> With eyes that watch the world and can't forget [...].
> And now I think I know what you tried to say to me,
> How you suffered for your sanity, How you tried to set them free.
> They would not listen, They're not, List'ning still, Perhaps they never will.
> *Vincent*, Don McLean

In this chapter, we have shown that the narratives and meanings located in *Frivillig tvang* and *Under en annen himmel* films provide evidence of the ways in which Norwegian society has and does makes sense of itself and its 'others' in relation to an enduring national fantasy of homogeneity. This fantasy purports to give consistency to the nation and its subjects and preserves it as a safely bounded whole. While assimilation through Norwegianisation policies appears to stand in contrast to contemporary integration policies, the difference between current policies and past assimilation thinking may not be so significant after all (Engen 2014, p. 122).

We argue that the story of the great grandmother in *Under en annen himmel* functions as a reminder of the personal, familial, and communal costs of assimilation policies. The story is also a reminder of the moral bankruptcy of fantasies of wholeness that underpin these policies. At the same time, the journey across time and space—which the story of the starry sky sets in motion—undermines the cultural essentialism this fantasy peddles by showing how culture is hybrid, moving, and ever-changing through time and space.

The great grandmother's starry night in turn interpellates Don McLean's lyrical tribute to Van Gogh's "sanity", which points to the world's lack of recognition of the artist's starry starry night, saluting "the eyes that watch the world and don't forget". McLean warns of a world that does not and may well never listen. This recalls the watchful eyes of the Kven narrator who is drawn to the starry night, as well as to the symbolic deafness of Norwegian policy-makers when faced with lessons from history, who instead allow paternalist fantasies of sameness to live on in their current manifestation. The consistently negative ways in which stories and practices of marriage and eldercare in Norwegian-Pakistani communities are framed in *Frivillig tvang* provides evidence of the ways in which acceptance into imagined communities is still perceived in mainstream culture as conditional on sameness (Gullestad 1992), and the exclusionary effects this thinking has. Norwegian-Pakistanis are collapsed into a community of more or less coerced individuals whose familial practices are perceived as inherently antithetical to those embraced by "free and good" Norwegians, as essentially incompatible with the values and norms of gender equality, and as fundamentally counter to the model of the dual carer-worker aligned with welfare strategies and thinking (Gullikstad et al. 2016).

Since *Frivillig tvang* represents Pakistani culture as the problem of integration, it cannot by default acknowledge the structural dimensions of racism within (Norwegian) home territory. On the other hand, the choice to avoid direct engagement with the structural dimensions of the Norwegianisation policy in *Under en annen himmel*, may relate to Mikkelsen not wanting to showcase Kvens as victims. Not pitting Kvenness and Norwegianess against each other is also a way of making a positive Kven identity more accessible to Norwegians with Kven backgrounds, something a "bitter" rehearsing of past wrongs may not have achieved. In doing this, *Under en annen himmel* expands the possibility of a more inclusive hybrid understanding of citizenship, extending a promise to Norway's new marginalised minorities. But while the Kven film stakes out this position in a context where Kvens are demobilised and de-politicised, Norwegian-Pakistanis still bear the brunt of symbolic ejection. At the same time, research on the everyday lives of Norwegian-Pakistanis points to their engagement with negotiations around identity as being much more in tune with the complex understandings of culture that the starry sky invokes, and which Rolfsen chooses to ignore (Östberg 2000).

Finally, *Under en annen himmel* contains a warning about the loss of language. Research suggests that the languages of new ethnic minorities are already disappearing within two or three generations in Norway (Berg 2003; Boyd et al. 1994). While mother tongue instruction is available in minority languages, it is offered only to those who have insufficient Norwegian language skills. Mother tongue instruction is thus not valued in itself, but is offered in the service of bettering Norwegian learning—in other words, for better assimilation (Vilbli.no 2018). We can wonder, along with Mikkelsen, not only what will happen to Børselv in 300 years, but what will happen to the Norwegian-Pakistani community, if the political pollution of exclusion continues to obscure the lights of the starry sky, and the multiple routes it illuminates.

Notes

1 Some people prefer the term Norwegian-Finnish over the term Kven. For the purpose of this article, we use the term Kven. For a discussion of the term, see for example, E. Niemi, *Kven—et omdiskutert begrep*, Varanger Årbok 1991, pp. 119–137.
2 The borders between the northern part of Norway and Sweden were drawn in 1751, between Russia and Norway in 1862, and between the northern part of Sweden and Finland in the Torne valley in 1809.
3 We use the term Norwegian-Pakistani for practical purposes—some may identify as Norwegian, as Pakistani, or as Norwegian-Pakistani or Pakistani-Norwegian.
4 The kantele has a very specific role in Finnish national mythology, and plays a key role in Finland's national epic, *Kalevala*.

References

Berg, H.J. (2003). *Språkbevaring eller språkbytte: en kvalitativ undersøkelse av språkvalg blant vietnamesere i Trondheim*. Trondheim: hovedfagsoppgave ved Institutt for nordistikk og litteraturvitenskap, NTNU.
Berlant, L. (1991). *The anatomy of National Fantasy: Hawthorne, Utopia, and Everyday Life*. Chicago: The University of Chicago Press.
Berlant, L.G. (1997). *The Queen of America Goes to Washington City: Essays on Sex and Citizenship*. Durham: Duke University Press.

Bjørklund, T. and Bergh, J. (2013) *Minoritetsbefolkningens møte med det politiske Norge*. Oslo: Cappelen Damm Akademisk.

Bowen, J.R. (2010). *Why the French Don't Like Headscarves: Islam, the State, and Public Space*. Princeton: Princeton University Press.

Boyd, S., Holman, A. and Jørgensen, J. (eds.) (1994). *Sprogbrug og sprogvalg blandt indvandrere i Norden*. Aarhus: Aarhus University Press.

Bredal, A. (2006a). 'Utlendingsloven mot tvangsekteskap: Om kunnskapsgrunnlaget for menneskerettslige avveininger'. *Nordic Journal of Human Rights*, 24, pp. 218–231.

Bredal, A. (2006b). *"Vi er jo en familie": arrangerte ekteskap, autonomi og fellesskap blant unge norsk-asiater*. Oslo: Unipax Institutt for Samfunnsforskning.

Bredal, A. (2013). 'Tackling forced marriages in the Nordic countries: Between women's rights and immigration control', in L. Welchman and S. Hossain (eds.) *'Honour': Crimes, Paradigms, and Violence Against Women*. London: Zed Books.

Bredström, A. (2003). 'Gendered racism and the production of cultural difference: Media representations and identity work among "immigrant youth" in contemporary Sweden'. *NORA—Nordic Journal of Feminist and Gender Research*, 11, pp. 78–88.

Clifford, J. (1997). *Routes: Travel and Translation in the Late Twentieth Century*. Cambridge: Harvard University Press.

Daugstad, G. (2009). *Søker krake make? Ekteskap og pardannelse blant unge bakgrunn fra Tyrkia, Pakistan og Vietnam. Rapport nr. 33, 2009*. Oslo: Statistisk sentralbyrå.

Døving, C.A. (2009). 'Migration: Ritual attrition or increased flexibility? A case study of Pakistani funeral practices in Norway', in V.S. Karla (ed.) *Pakistani Diasporas: Culture, Conflict, and Change*. Oxford: Oxford University Press.

Eldia (2013). European Language Diversity for All [Online]. Available: http://www.eldia-project.org/index.php/et/uudised-suendmused-vaeljaanded/press-releases/453-eng-eu-project-looking-at-finno-ugric-minority-languages-completed [Accessed 8 October 2018].

Engen, T.O. (2014). 'Enhetsskolen og minoritetene' in A.B. Lund and B.B. Moe (eds.) *Nasjonale minoriteter i det flerkulturelle Norge*. Bergen: Fagbokforlaget.

Erdal, M.B. and Oeppen, C. (2013). 'Migrant balancing acts: Understanding the interactions between integration and transnationalism'. *Journal of Ethnic and Migration Studies*, 39, pp. 867–884.

Eriksen, T.H. (2013). *Immigration and National Identity in Norway*. Washington, DC: Migration Policy Institute.

Fortier, A.M. (2008). *Multicultural Horizons: Diversity and the Limits of the Civil Nation*. Milton Park: Taylor & Francis.

Garner, S. (2014). 'Injured nations, racialising states and repressed histories: Making whiteness visible in the Nordic countries'. *Social Identities*, 20, pp. 407–422.

Goldberg, D.T. (2011). *The Threat of Race: Reflections on Racial Neoliberalism*. New Jersey: Wiley.

Gullestad, M. (1992). *The Art of Social Relations: Essays on Culture, Social Action and Everyday Life in Modern Norway*. Oslo: Scandinavian University Press.

Gullikstad, B., Kristensen, G.K. and Ringrose, P. (2016). *Paid Migrant Domestic Labour in a Changing Europe: Questions of Gender Equality and Citizenship*. Basingstoke: Palgrave Macmillan UK.

Hübinette, T. (2012). '"Words that wound": Swedish whiteness and its inability to accommodate minority experiences', in K. Loftsdóttir and L. Jensen (eds.) *Whiteness and Postcolonialism in the Nordic Region: Exceptionalism, Migrant Others and National Identities*. Farnham: Ashgate.

Hübinette, T. and Lundström, C. (2011). 'Sweden after the recent election: The double-binding power of Swedish whiteness through the mourning of the loss of "old Sweden" and the passing of "good Sweden"'. *NORA—Nordic Journal of Feminist and Gender Research*, 19, pp. 42–52.

Keaton, T.D. (2006). *Muslim Girls and the Other France: Race, Identity Politics, & Social Exclusion*. Bloomington: Indiana University Press.

Keskinen, S. (2009). '"Honour–related violence" and Nordic nation–building', in S. Keskinen, S. Tuori, S. Irni, D. Mulinari (eds.) *Complying with Colonialism: Gender, Race and Ethnicity in the Nordic Region*. Farnham, England: Ashgate.

Keskinen, S. (2017). 'Securitized intimacies, welfare state and the "other" family'. *Social Politics: International Studies in Gender, State & Society*, 24, pp. 154–177.

Kristin, W. and Åse, S. (2014). 'Young Norwegian-Pakistani women and sport: How does culture and religiosity matter?' *European Physical Education Review*, 20, pp. 489–507.

Lentin, A. and Titley, G. (2011). *The Crises of Multiculturalism*. London: Zed Books.

Lindqvist, J. (2009). 'Reindeer herding: A traditional indigenous livelihood'. *Macquarie Journal of International and Comparative Environmental Law*, 6(1), pp. 83–127.

McIntosh, L. (2015). 'Impossible presence: Race, nation and the cultural politics of "being Norwegian"'. *Ethnic and Racial Studies*, 38, pp. 309–325.

Melby, K., Rave, A.B. and Wetterberg, C. (2009). 'A Nordic model of gender equality? Introduction', in K. Melby, A.B. Rave and C. Wetterberg (eds.) *Gender Equality and Welfare Politics in Scandinavia: The Limits of Political Ambition?*Bristol: The Policy Press.

Under en annen himmel (2011). Directed by A. Mikkelsen: NRK TV.

Narayan, U. (2001). 'Minds of their own: Women, veiling and state intervention into cultural practices', in L. Antony and C.E. Witts (eds.) *A Mind of One's Own: Feminist Essays On Reason And Objectivity*. Milton Park: Taylor & Francis.

Niemi, E. (2005). 'Border minorities between state and culture', in T.N. Jackson and J. P. Nielsen (eds.) *Russia—Norway. Physical and symbolic borders*. Moscow: University of Tromsø and Russian Academy of Science.

Niemi, E. (2010) 'Kvenene – Fra innvandrere til nasjonal minoritet', in A.B. Lund and B.B. Moen (eds.) *Nasjonale minoriteter i det flerkulturelle Norge*. Tapir Akademisk Forlag, pp. 143–162.

Norske kveners forbund (NKF) [The Norwegian Kven Association]. (2018). Sannhetskommisjon [Online]. Available: http://kvener.no/sannhetskommisjon/ [Accessed 8 October 2018].

NRK (2017). A World-Class Publisher [Online]. Available: https://www.nrk.no/about/a-world-class-publisher-1.4029931 [Accessed 8 October 2018]

Olwig, K.F. (2011). '"Integration": Migrants and refugees between Scandinavian welfare societies and family relations'. *Journal of Ethnic and Migration Studies*, 37, pp. 179–196.

Östberg, S. (2000). 'Islamic nurture and identity management: The lifeworld of Pakistani children in Norway'. *British Journal of Religious Education*, 22, pp. 91–103.

Frivillig tvang (2014). Directed by U.I. Rolfsen: NRK TV.

Rose, J. (1998). *States of Fantasy*. Oxford: Clarendon Press.

Sernhede, O. (2001). 'Svart macho eller vit velour: utanförskap, hiphop och maskulinitet i det nya Sverige [Black macho or white velour: Estrangement, hip-hop and masculinity in the new Sweden]', in C. Ekenstam, T. Johansson and J. Kuosmanen (eds.) *Sprickor i fasaden—manligheter i förändring* [Cracks in the facade—transforming masculinities]. Hedemora: Gidlund.

Sollid, H. (2013). 'Ethnolects and language emancipation in Northern Norway'. *Sociolinguistic Studies*, 7.

Statistisk sentralbyrå [SSB] (2018). 'Immigrants and Norwegian-born to immigrant parents'. https://www.ssb.no/en/innvbef [Accessed 3 March, 2019]

Staunæs, D. (2003). 'Where have all the subjects gone? Bringing together the concepts of intersectionality and subjectification'. *NORA—Nordic Journal of Feminist and Gender Research*, 11, pp. 101–110.

Turner, G. (2006). *Film as Social Practice*. Milton Park: Taylor & Francis.

Tvedt, T. (2017). *Det internasjonale gjennombruddet. Fra «ettpartistat» til flerkulturell stat*. Oslo: Dreyers Forlag.

Vilbli.no (2018). Language Education for Language Minorities [Online]. Available: https://www.vilbli.no/en/en/no/language-education-for-language-minorities/a/025585 [Accessed 8 October 2018].

Walle, T. (2011). *A Passion for Cricket. Masculinity, Ethnicity and Diasporic Spaces in Oslo*. PhD dissertation. Oslo: UiO.

Walseth, K. and Strandbu, Å. (2014). 'Young Norwegian-Pakistani women and sport: How does culture and religiosity matter?' *European Physical Education Review*, 20, pp. 489–507.

Wikan, U. (2002). *Generous Betrayal: Politics of Culture in the New Europe*. Chicago: University of Chicago Press.

Yuval-Davis, N. (1997). *Gender and Nation: SAGE Publications*. London: SAGE Publications Ltd.

# Part 3
Questioned homogeneity and securitisation

9 From welfare to warfare

Exploring the militarisation of the Swedish suburb

Suruchi Thapar-Björkert, Irene Molina and Karina Raña Villacura

> It is not my most immediate measure to send in the military, but I'm prepared to do what it takes to ensure that serious organised crime goes away. (Stefan Löfven, Swedish Prime Minister, to TT News Agency [Jakobson 2018])

Introduction

The 2013 'suburban riots' which were triggered by the police (SWAT) shooting of Lenine Relvas-Martins, a 69-year-old man in the Stockholm suburb of Husby, brought debates on social polarisation, segregation, and gentrification to centre stage, as well as highlighting the role of state functionaries in contributing to violence. In the debates that followed, it became evident that the suburban areas of the Million Programme (including Husby) were specifically framed as an "anti-social and uncivilised [criminal] spatiality" (Ericsson et al. 2000, pp. 28, 29), and its residents as "violent political subjects" (de los Reyes 2016, pp. 164, 166). In fact, these areas were stigmatised from the moment the new housing development programme was launched by the Social Democrats at the beginning of the sixties, as a key project within the Swedish welfare state model. While the aim was to construct one million dwellings nationwide, located mostly in the Swedish cities' periphery, the sixties' fear of modern urbanism in Sweden (Molina 1997) accelerated the racialisation of these areas by the media, framing them as non-Swedish, less civilized, and more dangerous than other urban neighbourhoods (Ericsson et al. 2000).

A 2014 police report—'A national overview of criminal networks that have a major impact within local communities' (Rikskriminalpolisen 2014)—put forward the Swedish police's identification of 55 areas (all part of the Million Programme) in which they considered local criminal networks to have a major negative impact on local spaces and communities. The report—which is devoid of any local perspectives—frames the suburbs through representations of criminality and vulnerability. There is also an unexplained assertion of the existence of "parallel" societies with associated implications of self-segregation, isolationism, and failing citizens (Grundström and Molina 2016; also see Rikskriminalpolisen 2015). A 2015 follow-up report called 'Vulnerable areas—social risks, collective ability and undesired events', emphasises criminal vulnerability (associated mainly with violence and open drug dealings) and "criminal energy" (2015, p. 21), suggesting it be managed by a "high police presence" and "hotspot patrolling" in selected areas (Rikskriminalpolisen 2015, p. 23)[1].

Associating these "vulnerable" areas (Rikskriminalpolisen 2015) with being controlled by criminals, and as spaces in which law and order needs to be re-established, becomes a "rallying slogan based on a fantasy of danger as well as reconquest, the image of danger magnifying the courage of those who face it, and that of reconquest justifying the action aimed at realizing it" (Fassin 2013, p. 37). In this regard, such a fantasy is propelled by the role assigned to disciplinary authorities (police, penal system, intelligence) as legitimate interpreters of social reality, and which has—in the post Keynesian global era—led to the "upsizing" of the penal sector at the cost of "downsizing" of the welfare sector (Wacquant 2009, p. 3).

Furthermore, several government initiatives (in close collaboration with local councils, real-estate establishments, the District Administration Office (Stadsdelsförvaltingen), and the police) have been foregrounded in the Järva region, in the North West of Stockholm;[2] a) installation of a "sound scare" system (*SVT* 25 November, 2016), initially in two of the neighbourhoods in the Järva region (Tensta and Husby), arguably to keep drug dealers at bay; b) the potential creation of "zones of frisking" (Tronarp 2017); c) strengthening surveillance through microphones and body cameras (Stockholm Direkt 2017); and d) bolstering the presence of police numbers with private security guards patrolling the region (Rinkeby-Kista Stadsdelsförvaltning 2017). These proposals are closely related to similar developments in other Nordic countries, for example, the recent 2017 decision made by the Danish government on the deployment of military forces to patrol borders and special places such as synagogues (Bülow 2017), in order to release police forces to combat gangs and organised crime in the cities (Rasmusson 2017).

In this chapter, we argue that the suburban landscape is steadily being shaped through a shift in political discourse—from welfare to warfare—leading to a steady militarisation of the suburbs. A central theme that governs this process is the monitoring and management of 'problem' ethnic collectives and urban peripheries that adhere to an "alternate social order" through disciplinary regimes, and different forms of (im)mobilisation such as racial, ethnic, and religious profiling; identity controls; and draconian immigration laws (see Polisen 2017). Thus, processes of militarisation operate in tandem with practices and processes of securitisation, which entails the "production of security and security-related technologies and assemblages at various [socio-spatial] scales" (Low 2017, p. 367; Gluck and Low 2017). We extend this idea to argue that these modalities of security/insecurity in racialised residential areas inadvertently create a culture of impunity,[3] which can be analysed through the lens of structural violence. Structural violence is rendered invisible as it is "perceived" as the status quo, but "experienced" (see

Price 2012) as stigmatisation; assaults on dignity and integrity; and the steady erosion of individual agency.

Our arguments draw on in-depth interviews conducted during four months of intensive qualitative fieldwork in the Järva region in Stockholm, in 2018, by co-author Karina Raña Villacura. The respondents were identified through the snowball method, initiated through our contact with Husby Träff, a civil society organisation. We also accessed several other networks, which enabled us to have a more heterogeneous selection of respondents. The key actors were six official representatives from local authorities: the local housing company (1), the Police (3), the municipal Library (1), and the local administration office (1); five members of civil society organisations (Förörten I Centrum, Husby Träff, Rädda Barnen, Förorten mot Våld, Reactor); and 13 local residents. The interviews were taped, transcribed, and codified with the aid of the Atlas.ti software. The interviews were coded in relation to the main theoretical aims of the project, and its subsequent interview questionnaire. The main themes emerged from an analysis of the interview data through a "grounded theory approach" (Strauss and Corbin 1999). To maintain anonymity, our respondents have been coded as: O–from an Organisation, L–local resident, and AO–Authorities/Officials working in the suburbs. Working in the field presented some methodological challenges, due to the current climate of fear and suspicion, which has been shaped through ongoing processes of racialisation and objectification (Patel 2012; De Leeuw, Cameron and Greenwood 2012). The interview material was analysed together with a total of ten articles in broadsheet and local newspapers,[4] and seven official reports. Using interpretive content analysis, we identified both the "latent" (implicit) and "manifest" (literal) meanings in the texts (Krippendorff 2013). In addition, field notes were kept—these observations, experiences, and conversations further informed our qualitative enquiry. They served to describe situations and make sense of them during the analysis stage.

Globalisation of urban militarisation

Scholars' interest in the general relationship between militarism and welfare can be traced to the 1920s and 1930s, when the warfare industry was a central source of income for the national economy of the United States (Eisner 2000). Wehrle (2003) writes on the same matter, indicating that warfare more or less financed welfare, but as Gilmore (1998) notes, pressures from the capitalist class to minimise their contribution to social expenditures and welfare through taxes, marked the final shift at the end of the sixties: "With diminishing options for a social Keynesian spending program, the mainstream of organized labor embraced military Keynesianism" (Wehrle 2003, p. 527). Gilmore (2007, p. 78) refers to the political–economic changes of the American Keynesian state as a shift from the Keynesian "workfare"[5] state to the Keynesian militarised "warfare" state. In the case of the US at that time, we have observed a circular sequence of transformations, from warfare to welfare, and back to warfare. This sequence of transformations seems to be applicable to the Swedish context, though from a different perspective. In Sweden, the military industry has supported a welfare system that was fortified after the Second World War, through generating an income for the national Treasury (Glimell 2012); in other words, welfare provision has been sustained by warfare. In spite of the obvious differences between the two countries, these examples from the US and Sweden reveal that the relationship between welfare and militarism can transform and shift in different manners at different points in time, which reinforces Gilmore's statement that militarism is a global phenomenon. We conceptualise this shift as being a part of the Swedish state's process of transitioning from welfare to warfare, by which we mean that the proposal for addressing social problems through more welfare services (for example, providing employment and educational possibilities, and youth day centres) is being replaced with more police officers, more surveillance, and harsher punishments. This transition towards steady militarisation has not only occurred in the realm of public discourse but is being experienced by the residents of stigmatised neighbourhoods as an everyday lived reality.

The scene for militarisation that we refer to here is located in urban areas within an apparently calm and fully democratic society, whose societal institutions are working normally. Militarisation normalising warfare—that is, the military patrolling the streets of cities in times of peace—seems to be a global trend, since many urban residents worldwide have shared these experiences. In countries suffering from civil wars, such as Colombia and Nicaragua, the presence of the military on the streets has been an everyday phenomenon for a long time. Graham (2011) refers to the phenomenon of "military urbanism", which justifies the demonisation of populations and assaults against an urban, racial, or class enemy, by regularly invoking states of "exception and emergency" (Graham 2011, p. 83). Graham suggests that a process of "'policization of the military' proceeds in parallel with the 'militarization of the police'" (Graham 2011, p. 96). Militaristic policies nowadays operate in urban spaces, in specific neighbourhoods, and public spaces. The phenomenon implies that an organisation—the most common of which would be the police—acquires attributes characteristic of the military (Haggerty and Ericson 2006). Dikeç and Swyngedouw (2017) use the term "disruptions of the urban space" to refer to the effects that uprisings and riots can have in the practices of policing the city. Building upon Rancière, who distinguishes "between 'the police' and politics, where the former refers to established orders of governance, and the latter to disruptive episodes in the name of equality", the authors conclude that this process of disruption can sometimes lead to either more democratic participation (as in Spain, with the consolidation of the *Podemos* movement), or to more repression and increasing levels of violence and militarisation (Dikeç and Swyngedouw 2017, p. 14).

Inspired by the aforementioned international literature, we use the concept of militarisation to refer to increased levels of police violence in the deprived suburbs in Swedish cities, and to the normalisation of the rhetoric of warfare in public debates, rather than to the actual presence of the army on the streets. The presence of well-armed and heavily equipped police special forces who wear military-in-war style uniforms has been observed in Swedish cities since the 2000s and is steadily becoming part of everyday life for the residents of some Swedish suburbs, especially the stigmatised and demonised suburbs of the Million Programme (Dikeç 2017; Molina 2013). Researchers have also denounced an exaggerated use of violence by the SWAP police forces in the suburbs, both during uprisings such as in Husby in 2013 and in Gottsunda in 2009, but also independent of those (de los Reyes 2016; Sernhede, Thörn and Thörn 2016; Dikeç 2017). As we will soon illustrate, the demonisation of particular areas via media stigmatisation has been a key aspect in the initial racialisation and subsequent militarisation processes of the Million Programme's urban areas; among them is our case study area of Järva in the Stockholm region. It seems necessary to use the language of geopolitics and warfare by employing the term militarisation to better understand what is happening in the Million Programme suburbs regarding control, surveillance, and police violence. We also question if this is occurring at the same time, or rather *because* of the withdrawal of the welfare state in this era of neoliberalism and austerity policies. With the help of local voices, we will describe what this process currently looks like in Järva.

From welfare to warfare: The role of state violence

In our understanding of the concept of militarisation, state politics, and shifts in welfare politics play a central role in shaping processes of militarisation; these are not necessarily represented by the presence of the military on the streets, but on the more violent uses of force by the police (see Graham 2011). Building on the work of several authors such as David Harvey, Neil Smith, Jamie Peck, and others, we refer to the neoliberal turn in the Swedish welfare state, which was initiated at the end of the eighties (Grundström and Molina 2016), and dramatically intensified at the beginning of the nineties. A key consequence from this political, economic, and ideological shift has been the withdrawal of public welfare services, and a simultaneous proliferation of private firms instead. One local voice, a young male resident of Husby and youth club worker, also reaffirmed the trend towards a withdrawal of welfare that we have identified in literature:

> Then, it was a couple of years where they started, a lot of closing downs in the neighbourhood. A Health-Care Centre, a Youth Centre for kids was already closed down, schools, the school closed down also. (Interview L1)

The rationalisation commonly offered for diminishing public facilities is to place blame on the suburb itself, since "there is none who are willing to go to [Rinkeby, a neighbouring suburb] and work there ... [and] those who want to work there will run away from the area" (Interview AO3); this was invoked by a male police officer. Representing a suburb as lacking "safety" can be understood as one reason for the understaffing of public social service departments, despite a recent proposal (Stockholms Stad 2016) by the City of Stockholm Municipality to improve working conditions and increase the number of applicants to social workers positions within these offices. Nonetheless, the privatisation of welfare services more generally has implications such as reducing the presence of the local state via social services in deprived neighbourhoods of Sweden. For example, during the last three decades, the City of Malmö has privatised health-, child-, and elderly care services, significantly affecting its population's quality of life (Salonen 2012). Similarly, in Stockholm, residential segregation has led to a concentration of poverty in certain areas of the city, particularly those with a relatively high proportion of residents with migrant backgrounds. Precarious labour market conditions (especially in service branches), together with high unemployment levels, have contributed to an increasing income inequality between rich and poor.[6] The average income of Stockholm in 2015 was four times higher in the rich parts of the city than in the poorest ones, nearly double the 1990 statistics (Bremberg et al. 2015), the year in which welfare privatisation and deregulation of welfare began.

At the same time, the Swedish state *seemingly* substitutes social services with policemen, through constantly increasing the budget for police officers in racialised neighbourhoods. The ideological shift from welfare to warfare legitimises and normalises the police's use of force by employing the rhetoric of "we need more police officers in the area" (Molina 2013). Following the lead of the Danish Police Force, the Swedish government has advocated for reinforcing police power through increasing their resources, most noticeably since the increase of shootings and shooting-related deaths in Järva. In a 2017 press conference, prime minister Stefan Löfven announced that the government would allocate additional resources of 7.1 billion SEK to the police during the next three years. The budget proposal (which includes 300 million SEK more than the police originally requested), is the biggest police-focused increase since 2000, and can be understood as an attempt to "improve working conditions for police in order to get more people to stay in the profession" (Lindström and Svensson 2017). More recently, as we indicated in the quotation above, Löfven declared that he might consider putting the military on the streets (Jakobson 2018).

Furthermore, substantial changes in the character of the police forces sent to residential suburban neighbourhoods have been observed, which differ from the dispositions of those patrolling city streets in the seventies. The officers who arrive to investigate an incident—particularly one perceived as 'violent' (such as a burning car, stone throwing by youngsters, or a murder)—often conduct themselves as if preparing for battle, as if the suburb was a wartime battlefield. Moreover, the police seem to be increasingly dominant within how public debates on "policing the suburbs" are articulated.[7] This could be partly attributed to the fact that most Swedish newsrooms rely on a central news wire agency for their content, which in the case of the Husby shooting, unquestioningly accepted the police narrative as the "truth", and disseminated it across all media channels (Djalaie, 2016). Invoking the "deviant focus" of this journalism, a respondent from *Tensta Konsthall* [Tensta Art Hall] (Interview O5) mentioned how journalists "sometimes [...] do not even come here—they just write from the police reports that are sent out [...] which lack the perspective of the residents who live here". Furthermore, internal transformations within the police institution entails processes of centralisation, decentralisation, and a combination of both within decision-making processes. Decentralisation processes started in 1993, and fostered a shift in police working methodologies, transitioning from reactive duties against already perpetrated crimes, to more crime prevention work (Lindström et al. 2001). The emphasis on preventive measures was strengthened in 2014, when it was highlighted in the government's budget proposal and reinforced via institutional reorganisation in 2015. This restructuring engaged different local actors in preventive work methodologies that employed centralised and decentralised dimensions, together with more local strategic directions to guide the police's work (Elgemyr et al. 2017).

Understanding militarisation as processes of exclusion that are accompanied by a harder police presence in deprived suburbs subsequently creates the conditions for the emergence of, and increasing violence within, disempowered groups. Nevertheless, this form of violence—which is the only one mentioned in the media and dominant public discourses as "problematic", despite the existence of other forms of violence (and the power it sustains) exerted by unholy alliances between the state and capitalist exploitation (Listerborn et al. 2011)—neither explains nor justifies processes of militarisation. Violence cannot be explained by focusing on specific individuals and deviant pathologies but should be understood as an effect of social relations. For example, youngsters throwing stones or burning cars is not the breakdown of social order, but rather is a power struggle against the ways in which the current social order is maintained. As Ray (2000) points out, violence—like other forms of behaviour—is embedded in durable forms of sociality, or in routine social relationships (Ray 2000). What should be at stake in one's analysis is the role played by state violence in its varied forms—that is, subjective, systemic, and structural, but also symbolic, as in the media's stigmatisation of deprived suburbs and their residents (Listerborn et al. 2011). Stigmatised places become natural places for locating state violence. Several public and official voices claim there is a need to augment poor suburbs with the presence of more police officers, and the introduction of the military. This becomes justified through the dissemination of images of deprived neighbourhoods framed as sites of gang criminality and Islamic radicalisation. We will now analyse practices of police militarisation through the narratives articulated by the residents of Järva.

Distrust and denial in the everyday

One outcome of the normalisation of militarised discourses on policing the suburbs is the Islamophobic creation of the violent male resident trope, who may also be an Islamic terrorist. In 2014, the government created "The National Coordinator to Safeguard Democracy against Violent Extremism" (their translation).[8] According to some respondents, this national policy—which aims to protect democracy and prevent violent extremism—has trickled down to the local level, affecting everyday life in Husby. A member of one of the biggest civil society organisations in Husby mentioned how, when asked about issues of Islamic radicalisation within the youth activity centre he was working at, he was disbelieved; in that instance, the administrator in charge of the investigation did not believe his claim "that such issues were rarely seen in the youth activity centre" (Interview O2). In another instance, a female respondent who works as a process developer for an NGO operating in the region, commented: "When it comes to social services, the people are terrified because there are really bad stories about how they [social services] have treated children" (Interview O4). In fact, there is a dominant perception among the social services that parents need to bear the blame for not being "strict enough" towards their children (Field notes, June 13, 2017). Thus, we see responsibilities shifting from being ascribed through a structural level, to the increasing scrutiny of the individual, which then becomes a justification for "assigning 300 policemen more only in Rinkeby" (Interview L5), as described by a young male from a civil society organisation dealing with violence. Instead of offering equal and effective social freedom through education, work, and inclusion (for example, directing efforts to integrate youths in the labour market), and instead of implementing a much needed "structural analysis"[9] (as suggested by a local resident, Interview L5) to address systemic injustice, efforts have been (mis)placed via investment in police resources.

These experiences are embedded within the broader structures of cultural and social institutions, which goes beyond individuals (Menjívar 2008), while at the same time constituting their 'everydayness'—their lived realities. The prevailing environment of distrust and fear on the one hand, together with the respondents' lack of belief in the institutional legitimacy of social services, police, and local and national authorities on the other, combines to support a culture of impunity. We conceptualise this culture of impunity through the lens of structural violence, which, in the context of the neighbourhoods included in this study, comprises an array of offences against human dignity: poverty, social inequalities including racism, and more generally, human rights abuses (Galtung 1996). These "multi-axial models of suffering" shape a political economy of brutality (Farmer 1996, p. 274). Those who seek to resist often find that they are punished further for challenging the status quo, and that the punishment (often through subjective but also systemic and symbolic violence) is considered to be legitimate. Thus, it comes as no surprise that the increasing presence of the police is justified through a sustained process of targeted stigmatisation, where human beings become expendable commodities, and the presumed safety of society occurs through the erosion of their humanity. Their dignity is undermined by constructing them as insignificant and unworthy of consultation; as objects of deceit and intimidation; and of criminalisation. This is best exemplified through an account by a young male respondent and resident of Husby, who is an employee of a youth activity centre in the neighbourhood.

> There was a shooting at the parking lot here in Husby. It was aimed at other people, but we were travelling in a car, my friends and I, and they thought we were those people they had fought with (…) So a motorcycle and a car came right next to us and started to shoot. We were four and two got struck. I and another friend got fragments in our eyes (…) then we called the ambulance (…) Then she was "no, we won't send anyone", I took the phone and said, "come to Oslogatan", and I said he got *flaskad* [fragments of a bottle], a bottle because I already knew, in advance, if they see that I got shot so I would wait for another additional hour. I said I got *flaskad* and she refused to believe in me. (Interview L1)

As Farmer argues, "the 'texture' of dire affliction is (…) best felt in the gritty details of biography" (Farmer 1996, p. 263)—in this case, our respondent subsequently lost vision in one of his eyes (Interview L1). The silencing of suffering casts sufferers out of the public's moral compass, it "muffles" suffering, rendering it barely noticeable (Opotow 2001), and changes the moral colour of an act from "red/wrong to green/right or at least to yellow/acceptable" (Galtung 1990, p. 292). Furthermore, it manifests reality as 'opaque', so that others are unable to understand the gravity of a specific situation. To use Scheper-Hughes's (1996) powerful metaphor, this—together with forms of institutional inefficiency illustrated in the narrative above—constitutes a form of "invisible genocide"; it's invisible not because it's hidden, but precisely the opposite—it's harder to perceive because it's right before our eyes, yet its effects can be seen within many people's lives. These invisible acts are conducted in the "normative social spaces" of schools, clinics, streets, and prisons (Scheper-Hughes 2004, p. 14), leading to death and injury (as we see in the example of the shooting). We observed that the main mural in the centre of Husby bears the acronym RNHRAM, which represents the initials of the names of young people from Järva who have died (due to illness, gang violence, shooting, or political violence), whose lives remain 'invisible' to the State, but visible to those who live in Järva (Field notes—Graffiti in Husby, 7 June, 2017). This invisibility also hides what Arendt (1964) describes as the "banality of evil", whereby supposed normal, decent people become "technicians of genocide"—like the lady from the 112 emergency line who responded, "no, we won't send anyone", despite knowing that the caller had been pierced by bottle fragments due to a shooting. This is further illustrated by Italian psychiatrist Franco Basaglia, who in drawing links between "war crimes" and "peace-time crimes", argues that "ordinary" people could practice torture, terror, and "genocidal practices", especially in a culture where institutional inefficiency and indifference is pervasive. In the Swedish state, which can be seen as the epitome of institutional efficiency, this narrative arguably stands out even more.

In another instance, a respondent working in *Tensta Konsthall* [Tensta Art Hall] narrated a shooting in Tensta in which one person was injured and another killed in the summer of 2016.

> And the police arrived here maybe in half an hour, or maybe earlier than that, but they [the police] left him totally uncovered on the street, there were so many kids around, many relatives, people who knew him. This is traumatic for the whole neighbourhood. The ambulance came too late, so it was impossible to save him, and it is an issue, the ambulance must be escorted by the police to get here, which means that the ambulance comes always too late. Then, when it happened, there were many children who could see this, and it is also a traumatic experience for those kids. But, the District Administration Office was not here and that shows, you know, if this would happen in another place in Stockholm, then the help would have been there at once. (Interview O5)

Philosopher and political theorist Achille Mbembe has put forward the idea of "necropolitics", by which he names the violence that resides within the logics of European modernity (also see da Silva 2009). Arguably, in the "repressed topographies" of the suburbs, the expendable racial others are subjected to conditions of life which are similar to the status of the "living dead" (Mbembe 2003, p. 40). The "uncovered" body on the street is not only symbolic of a racialised state of expendability, an ultimate expression of sovereignty which dictates, "who may live and who must die" (Mbembe 2003, p. 11), but also who deserves dignity in death, and who does not. It furthermore reinforces the idea of the "inevitability" of violence and tragedy in the suburbs.

Frisking, body searches, and racial profiling

In a recent policy development, the Swedish Justice Minister, Morgan Johansson, advocated for introducing "search zones where the police can frisk people, even though they suspect no crime", in search of, for example, firearms or drugs. Despite knowing with certainty that the method has been criticised for violating personal integrity, Johansson stated: "of course, it should always be weighed against the integrity aspects, but as I understand, it has had an impact in Denmark, and I will watch with interest what evaluations [of the method] become available" (Aftonbladet, 1 September, 2017).

Local residents in this study mention the increasing frequency of body searches without particular motives, as if the bodies of the racialised migrant population were the property of the state and the police. These experiences produce fear in response to the police, and a feeling of permanent unsafety.

> You look at the positive so you can move on, but there are so many negatives, that is not possible to ignore. It could happen suddenly, "Okay, all of you against the wall, show your ID", just because something has happened and we look like them, but what does it have to do with us? What can we do? We look like [their target], that is all. (Interview L6)

At times, to "look like them" (in regard to race or ethnicity), becomes the central criterion for the police to stop and search, and can also be understood as an "effect of racializing practices" (Keskinen et al. 2018, p. 7). In the report 'Randomly Selected' [*Slumpvis Utvald*] (Schclarek Mulinari 2017; also see Dikeç 2017), the author conducted a series of interviews with young residents of stigmatised neighbourhoods in several Swedish cities. The interviewees came from Afro-Swedish, Roma and Muslim communities, and explained that being stopped by the police is a common experience. The victims reported being criminalised and treated as suspicious, even in situations when they themselves have been victims of crime. Interestingly, police officers who were interviewed categorically denied racial profiling. They referred to racial profiling as occurring casually and in isolated cases, or alternatively as inevitable, due to the nature of the practice at national borders. Or, in the words of one interviewed police officer respondent, who explained why frisking happens within certain racialised neighbourhoods: "you shouldn't claim that it is racist. We have to be there. It is there where crime occurs and where people feel unsafe, which shows that this [the area] is a hotspot. It is there that we have to be" (Schclarek Mulinari 2017, p. 32). The police rationalise that stop searches and frisking are predominant within particular suburbs, since they house mostly immigrant populations—a problematic linking of race and place. Thus, these racial profiling practices questionably link racial markers to discourses of "criminality" (Goodey, 2006, p. 209) and (in) security, while justifying the intensive policing of marginalised communities that face racial discrimination.

The police force's denial of racism and racial profiling is especially problematic in light of statistics that prove that only a minority of all reported cases of police violence are followed up by the courts (UNT, 1 January, 2017). Living in a racialised body with the stigmatisation of 'dark skin' seems to make individuals intrinsically suspicious, and a legitimate subject for being frisked. Thus "the body itself is inscribed with, and demarcates, a continual crossing of multiple encoded borders—social, legal, gendered, racialized and so on" (Amoore 2006, p. 337). The assertion of this border is found not only in distinctions between citizens and non-citizens, but also in the boundaries of social and political otherness (Balibar 2005).

Surveillance of racialised suburbs

In neoliberal times, even the phenomena of surveillance must be analysed as another feature of the general trend to privatise and decentralise; this is concomitant with the normalisation of stigmatisation that suburban residents face, and their subsequently being understood as lacking credibility. Surveillance technologies are contingent upon ways of knowing, managing, and controlling suspect populations (also see Haggerty and Ericsson 2006). Inspired by Foucault amongst others, Uitermark (2014) refers to the trend of applying selective repression in the neighbourhoods of European cities as "governmentality in situ", asserting that the intensification of repression responds to new forms of territorialised surveillance and boundary enforcement that is "used to keep marginalised populations in check" (Uitermark 2014, p. 1420). In Uitermark's argument, the participation of these "other actors" that we recognise in the Swedish case includes the very projects that purport to assist migrant populations with integration (and counteracting spatial segregation). Again, processes of neoliberal (anti-welfare) racialisation, with their tendency towards militarisation, result in the staging of state repression in the suburbs through particularly racialised politics of violent urban control.

With the increasing decentralisation of surveillance comes new forms of indirect surveillance *by* chosen citizens *about* other citizens, played out through Citizen Hosts [*medborgarvärdar*].[10] As a potential bridge between authorities and residents in the suburbs, Citizen Hosts or 'security watches' operate through a citizens' office in a central suburban location, and are local residents hired by the District Administration Office to walk around the neighbourhood, meet people, and answer practical questions about the local government institution. Nonetheless, their role remains contentious. While the District Administration Office itself is framed by a local resident as "a prison, [where] every single door is locked because they do not want someone going in and bothering them" (Interview L1), the void left from the municipal office's departure seems to have arguably been bridged, to some extent, by the Citizen Hosts. A mistrust of this infrastructural development was articulated by many respondents and local residents on multiple occasions. They [local residents] felt that first, the Citizen Hosts did not constitute a legitimate voice in the suburbs, as they were meant to fill the void left by removing the state's presence in the suburbs. Second, the residents deem the Citizen Hosts—and its whole District Administration Office supporting structure—as a reflection of exclusionary and discriminatory practices.[11] Though the positions of Citizen Hosts/fieldworkers who patrol the neighbourhood are mainly awarded to residents of immigrant backgrounds with 'foreign names', they are not given the agency to be part of decision-making processes.

Racialised practices of surveillance relate to the production of norms that pertain to specific groups, or as John Fiske argued, "surveillance is not applied equally to all, [...] for it is a way of imposing norms, [on]...those who have been othered into the 'abnormal'" (Fiske 1998, p. 81). This is corroborated by the depiction of the aforementioned suburban areas as deviant, as a place where "normal situations do not exist" (Interview AO3), as suggested by a local police officer. This inadvertently becomes a justification for state institutions to withdraw, leading to a steady "abandonment of the suburb". Drug-related crime, drug use among youth, and associated criminal activities have all uniformly informed the rationalisation to increased surveillance, whether it be the "sound scare system", surveillance cameras, body cameras,[12] or the more recent use of microphones (Stockholm Direkt 2017) that aimed to strengthen surveillance in order to control criminals and gangs, who were framed by Mikael Cederbratt of the Conservative Party *Moderaterna* as "cancerous tumors in our country" (Aftonbladet, 19 October, 2017). As an NGO respondent who lives and works in Järva put it:

> It has been presented as: this violence among foreign people that kill each other, they are gang members, and we should do something about security, safety, and increase the police efforts, we need to set up surveillance cameras. (Interview O4)

Surveillance and control thus operate in a synchronised manner, which has direct consequences on the well-being of residents; as one respondent from a civil society organisation put it: this "creates a psychosocial environment that is very unhealthy" (Interview O1), rather than an environment that expands their individual and social capabilities.

Paradoxically, the suburbs are increasingly discussed as nodes for the building of participatory spaces through deliberative democracy models. Nonetheless, instead of being recognised as subjects in political processes, young people are subjected to various forms of surveillance, which in the very least, erodes these spaces of political deliberation. It reinforces a democratic deficit, which encompasses a lack of acknowledgement of local voices in public discourse, including consulting and actively involving them in local developments (see de los Reyes et al. 2014). As a respondent from a civil society organisation noted,

> If you feel that your voice has no value when you look at the representatives of the official society, and then you get threatened by the organisations that represent the official society, like police and stuff like that. And then you have this picture in the media that people like you are this and that. It's a lot of things. It adds up. (Interview O1)

The socially dominant often claim a sense of entitlement to speak, but also to shape interactions, as "their speech and opinion are judged [the] most legitimate" (Olson, 2011, p. 537). Hayward (2004, p. 4) argues that besides inequalities in resources for "effective decision-making influence" (within spheres such as education, information, and skills), and inequalities in resources for "effective participation" in deliberations (related to disparities in income, wealth, and social status), cultural inequality can devalue and delegitimise the "communicative tendencies" of subordinated groups. Furthermore, within the context of everyday interactions, deliberative practices are often dominated by those equipped with symbolic capital, who can not only repress challenges from competing opinions, but can also make social agents accept the existing order as 'natural'. This arguably often leads to processes of internalisation by 'subaltern' subjects (in our case, residents of immigrant suburbs) who understand their exclusion(s) to be caused by, and a consequence of their very existence. As two local respondents mentioned:

> It is a good country (Sweden), we have democracy. If you are good, aware and smart and you wake up early in the morning, you can get a job. (L4)
>
> First of all, we are not smart, we are immigrants. We do not participate in Swedish democracy. Instead of being involved, we choose exclusion in certain ways. (L3)

The paradox for second-generation suburban youth—"being born in Sweden, but called an immigrant"—and an internalised identity that operates as an antithesis to Swedish values of being "good", "aware", and "smart", inadvertently relegates them to the margins of Swedish democracy, and forecloses all possibilities for deliberation. In this way, processes of deliberation arguably still remain the preserve of those who are dominant (white), whose claims for supporting an inclusive deliberative democracy still rests on the exclusion of the 'Other'. This subsequently erodes possibilities for deliberation, makes deliberative processes a hollow rhetoric, and reproduces the existing political (white) order. If our aim is to bring marginalised voices into public discourse, then from a deliberative equality perspective, we need to acknowledge the unequal possibilities, positionalities, and opportunity structures that prevent marginalised voices from informing dominant frames of interpretation.

Concluding discussion

In our chapter, we demonstrate that since the Second World War, Sweden's welfare rhetoric has been transformed into a rhetoric of warfare, which places repression at its centre. We refer to this process as the militarisation of the Swedish suburbs. Through a constructed narrative of a racialised, stigmatised, and demonised suburb—and with Järva as only one of many examples in Swedish urban geography—a justification for the withdrawal of state (public) institutions and infrastructure is established. Thus, the shift from welfare to warfare not only shapes the material contexts people inhabit, but also signals that the indigent do not merit public support. Moreover, the political rhetoric of almost all parties in parliament reiterates a discourse of militarisation in relation to public space, through an increase in state expenditure on police resources, and in the number of police officers located in poor and racialised residential areas. Increased levels of acceptable state violence, and the declaration of a "state of exception" for stigmatised residential areas, then work to legitimise the already prevailing high levels of 'exception' and policing within which the citizens of these areas are subject to; this becomes a justification for more rigid surveillance. This is despite the paradox that behind every case of uprising in Sweden during the last eight years, lies the preceding provocative action carried out by the police (Hallin et al. 2010; Molina 2013; de los Reyes 2016; Sernhede, Thörn and Thörn 2016; Dikeç 2017; Boréus and Flyghed, 2016). This has resonances with other cases reported by scholars elsewhere, as in the report on the 2011 Tottenham riots in the United Kingdom—'Reading the Riots'—where of the 270 people interviewed who were directly involved, 85 percent said that "policing" was an important factor in why the riots happened (Lewis et al. 2011).

Similarly, postcolonial research has focused on the trends related to increasingly violent repressions of subordinated racialised subjects. An emblematic example of this is the work of Soja (2000) on the 1992 Rodney King case in Los Angeles, where a group of white policemen brutally beat an African-American taxi driver. The incident was filmed, and the video was disseminated by the media, leading to the Los Angeles riots that same year. Police brutality against the bodies of African-Americans, especially in deprived neighbourhoods, must be read within the logics of a racial state (Goldberg 2002), that operates under the neoliberal conditions of capitalism (Wacquant 2008; Dikeç 2017). The processes of militarisation that we can nowadays observe in the rhetoric of Swedish officials—who ask for more police officers and military forces to "control" the suburbs, and to some extent, the actions and abuse of the police on civilian populations in Swedish neighbourhoods—must be read through the intersecting lens of racism and neoliberalism. To understand this new urban geopolitics, it is necessary to look at how technologies of warfare used by states against cities (or city-regions) have been normalised now and in the past (Sidaway 2009).

Studying state violence on the bodies of racialised individuals in suburban Sweden, "do[es] not unleash an ethical crisis because these persons' bodies and the territories they inhabit always already signify violence" (da Silva 2009, p. 213; Listerborn, Molina and Mulinari 2011). This "racial state of expendability" nurtures what we call a culture of impunity for the racialised subaltern subjects (Marquez 2012), where feelings of fear in relation to the police, as well as the sense of helplessness, can be associated with a normalisation of state terror and violence. Our analysis highlights the ways in which political, economic, and institutional power sows the seeds of social suffering, by installing and normalising state violence in the racialised neighbourhoods of the Million Programme. The suffering inflicted by structural violence is often silenced so as to quash opposition. Suffering is not effectively conveyed by statistics; qualitative research on the intersections between varied forms of power on the one hand, and the varied forms of violence on the other, are important for understanding these processes of militarisation globally.

Notes

1 With reference to urban policy measures in the Netherlands, Schinkel and van den Berg (2011) refer to Intervention teams operating in Rotterdam in so called "Hotspot zones", which are selected on the basis of the "Rotterdam Safety Index". Inhabited by mainly non-native Dutch people, these areas are perceived by the authorities to be in a state of decline, with crime identified as one of the causes for this urban degeneration.
2 Stockholm is administratively divided into districts. The district division came into operation in 1997 with 24 areas, but it was reduced to the current 14 in 2007. The area concerning our study is popularly known as Järva, and contains two different administrative districts: Rinkeby-Kista comprises Husby, Kista, Rinkeby, Akalla and Hansta, while Spånga-Tensta includes Spånga, Tensta, Hjulsta, Bromsten, Flysta, Solhem, and Sundby. Both districts are associated with Stockholm Stad, but they oversee social services oriented to the residents of the given area. The district is driven by an elected political board, and some of their areas of responsibility include nursery schools; elderly care; individual and family care; culture; and spare time activities. (Stockholm Stad 2016).
3 This notion shares similarities with the *Västgötalagen* [the Westrogothic law], which is one of the oldest Swedish provincial laws from the thirteenth century. Nonetheless, this code of law sanctioned compensations which varied with the region one hailed from. For example, if one killed a free man (one from Västergötland) one would pay a fine of 21 marks. The fine for killing a Swede (a man from Svealand) was 13 and 1/3 marks, and for killing a Dane or a Norwegian, it was nine marks. This reference was provided by Shahram Khosravi.
4 *Dagens Nyheter, Svenska Dagbladet, Aftonbladet,* and *Expressen,* and local media outlets located in the Järva region such as *Norra Sidan*.
5 Workfare denotes that welfare entitlements are based on work.
6 OECD reports (2011, 2015) highlight that in traditionally egalitarian countries— such as Germany, Denmark, and Sweden—the income gap between the rich and poor is widening, from 5 to 1 in the 1980s, to 6 to 1 today.
7 This is part of ongoing research on media stigmatisation of the suburb by Molina and Backvall at the Institute for Housing and Urban Research (IBF) at Uppsala University.
8 Nationella samordnare för våldsbejakande extremism.
9 The youth tend to have a sense of disbelief in their own power to make a better future for themselves, and illegal criminal and drug-related activities may become a route for acquiring a sense of importance, especially when other paths seem unachievable. If young people can imagine change or alternative realities, then the attractiveness of criminality as an option will hold low salience for the youths (Field Notes, 10 May, 2017).
10 In a decision taken in 2008 by the District Administration Council (Rinkeby-Kista Stadsdelsnämnd 2008), the District Administration Office in charge of Kista-Rinkeby suburb moved (2008) from its existing location in the Husby neighbourhood, to new premises located in the "innovation" area of Kista Science City. (https://insynsverige.se/documentHandler.ashx?did=111773). Similarly, the District Administration Office of Spånga-Tensta moved out (2008) from its former building in the Tensta neighbourhood to Lunda, Spånga (https://insynsverige.se/stockholm-spanga/protokoll?date=2009-06-11#record-6).
11 Ironically, a former police officer, Ditte Westin, was appointed as head of culture and democracy issues in the District Administration Office (Spånga Tensta) at the moment of our inquiry (Interview O5), though subsequently removed to the Security Office in Spånga Tensta after strong criticism: (http://www.stockholmdirekt.se/nyheter/kritiserade-chef-byter-arbetsuppgifter/repdpnrav!YneSwsSljQ7dBqkyn4JBw/).

12 One further expression of the decentralised nature of surveillance is the recently approved use of 'body cameras' in public transport drivers, who have thus become vehicles of surveillance. This pilot intervention described as a "preventive security measure" by the security chief of Arriva (a private transport company) was enacted to work in conjunction with the existing surveillance cameras on buses (https://www.arriva.se/blog-post/kroppsburna-kameror/).

Acknowledgements

We would like to thank Husby Träff, Rädda Barnen, Tensta Konsthall, and Förorten i Centrum for facilitating our fieldwork. Preliminary ideas in this chapter were presented at the 'Kunskapskonferens om det Civila Samhället' (2017) organised by the Swedish Agency for Youth and Civil Society (MUCF). We thank Ailin Moaf Mirlashari (Streetgäris), Maria Sundbom Ressaissi (MUCF), and Åsa Ljusberg (MUCF), for their critical interventions. We are very grateful for the insightful comments by Suvi Keskinen, Unnur Dís Skaptadóttir, Mari Toivanen, Helga Tryggvadóttir, Markus Himanen, and Rene León Rosales, which helped shape the chapter in its current form. This research was funded by Vetenskaprådet (2014-1768)

References

Amoore, L. (2006). 'Biometric borders: Governing mobilities in the war on terror'. *Political Geography*, 25, pp. 336–351.
Arendt, H. (1964). *Eichmann in Jerusalem: A report on the banality of evil*. New York: Viking Press.
Balibar, E. (2005). 'Difference, otherness, exclusion'. *Parallax*, 11(1), pp. 19–34.
Boréus, K. and Flyghed, J. (2016). 'Poliskultur på kollisionskurs', in P. de los Reyes and M. Hörnqvist (eds.) *Bortom Kravallerna. Konflikt, Tillhörighet och Representation i Husby*. Stockholm: Stockholmia.
Bremberg, E., Slättman, H. and Alarcón, P. (2015). Inkomstskillnadernas Stockholm. Rapport från Kommissionen för en socialt hållbart Stockholm. Stockholms stad.
da Silva, F. (2009). 'No-bodies: Law, raciality, and violence'. *Griffith Law Review*, 18(2), pp. 212–236.
de Leeuw, S., Cameron, E. and Greenwood, M. (2012). 'Participatory and community-based research, indigenous geographies, and the spaces of friendship: A critical engagement'. *The Canadian Geographer/Le Géographer Canadien*, 56(2), pp. 180–194.
de los Reyes, P., Hörnqvist, M., Boréus, K. and Estrada, F. (2014). *'Bilen brinner men problemen är kvar'. Berättelser om Husbyhändelserna i maj 2013*. Stockholm: Stockholmia Förlag.
de los Reyes, P. (2016). 'Husby, våldet och talandets villkor', in P. de los Reyes and M. Hörnqvist (eds.) *Bortom kravallerna. Konflikt, tillhörighet och representation i Husby*. Stockholm: Stockholmia Förlag.
Dikeç, M. (2017). *Urban Rage. The Revolt of the Excluded*. New Haven & London: Yale University Press.
Dikeç, M. and Swyngedouw, E. (2017). 'Theorizing the politicizing city'. *International Journal of Urban and Regional Research*, 41(1), pp. 1–18.

Djalaie, R. (2016). 'The Police are the main source of information in such events?', in N. Sadr Haghighian *Fuel to the Fire*. Stockholm: Tensta Konsthall, November.

Eisner, M.A. (2000). *From Warfare State to Welfare State. World War I, Compensatory State Building and the Limits of the Modern Order*. Pennsylvania: University of Pennsylvania Press.

Ericsson, U., Molina, I. and Ristilammi, P.M. (2000). *Miljonprogram och media. föreställningar om människor och förorter*. Stockholm: Riksantikvarieämetet & Migrationsverket.

Farmer, P. (1996). 'On suffering and structural violence: A view from below'. *Daedalus*, 125(1), pp. 261–283.

Fassin, D. (2013). *Enforcing Order. An Ethnography of Urban Policing*. Cambridge, Malden: Polity Press.

Fiske, J. (1998). 'Surveilling the City: Whiteness, the Black Man and Democratic Totalitarianism'. *Theory, Culture and Society*, 15(2), pp. 67–88.

Galtung, J. (1990). 'Cultural Violence', *Journal of Peace Research*, 27(3), pp. 291–305.

Galtung, J. (1996). *Peace by Peaceful Means. Peace and Conflict, Development and Civilization, International Peace Research Institute*. Oslo: Sage Publications.

Gilmore, R.W. (1998). 'Globalisation and US prison growth: From military Keynesianism to post-Keynesian militarism', *Race and Class*, 40(2–3), pp. 171–188.

Gilmore, R.W. (2007). *Golden Gulag: Prisons, Surplus, Crisis, and Opposition in Globalizing*. California: University of California Press.

Glimell, H. (2012). 'The Swedish welfare-warfare nexus and the new security architecture', in B. Larsson, M. Letell and H. Thörn (eds.) *Transformations of the Swedish Welfare State: From Social Engineering to governance?* New York: Palgrave MacMillan, pp. 41–55.

Gluck, Z. and Low, S. (2017). 'A sociospatial framework for the anthropology of security', *Anthropological Theory*, 17(3), pp. 281–296.

Goldberg, D.T. (2002). *The Racial State*. Massachusetts/Oxford: Blackwell Publishers.

Goodey, J. (2006). 'Ethnic profiling, criminal (in)justice and minority populations'. *Critical Criminology*, 14, pp. 207–212.

Graham, S. (2011). *Cities under Siege: The New Military Urbanism*. London/New York: Verso.

Grundström, K. and Molina, I. (2016). 'From Folkhem to lifestyle housing in Sweden: Segregation and urban form, 1930s–2010s'. *International Journal of Housing Policy*, 16(3), pp. 316–336.

Haggerty, K. and Ericson, R. (2006). *The New Politics of Surveillance and Visibility*. Toronto: University of Toronto Press.

Hallin, P.O., Jashari, A., Listerborn, C. and Popoola, M. (2010). *Det är inte stenarna som gör ont. Röster från Herrgården, Rosengård—om konflikter och erkännande*. Publications in Urban Studies (MAPIUS) 5. Malmö: Malmö University.

Hayward, R.C. (2004). 'Doxa and deliberation', *Critical Review of International Social and Political Philosophy*, 7(1), pp. 1–24.

Keskinen, S., Alemanji, A., Himanen, M., Kivijärvi, A., Osazee, U., Pöyhönen, N. and Rousku, V. (2018). The Stopped—Ethnic Profiling in Finland. SSKH NOTAT/ SSKH Reports and Discussion Papers No.1/2018. Helsinki: Swedish School of Social Science, University of Helsinki.

Krippendorff, K. (2013). *Content Analysis: An Introduction to its Methodology* (3rd edition). Los Angeles, CA: Sage.

Lewis, P., Newburn, T., Taylor, M., Mcgillivray, C., Greenhill, A., Frayman, H. and Procter, R. (2011). *Reading the Riots: Investigating England's Summer of Disorder*. London: The London School of Economics and Political Science & The Guardian.

Listerborn, C., Molina, I., and Mulinari, D. (2011). *Våldets topografier: betraktelser över makt och motstånd*, 1. utg. edn, Stockholm: Atlas.

Low, S. (2017). 'Security at home: How private securitization practices increase state and capitalist control'. *Anthropological Theory*, 17(3), pp. 365–381.

Márquez, J.D. (2012). 'Latinos as the Living Dead: Raciality, expendability, and border militarization'. *Latino Studies*, 10(4), pp. 473–498.

Mbembe, A. (2003). 'Necropolitics'. *Public Culture*, 15, pp. 11–40.

Menjívar, C. (2008). 'Violence and women's lives in Eastern Guatemala: A conceptual framework'. *Latin American Research Review*, 43(3), pp. 109–136.

Molina, I. (1997). *Stadens rasifiering: Etnisk boendesegregation i folkhemmet* [Ethnic Residential Segregation in the Swedish Folkhem].Uppsala: Acta Universitatis Upsaliensis.

Olson, K. (2011). 'Legitimate speech and hegemonic idiom: The limits of deliberative democracy in the diversity of its voices'. *Political Studies* 59(3), pp. 527–546.

Opotow, S. (2001). 'Social injustice', in D.J. Christie, R.V. Wagner, and D.D. Winter (eds.) *Peace, Conflict and Violence: Peace Psychology for the 21st Century*. New York: Prentice-Hall.

Patel, T. (2012). 'Surveillance, suspicion and stigma: Brown bodies in a terror-panic climate', *Surveillance & Society* 10(3/4), pp. 215–234.

Price, J.M. (2012). *Structural Violence: Hidden Brutality in the Lives of Women*. Albany, New York: State University of New York Press.

Ray, L. (2000). 'Memory, violence and identity', in J. Eldridge, J. MacInnes, S. Scott, C. Warhurst, and A. Witz (eds.) *For Sociology, Legacies and Prospects*. Durham: Sociology Press, pp. 145–159.

Salonen, T. (2012). *Barns ekonomiska utsatthet i Sverige*. Stockholm: Rädda Barnen.

Schclarek Mulinari, L. (2017). *Slumpvis Utvald*. Stockholm: Civil Rights Defenders.

Scheper-Hughes, N. (1996). 'Small wars and invisible genocides'. *Social Science and Medicine*, 43(5), pp. 889–900.

Scheper-Hughes, N. (2004). 'Dangerous and endangered youth: Social structures and determinants of violence'. *Annals of the New York Academy of Sciences*, 1036(12), pp.13–46.

Schinkel, W. and van den Berg, M. (2011). 'City of exception: The Dutch revanchist city and the urban homo sacer'. *Antipode*, 43(5), pp. 1911–1938.

Sernhede, O., Thörn, C., Thörn, H. (2016). 'The Stockholm uprising in context: Urban social movements in the rise and demise of the Swedish welfare-state city', in M. Mayer, C. Thörn and H. Thörn (eds.) *Urban Uprisings*. London: Palgrave Macmillan, pp. 149–173.

Sidaway, J. (2009). 'Shadows on the path: Negotiating geopolitics on an urban section of Britain's South West Coast Path', in *Environment and Planning D: Society and Space*, 27(6), pp. 1091–1116.

Soja, E. (2000). *Postmetropolis: Critical Studies of Cities and Regions*. Oxford: Basil Blackwell.

Strauss, A. and Corbin, J. (1999). *Basics of Qualitative Research: Techniques and Procedure for Developing Grounded Theory*. London: Sage.

Uitermark, J. (2014). 'Integration and control: The governing of urban marginality in Western Europe'. *International Journal of Urban and Regional Research*, 38(4), pp. 1418–1436.
Wacquant, L.J.D. (2008). *Urban Outcasts: A Comparative Sociology of Advanced Marginalit*. Cambridge: Polity.
Wacquant, L.J.D. (2009). *Prisons of Poverty*. Minneapolis/London: University of Minnesota Press.
Wehrle, E.F. (2003). 'Welfare and warfare: American organized labor approaches the military-industrial complex, 1949–1964'. *Armed Forces & Society*, 29(4), pp. 525–546.

Internet resources

Aftonbladet (2017). 'Moderater vill sätta in militär i förorten'. Available at: https://www.aftonbladet.se/senastenytt/ttnyheter/inrikes/article26296706.ab [Accessed 8 October 2018].
Bülow, A. (2017). Dansk militär tar över en del av polisens uppgifter—bland annat bevakningen av synagogan i Köpenhamn. YLE-Svenska. Available at: https://svenska.yle.fi/artikel/2017/09/29/dansk-militar-tar-over-en-del-av-polisens-uppgifter-bland-annat-bevakningen-av [Accessed 8 October 2018].
Elgemyr, M., Hollari, S., Hansson, M., Alvant, P., Svanberg, K. and Gustafsson, C. (2017). Nationellt och lokalt brottsförebyggande arbete [Online]. Brå, Brottsförebyggande rådet. Available at https://www.bra.se/publikationer/arkiv/publikationer/2017-11-27-nationellt-och-lokalt-brottsforebyggande-arbete.html
Jakobson, H. (2018). 'Löfvens besked om militärer mot kriminella'. *Expressen*. Available at: https://www.expressen.se/nyheter/lofvens-besked-om-militarer-mot-kriminella/ [Accessed 8 October 2018].
Lindström, P., Pauloff, A. and Granath, S. (2001). Hur-Var-Närpolis En granskning av närpolisreformen, [Online] Brottsförebyggande rådet. Information och förlag. Available at: https://www.bra.se/publikationer/arkiv/publikationer/2001-06-08-hur—var—narpolis.html
Lindström, E. and Svensson, O. (2017). Regeringen storsatsar på polisen. [Online] Available at: https://www.aftonbladet.se/nyheter/a/kkRqA/regeringen-storsatsar-pa-polisen. [Accessed 8 October 2018].
Molina, I. (2013). Vi måste prata om polisens upptrappade Husbyvåld. *SVT Nyheter* [Online] Available at: https://www.svt.se/opinion/vi-maste-prata-om-polisens-upptrappade-husbyvald. [Accessed 8 October 2018].
OECD (2011). *Divided We Stand: Why Inequality Keeps Rising*. Paris: OECD Publishing. http://dx.doi.org/10.1787/9789264119536-en [Accessed 8 October 2018].
OECD (2015). *In It Together: Why Less Inequality Benefits All*. Paris: OECD Publishing. http://dx.doi.org/10.1787/9789264235120-en [Accessed 8 October 2018].
Polisen (2017). *Utsatta områden. Social ordning, kriminell struktur och utmaningar för polisen*. Stockholm: Nationella operativa avdelningen. Available at: https://polisen.se/siteassets/dokument/ovriga_rapporter/utsatta-omraden-social-ordning-kriminell-struktur-och-utmaningar-for-polisen-2017.pdf [Accessed 8 October 2018].
Rasmusson, D. (2017). Militär tar över polisuppgifter i Danmark'. Sveriges Radio. [Online] Available at: https://sverigesradio.se/sida/artikel.aspx?programid=83&artikel=6788321 [Accessed 8 October 2018].

Rikskriminalpolisen (2014). *Kriminella nätverk med stor påverkan i lokalsamhället 141020 sekretessprövad*. Stockholm: Polisen.

Rikskriminalpolisen. (2015). Utsatta Områden- sociala risker, kollektiv förmåga och oönskade händelser. Available at: https://polisen.se/siteassets/dokument/ovriga_rapporter/utsatta-omraden-sociala-risker-kollektiv-formaga-och-oonskade-handelser.pdf [Accessed 8 October 2018].

Rinkeby-Kista Stadsdelsnämnd (2008). Sammanträdesprotokol. [Online] Available at: https://insynsverige.se/documentHandler.ashx?did=111773 [Accessed 8 October 2018].

Rinkeby-Kista Stadsdelsförvaltning (2017). Tjänsteutlåtande. [Online] Available at: http://insynsverige.se/documentHandler.ashx?did=1882043&rt=0&t= [Accessed 8 October 2018].

Stockholm Direkt. (2017). Kameror och mikrofoner övervakar Järva. Available at: https://www.stockholmdirekt.se/nyheter/kameror-och-mikrofoner-overvakar-jarva/repdpnqkq!dGx1glsN1ItP44sCiPYPFQ/ [Accessed 8 October 2018].

Stockholm Stad. (2016). 'Handlingsplan för en förbättrad arbetssituation'. [Online] Available at: http://www.stockholm.se/Arbete/Att-arbeta-i-Stockholms-stad/Socionom-i-Stockholms-stad/Handlingsplan-for-forbattrad-arbetsmiljo/ [Accessed 8 October 2018].

Stockholms Stad. (2016). Områdesfakta. [Online] Available at: http://statistik.stockholm.se/omradesfaktax [Accessed 8 October 2018].

SVT Nyheter. (2016). Knarkskrämma" plockas bort i Tensta—efter kritik. [Online] Available at: https://www.svt.se/nyheter/lokalt/stockholm/knarkskramma-plockas-bort-i-tensta-efter-kritik. [Accessed 8 October 2018]

Tronarp, G. (2017). 'Justitieministern öppnar för att införa visitationszoner'. *Aftonbladet*. [Online] Available at: http://www.aftonbladet.se/nyheter/a/MQdpr/justitieministern-oppnar-for-att-infora-visitationszoner [Accessed 8 October 2018].

UNT (2017). Anmälningar mot polis utreds sällan. [Online] Available at: http://www.unt.se/nyheter/uppsala/anmalningar-mot-polis-utreds-sallan-4685055.aspx [Accessed 8 October 2018].

10 "Living in fear"

Bulgarian and Romanian street workers' experiences with aggressive public and private policing[1]

Markus Himanen

Introduction

This chapter is a case study of public and private policing of vulnerable and marginalised minorities in the Nordic context. The research is based on extensive interviews with precarious street workers from Romania and Bulgaria living rough in the Helsinki metropolitan area, in addition to individual interviews with officers of the Helsinki Police Department, and third-sector experts working with migrant workers. Disadvantaged migrants from Romania and Bulgaria—many of whom belong to the Roma minority—have worked in the streets of Helsinki since 2007, when these countries joined the European Union. They earn their income through begging, peddling, collecting cans for recycling, and other types of informal street work, and they usually sleep rough or in homeless shelters. The main reasons for this form of migration are economic marginalisation, poor living conditions, and discrimination concerning members of the Roma minority in Southeast Europe (Djuve et al. 2015, pp. 33–54; Duval and Wolff 2016; Tervonen and Enache 2017, pp. 1121–1127). Although it is the free movement framework of the European Union that makes these types of migrations possible, instead of rights-based solutions, EU countries have reacted to these migrations mainly with negligence and indifference, or with criminalising and securitising policies (Cahn and Guild 2008; Sigona 2011; van Baar 2011). Empirical research on the policing of precarious street workers and Roma migrants indicates that these groups face arbitrary surveillance, regular police stops, ethnic profiling, degrading treatment, and frequent evictions by the police or security guards—although estimates differ on how widespread discriminatory and abusive policing is in different countries and cities across Europe (Cahn and Guild 2008, pp. 63–67; Davis and Ryan 2017; Djuve et al. 2015, pp. 97–108; Fassin 2013, pp. 161–164; FRA 2017, pp. 68–75; NIM 2015).

Recent European criminological research has highlighted how the policing of social groups in precarious and unsecure positions—such as undocumented migrants, asylum seekers, and Roma migrants—is linked to the merging of crime control and immigration control regimes (Fekete and Webber 2010; Franko Aas and Bosworth 2013; van der Woude, van der Leun and Nijland

2014). However, the experiences of marginal communities—such as asylum seekers or Roma—are often excluded from criminological research, therefore it is important to develop research strategies that enable their perspectives on policing matters to be heard (Garland, Spalek and Chakraborti 2006). Ethnographic research has started to consider the experiences of Roma migrants navigating the policies of host countries, and the practices of control agents in different national contexts such as France (Clavé-Mercier and Olivera 2018), Great Britain (Grill 2017), and Italy (Ivasiuc 2015; Solimene 2013). At the same time, most of the current research on the securitisation of Roma migration concentrates on the interpretation of more general policy-level changes, and on the political framing of the phenomenon of trans-European mobility of marginalised and vulnerable EU citizens (Leggio and Matras 2018, p. 10). Less attention has been paid to the experiences and understandings of disadvantaged migrants themselves, or to the point of view of the control agents enforcing these policies.

Recent sociological work in the Nordic countries has shown that control-oriented policies towards foreign homeless street workers contribute to the marginalisation of Roma migrants and other street workers from Southeast Europe, but no studies have focused exclusively on different forms of public and private policing (Barker 2017; Ciulinaru 2017; Djuve et al. 2015; Jokela 2017; Tervonen and Enache 2017). To explore the concrete practices and effects of the criminalisation of mobility, it is important to look at how they materialise in everyday interactions between the central protagonists: policemen, security guards, and, most importantly, the street workers themselves. In this chapter, I address the following question: how does the criminalisation of migration function through public and private policing of street workers from Romania and Bulgaria, in the context of Nordic societies? I respond to the research question by examining three interrelated themes concerning (1) the policing practices that street workers encounter in Helsinki, (2) the way that street workers experience these practices, and their effects on their everyday lives, and (3) the police's rationalisations of different kinds of control measures that are directed towards the street-worker population. Exploring these themes reveals information about police malpractice—such as ethnic profiling—in Nordic countries, especially in the context of policing precarious minority groups. It also poses the question of whether the dual commitments of the Finnish authorities to the equality of European citizens, and the politics of managing street workers, can really coexist without contradicting each other.

As has been suggested recently by European researchers, the concept of the criminalisation of migration should refer not only to the convergence of criminal and immigration law, but also to the intertwinement of crime control and migration control in a broader sense (Franko Aas 2011, p. 332; van der Woude, van der Leun and Nijland 2014, pp. 562–563). This has been demonstrated by recent public debates connecting crime and immigration, and practices of police and border guards that mix crime and immigration-based jurisdictions. According to criminological research, police use their powers in a socially differentiated manner. The police have a tendency to treat groups that are defined by the majority population as problematic, and who are to some extent excluded from the sphere of equal citizenship, as "police property" (Lee 1981, pp. 53–56; Reiner 2010, p. 25; Waddington 1999, p. 42). The lower strata of a particular society—often members of racialised communities—experience heavy-handed policing (see e.g., Reiner 2010, pp. 159–174). Because there is a clear risk that the criminalisation of certain migrant populations will increase the use of zero tolerance and stop and search type practices, it is important to research if vulnerable populations have experienced this kind of policing within the Nordic context.

Besides discussing the criminalisation of immigration, this chapter also contributes to research on the migration of Roma and other precarious groups from Southeast Europe. In addition to approaches that highlight the securitised framing of Roma people as social threats, and the criminalisation of the mobility of disadvantaged migrants, some researchers have emphasised the role of the European citizenship regime in the exclusion of the Roma. Hepworth has argued that the Italian policy of evictions and deportations of Romanian Roma has "constituted them as abject European citizens", resulting in a redefinition of the boundaries of European citizenship (2012, p. 442), while Barker has pointed out that the juridical non-membership of Roma migrants in the Swedish nation state has strongly influenced state policies towards them (2013, pp. 248–250). Examining how precarious EU migrants are treated is one way to analyse how the borders of a Nordic welfare state are redrawn when they apply to migrant groups that lack permanent membership status (Barker 2017; see also Keskinen 2016).

I will first present data and methods, then move onto the political context of the street-worker phenomena, and Roma migration in Finland, before presenting my analysis. In the first two parts of the analysis, I discuss the encounters of street workers from Romania and Bulgaria with control agents. I then analyse and interpret the police's views regarding the phenomena of the mobility of disadvantaged EU citizens, before concluding the results of the study.

Researching the criminalisation of street workers as an extreme case of Finnish policing

The research is based on a thematic analysis of semi-structured group interviews with precarious street workers, individual interviews with officers of the Helsinki Police Department, and third-sector experts working with migrants. The data was collected as part of the research project "The Stopped—Spaces, Meanings, and Practices of Ethnic Profiling", which examined ethnic profiling by the police in Finland (Keskinen et al. 2018).[2] This chapter builds upon a part of that project's data, and includes nine semi-structured group interviews (N = 26) with precarious street workers from Romania and Bulgaria living rough in Helsinki. Two interviewers (assisted by an interpreter) conducted the interviews between June and September 2016 using Romanian or Bulgarian languages. It is estimated that between 200 to 300 (Granqvist, Enache and Dorofte 2016, p. 4), or up to 400 (City of Helsinki 2011, p. 6) Bulgarian and Romanian Roma people stay in Helsinki. The street workers who participated in this study were contacted through the interpreters, who had previous contacts with street-worker families.[3] The age of the participants ranged from 19 to 49 years and consisted of seven men and seven women from Romania, and nine men and three women from Bulgaria. They had diverse educational and professional backgrounds, although were predominantly working class. All the participants earned their living through one or several of the following occupations: selling the magazine that supports homeless people, *Iso Numero* [*Big Issue*], in the city centre or shopping centres around Helsinki; by begging; selling flowers; and collecting bottles for recycling around the city. The participants were asked to discuss their experiences related to police stops and checks; interactions with security guards; and forced removals and evictions.

Of the 14 Romanians interviewed, 11 identified as Roma and of the 12 Bulgarians interviewed, ten identified as Roma. The question of ethnic Roma identity in Southeast Europe is a complex issue. For example, in Romania a large number of those who are identified as Roma by the authorities or by their compatriots do not consider themselves to be Roma (Ladányi and Szelényi 2001). I follow Djuve et al. (2015) by referring to this migrant group as street workers, as all research participants worked on the street, didn't have residency or a stable job in Finland, and were predominantly living rough (with some exceptions) in Helsinki.

The authorities interviewed worked at the Helsinki Police Department in the units responsible for public order and safety; preventive policing; crime investigation; and immigration ($N = 9$). The police were interviewed concerning themes of police stops; ID checks related to immigration law enforcement; ethnic profiling; and the policing of foreign nationals including Bulgarian and Romanian street workers. Besides these, five interviews were carried out with experts who have worked with street workers as lawyers, researchers, or social workers in the third sector ($N = 6$). They were asked to discuss the problems that street workers encountered with the police and security guards.

The policing of street workers in Helsinki can be seen as an extreme case (see Flyvbjerg 2006, pp. 230–231) of policing—this is because their presence in Finland is a highly politicised topic, and because of their precarious legal and social status. The case is not a representative sample of policing in Finland, but it enables us to identify the inherent risks in current policing practices that can lead to infringements of fundamental rights in similar circumstances. It is likely that both the number of groups living in comparable conditions, and this criminalising approach, will become increasingly common due to the so-called asylum crisis of 2015–2016, and due to Finland and other EU states' restrictive responses.

The interviews were coded and analysed thematically (Guest, MacQueen and Namey 2012). The interviews of the street workers were understood as narratives that combine both testimonial aspects that describe actual existing policing practices, and reflective aspects that provide information on how these practices are experienced and interpreted. Correspondingly, the themes were selected and organised, on the one hand, around the practical context of interactions such as ID checks or evictions, and on the other hand, around emotions and interpretations they evoked, such as feelings of stress or experiences of unfair treatment. Additionally, these accounts were compared with the descriptions that the NGO experts provided concerning the policing practices they had witnessed themselves, or discussed with street workers. The expert interviewees had accrued knowledge about the phenomena over an extensive period of time, and they had been in contact with a significant number of all the street workers from Romania and Bulgaria who had been staying in Finland during recent years.

As the Helsinki Police Department is the central actor responsible for controlling what they call the "beggar phenomena", the police interviews made it possible to examine the ways in which the officers understand the issues involved. The analysed themes first concerned what kind of security and safety issues the police think are related to the phenomena of Romanian and Bulgarian street worker migration, and second, how authorities connect street workers to different policing measures, such as ID checks.

Controlling the movement of "Roma beggars" in Finland

The criminalisation of the movement and migration of poor people has a long history that goes back to at least the formative period of the modern nation state and capitalist labour markets (e.g. Weber and Bowling 2008). In particular, Roma in Finland and in other Nordic countries have been victims of aggressive policing tactics, facing the criminalisation of their livelihoods (Pulma 2009, pp. 82–91; Engebrigtsen 2017, pp. 48–49). In Finnish public debates, the connection between migration and criminality is often constructed in a racialising manner in which the ethnic or religious background of the perpetrator functions as an explanation of the crime (Keskinen 2014). Similarly, in the European debates on Roma migration, survival strategies of Roma people—such as begging or trans-European mobility—are often attached to crime and explained through presupposed cultural characteristics (Grill 2017; Sigona and Trehan 2011). Also, in Finland and other Nordic countries, street workers from Romania and Bulgaria are usually perceived as a distinct and racialised group among the European labour migrants: they are categorised as "Roma" or "Romanian Roma" regardless of their self-identification, or stigmatised as "beggars" or "Roma-beggars" (see Tervonen and Enache 2017, pp. 1116–1117).

Street workers are situated in a liminal space in relation to the social and judicial structures of the Nordic welfare state, as they are included in the European area of free movement but excluded from accessing residence and its associated rights. They have a right to travel to Finland freely, and a right to stay in Finland for the duration of three months (although this time limit is, in practice, very rarely enforced). For residency, they would need to obtain a regular work contract, which due to the nature of their work, is practically impossible to come by. The European legal framework for free movement does not take into account the social rights of those workers unable to secure residency or regular labour contracts in a member state (Conant 2006, p. 93). This does not mean that homeless street workers would be outside of all protections, as their minimum social rights are guaranteed, in principle, by the European Human Rights Convention and the Finnish constitution. However, as Finland has a residence-based welfare system, there exist very limited institutional procedures that would guarantee the realisation of these rights (Tervonen and Enache 2017, p. 1117).

Before the eastern enlargement of the European union, Finland had already made restrictions to asylum legislation in response to the migrations of Romani asylum seekers from the candidate countries (Nordberg 2004). Unlike in Denmark and in some communes in Norway, begging is not criminalised in Finland, and municipalities do not have the legal authority to ban it. The government put forward a law proposal to criminalise aggressive begging and unauthorised camping in urban areas in 2010, after two national committees had discussed "the beggar phenomena", (HE 2010), but the law was never passed. Tervonen and Enache argue that instead of developing a coherent national policy towards Roma migration, Finland has left the issue to municipal authorities who have used different control agents—such as social workers and police—to implement "indirect bordering techniques" (2017, p. 1127).

In Finnish public discourse, Roma migration has been framed as a security issue (Jokela 2017, pp. 72–74). For example, Romanian and Bulgarian nationals have often been connected to human trafficking (Himanen and Könönen 2013, pp. 121–123). At the same time, the Finnish authorities have recognised that Roma migration is to a large extent caused by a combination of economic deprivation and ethnic discrimination in Romania and Bulgaria, and some state authorities have been critical of the discriminatory implications of a criminalising approach to begging and rough sleeping (see City of Helsinki 2011, pp. 44–49; Ministry of Interior 2010, pp. 46–52). Interestingly, the possibility that the securitised framing of begging and the transnational mobility of poor EU migrants would lead to policing practices that contradict and undermine legislative commitments to human and fundamental rights, is rarely discussed in public.

Stops, apprehensions, evictions, and removals: Encounters with control agents

The street workers testified that they faced frequent stops, questioning, searches, and identity checks by the police; apprehensions without criminal charges; evictions from their sleeping places by the police; and recurrent removals from semi-public spaces such as train stations and shopping centres by security guards.

All participants stated they had interacted with the police during the last 12 months, and almost everyone had been stopped by the police and asked for identity documents. A young Bulgarian Roma woman who had spent some weeks in Finland for three concurrent summers had been stopped for ID checks by the police approximately five to ten times. She mentioned one incident from spring 2016:

> Three or four of us were sitting on the benches near a shopping centre and drinking coffee. Two policemen approached us, they said that they came from Romania and Bulgaria. The Bulgarian one [...] asked from us, in Bulgarian, if we are sleeping outside and what are we doing here. He said that it is possible that sleeping in outside might result in trouble. You could get arrested and deported from Finland.

The reason why the woman and her friends met a policeman from their home country in the centre of Helsinki is due to an agreement between Finland, Romania, and Bulgaria that stipulates that Romanian and Bulgarian officers assist the Helsinki Police Department with supervisory and investigative tasks. According to her, the first question the officers asked was to see identification papers. The policing this Roma group experienced was typical in a sense, given there was no apparent justification for this control, or for the precise reason why they were targeted for this line of questioning and ID checks. In this particular situation, the legality of the police's actions is even more muddled, as the Romanian and Bulgarian officers do not have any jurisdiction in Finland but are merely assisting Finnish forces.

During some of these stops and questionings, the street workers described police officers inquiring about where they obtained their bike or mobile phone. Similar police practices were also reported in other Nordic cities such as Oslo and Copenhagen (Djuve et al. 2015, p. 107). The aforementioned Romanian and Bulgarian police officers would also occasionally 'instruct', or perhaps threaten them with sentiments like "you should not use bikes", as the local police would believe that the bicycles have been stolen. These accounts indicate that a generalised suspicion is directed towards begging migrants, and raises questions concerning the legal basis of selecting these targets for questioning. An interviewed expert who was born outside Finland, and whose work involved supporting street workers, had experienced a police ID check when speaking with street-worker clients by the railway station, and wasn't given any explanation for the reasons behind the check. The person started to always keep an employee ID badge visible when interacting with the street workers, to avoid getting "arrested based on my profile".

The participants testified that police stops also led to them being apprehended for periods of between a few hours to 12 hours. The most common street-worker complaint concerning these detentions was that the reason for their apprehension was not explained to them in a language they could understand. For example, one Romanian Roma man said he was detained when walking past the railway station and released the next day without any clarification. He speculated that he might have been arrested because the police thought he was "a drunken person or a drug addict". In one case, the reason was a suspicion of forged identity papers, and in another case, the legality of staying in Finland; some of the apprehensions were related to suspicions of crime.

During the aforementioned stop and questioning of the Bulgarian Roma woman and her friends, police threatened them with deportation if they subsequently camped illegally. The street workers challenged this: one of her female friends responded by asking, "well, could you then show us an apartment or someplace where we could sleep? Can you find us accommodation and work?". Indeed, besides issues of employment and income, the biggest concern for street workers was the possibility of finding a safe place to stay for a night. The problems they listed that related to rough sleeping were cold, damp, unsafe, and unhygienic conditions. They were also afraid of being attacked by other homeless persons or drug users. One Bulgarian man said that he had been hospitalised after a serious attack by an unknown person while sleeping in a park in Helsinki.

Most of the participants reported evictions from tents, cars, and abandoned houses, or of simply being woken up and told to leave when sleeping in a park. A Romanian couple had come to Finland several times to earn money for their children's education—they used to stay with other families in an abandoned building. The husband is in his forties and used to work manual jobs in Romania before becoming unemployed; at the time of the interview he sold *Iso Numero* [*Big Issue*] in Helsinki. He described a particular eviction in which the police used some kind of chemical spray or a gas grenade in the middle of the night to evict him and his family. The chemical made it impossible to inhabit the place for several days, but after that, the family could return. Indeed, hide and seek was a common theme in accounts concerning evictions. The street workers were forced to play a certain kind of game with the police: people were evicted but would return to the same place later, often during the same night. For example, one participant stated that the police forced him and his friends to dispose of their tent in a garbage bin, but that they were able to collect it afterwards.

Private security companies have a responsibility for the safety of several private and semi-public spaces—such as transport hubs and shopping centres in the city centre—that street workers often spend time in. The street workers testified that the behaviour of security guards caused them significant issues: first, their encounters with guards were frequent, and made their daily working life difficult; second, they felt that the guards behaved disrespectfully; and third, they were afraid of the guards being violent. The most common context of security guard interactions was their control of the use of some spaces, or certain facilities of these spaces, such as toilets or electricity. Romanian participants usually worked around the Helsinki central railway station selling the *Iso Numero* [Big Issue] magazine or flowers, or begging. Bulgarians worked around the Kamppi shopping centre a few blocks away. Reasons street workers needed to use the interior space were, for example, to rest, seek cover from rain or cold, use the toilet, get coffee, or charge mobile phones. They often complained about how they were constantly removed from the space without a justifiable reason, as a 27-year-old Romanian woman explained:

> They [guards] threw us out in the rain. All the time, they are coming to us and they say go, and it doesn't matter if it's raining. And on that day, it was raining so much that we were quite wet. We tried to stay inside the premises, but they came, and they threw us in the rain telling us to go. […] many other people were in railway station […] because it was raining. So, people came inside but guards told only to us to go but not to the other people.

As is clear from this account, the street workers felt in general that they were discriminated against by the guards. Often, they were told not to use the toilets of the centre nor to charge their mobile phones. Several of the Bulgarian participants complained that the shopping centre guards opened toilet doors even when they were inside using the toilet. Some complained that their phones were confiscated. Many of the street workers said that guards used unnecessary force when removing them from a place. Also, the expert interviewees had heard several accounts from the street workers about the needless use of force by the guards.

Effects of arbitrary, discriminatory and punitive policing

Although individual incidents cannot be verified, the recurring and similar testimonies of both Bulgarian and Romanian street workers and the expert interviewees imply that they faced the use of policing powers "as a harassing technique against marginal sections of the population" (Waddington 1999, p. 140). The concept of "police property" (Lee 1981 pp. 53–54) is widely used in police research, and can be used to describe the predicament of street workers—first they are marginalised through their intersecting legal status, class position, and ethnicity; second, the issue of begging has to a large extent been left to the police and security guards to deal with (see Tervonen and Enache 2017); and third, their presence on the streets is regularly linked to crime and security issues within public discourse (Himanen and Könönen 2013, pp. 121–123; Jokela 2017, pp. 72–74; Yuval-Davis et al. 2017, pp. 1157–1159). Their experiences are similar to those presented in other studies and confirm that aggressive policing tactics—such as zero tolerance or stop and search without reasonable suspicion—are universally experienced as discriminatory and punitive (Bradford 2015; Fassin 2013, p. 156; Reiner 2010, pp. 155–156). It can be argued that the experiences described by the street workers can be connected to the arbitrary, discriminatory, and punishing nature of policing practices. The experience of arbitrariness was related to the fact that the street workers were seldom informed about the possible legal reasons for the controls. The control agents did not indicate any sensitivity to or understanding of their situation—for example, the workers were told that they should sleep in a camping place that they could not afford. The street workers also said that these practices led them to experience constant stress and pressure, because they could never know when they would be evicted from their sleeping place by the police or removed from some public space by the guards.

The experience of being discriminated against was first connected to interactions in which the street workers felt that they were treated differently from others in similar situations. Guards would remove them from the railway station, but other people were allowed to stay, or the police would approach only them in public places to ask for their papers. Second, the street workers suspected that some of the guards and police officers were racist, and interpreted their actions as results of these attitudes. However, some thought that the aggressive attitude of the control agents had more to do with begging or criminality of other Romanian or Bulgarian nationals, or their constant visibility in the city centre. They connected racism to aggressive behaviour and the use of racist language, such as the guards telling them to "go home to Romania". The accounts of the use of hostile language by the police was not common in the data, but there were several accounts of improper language by the security guards. In sum, the accounts of street workers and experts indicate that police stops, checks, and questioning were related to profiling in which their perceived ethnicity or nationality, their continuous visible presence in urban spaces, their clothing, and their behaviour such as begging, combined to form a criminalised profile that triggered these controls.

The experiences of punitiveness were related to the sometimes-violent nature of the policing and accompanying humiliating encounters. Street workers described experiences of humiliation resulting from degrading treatment. For example, one man described his sudden apprehension by the police by saying that "I was just treated like a dog, a homeless dog". The data includes also descriptions of police practices with clearly punitive intentions: a Romanian woman was transported outside Helsinki in a police van and left by a road in the forest after an incident in a supermarket in which she was given a fine after minor shoplifting. The woman said that the drive took approximately 20 to 30 minutes on a freeway. According to two other accounts, this kind of transportation and dumping by the police had also happened inside city limits. Additionally, a similar but separate incident that included removal outside the city was described by one of the expert interviewees. A Norwegian research report testifies that this kind of dumping of street workers has been systematically implemented by the Oslo police (NIM 2015, pp. 35–36).

Besides humiliation, feelings of fear and stress were commonly expressed by street workers when describing their interactions with the police or security guards; these encounters also produced these after-effects. When discussing how his community was both unfairly targeted and left without police protection, one Romanian man stated that "we are all the time living in fear". In addition to this emotional burden, the type of policing that street workers and NGO workers described impact trust and confidence in authorities. Frequent and disproportionate police encounters generally lead to low levels of trust towards the police among members of ethnic minorities, as has been confirmed by previous research in other contexts (e.g. Bradford 2015, p. 108). Some of the street workers said that they did not trust the police and believed they would not be protected by them if they complained about the behaviour of the guards. At the same time, the accounts concerning the police did not focus exclusively on harassment: the street workers also had positive experiences with the police, especially in cases in which their behaviour came across as friendly or neutral. One Bulgarian street worker indicated that it was beneficial that the Bulgarian officer was in Helsinki, as he could speak their language and they could ask for advice. Some of the street workers stated that the guards would behave less aggressively if the police were present and nearby. In general, trust in the Finnish police authorities seemed to depend, at least partially, on how professionally the police had behaved towards the street workers, which corresponds to findings of recent research on police legitimacy (Bradford 2015, p. 106). At the same time, the criminalisation of their presence in Helsinki meant that the street workers felt that they were mostly excluded from broader European citizenship, and therefore they did not think that the policing they encountered was legitimate.

Management of begging: Supervision, transnational policing, and enforcing the ban on rough sleeping

The police interviewees understood begging as a multifaceted public safety issue that had to be managed. Police officers indicated that begging was connected to several security issues, such as citizens' experiences of their public safety, crime, immigration-related questions, and illegal camping. According to a Helsinki police officer, these concerns also motivated the cooperation between the Finnish police and Romanian and Bulgarian officials:[4]

> I don't know if it is the right term, but the suspicious loitering that especially Romanian and Bulgarians are doing has, besides criminality, been a [...] reason why there has been co-operation with these countries. We have to consider, how safe does a Finnish person or the average person living in Finland feel? [...]. This phenomenon around the Railway square is a very visible phenomenon for everyone, and it is so that one has to set boundaries to it, so that the average person doesn't feel threatened when being or moving there.

The officer interprets the "visibility" of begging as suspicious and relates the general public's assumed experiences of "feeling safe" or "threatened" to the begging phenomena. The reasons for police interventions seem to originate from the physical and visible presence of the street workers in the city space, although the officer does not articulate the exact factors that make them especially visible, and their visibility especially threatening compared to other groups occupying the city space. Similar concerns are also repeated in existing Ministry of Interior (HE 2010) and City of Helsinki (2011) policy documents. The police officer indicated that this preventive approach aims to tackle issues related to begging by "setting boundaries" to it—"before the matters are at the level of a criminal complaint"—and that this was an important way to keep foreigner crime at a relatively low level in Finland.

A central concern of the Romanian street workers was that they would be mistakenly identified as criminals, and that it would affect their reputation in Finland, thus also their earnings.[5] The police discussed the criminality of Romanian and Bulgarian citizens in the framework of "mobile criminality" or "foreign criminal groups" who come to Finland to enact property crimes such as theft. Police estimated that "beggars" had "different motivations" to come to Finland, and did not form a "homogenous group", indicating that not all but some beggars committed crimes. Considering that on the one hand, authorities identified a strong connection between street work and crime, and on the other hand, believed that begging itself indicated a "safety issue", there is an obvious risk that street workers are collectively held responsible for the crimes committed by their compatriots.

In the context of immigration policing, police officers considered begging to be a signifier that "people are not able to take care of themselves", which in the case of foreign nationals, was seen as grounds for stops, identity checks, and police questioning. In Finland, the police have the jurisdiction to control the identity of a person to check their immigration status. An interviewed police officer indicated that European citizens from other member states are considered to be foreigners from the perspective of the police, and that immigration powers are also useful when stopping foreign criminal groups. Although internal immigration controls should—according to the law—primarily target suspected undocumented immigrants and non-EU citizens, the interview data indicates that police also rely on the jurisdiction for immigration law enforcement when carrying out ID checks for street workers. Police also said that they were protecting the street workers themselves from human trafficking, which made checking IDs necessary.

According to the City of Helsinki, camping is not allowed in Helsinki, and they have thus given the Helsinki Police Department a warrant to evict all camps from city-owned land (City of Helsinki 2011, p. 6). This policy is largely based on police discretion, as the City of Helsinki does not have the jurisdiction to ban short-term camping or rough sleeping on common places, irrespective of if the land is owned privately or by the City: every person has the right to sleep temporarily in common places if they are not causing a disturbance (HE 2010, p. 9). The police argue, on the one hand, that evictions and removals are legitimate because of their agreement with the City of Helsinki, and on the other hand, that—using preventive logic—the camps have to be evicted before they grow too big. The police were unable to provide a clear distinction between legal, temporary camping, and camping that causes a disturbance. Nevertheless, based on testimonies from street workers and NGO workers, the camping ban was communicated to the street workers as a rule that concerned all those rough sleeping in Helsinki, without any qualification. A ban on rough sleeping was not made part of the criminal code or public order code, although it is heavily controlled. The street workers were forced to relocate frequently, but they were not served official criminal charges. Thus, the policy of the City of Helsinki and the Helsinki Police Department has led to a process of criminalisation that is not based on criminal or public order legislation, but on quasi-official practices that exploit a grey area within the current legislation.

To a certain extent, police interviews confirmed that the police consider street workers as their "property" and indicated that the police were responsible for controlling begging in response to fears and prejudice that the general public had towards foreign street workers and begging practices. The police responded to these public safety concerns by evicting rough-sleeping street workers, transnational policing strategies, and supervision through ID checks and questioning. The practices were seen as preventive and were based on exploiting a legal grey area—instead of the official criminalisation of street workers, the police used a mixture of different juridical rationales when implementing these measures, such as immigration policing, public order policing, and crime prevention. This tendency of law enforcement officials to alternate between criminal and immigration law powers has been identified as a central tenet of criminalising processes (van der Woude and van der Leun 2017, p. 32).

Conclusions

The interviewed Bulgarian and Romanian street workers reported frequent stops, ID checks, and questioning by the police (that sometimes led to apprehensions); evictions from sleeping places including small campsites and parked cars by police and security guards; and frequent removals from different semi-public spaces by security guards. Based on the interview data, the experiences caused by these criminalising interactions with control agents were identified as arbitrary, discriminatory, and punitive. The street workers felt that the control agents failed to consider their actual social position that forced them to beg, find shelter in semi-public space, and sleep rough; that they were unfairly targeted; and that they were treated disrespectfully and in an aggressive manner. Their encounters with control agents caused emotions of fear, stress, and humiliation, and decreased trust towards policing practices. These experiences of disadvantaged migrants coming from Romania and Bulgaria correspond with what has been reported about policing practices in other Nordic countries (Djuve et al. 2015, pp. 97–108; NIM 2015), and support research evidence concerning both policing "Roma minority" (FRA 2017, pp. 68–75) and "Romani migrants" (Cahn and Guild 2008, pp. 63–67) in Europe in general. Further research is required to estimate how widespread this kind of harassment is in Helsinki, the rest of Finland, and the Nordic countries. However, it is highly likely that current practices of public and private policing in Finland pose a risk to the fundamental rights of mobile and poor European citizens.

The data indicates that the Helsinki Police Department considers street workers as part of a public order phenomenon centred around visible begging in urban space, and that this has to be managed with different policing practices, such as the implementation of a quasi-formal ban on rough sleeping; trans-European policing cooperation; and the supervision of beggars through stops, ID-checks and questioning. These practices reflect general tendencies of criminalisation around European mobility (Fekete and Webber 2010; van der Woude, van der Leun and Nijland 2014). Although in Finland, unlike in Denmark or Norway, migrant street work or rough sleeping was not criminalised through legislation, these current policies and policing practices had similar criminalising effects, as they placed the street workers into a position of police property (Lee 1981), outside the sphere of equal citizenship. Further research is needed to understand the role of the private security guards, because their centrality in the accounts of the street workers could indicate that the rise of private policing has a significant impact on how excluded minorities are policed. While the abusive behaviour of the guards cannot be directly attributed to local or national policies, these current broader securitised discourses could legitimise more heavy-handed private policing now and in the future.

Policing practices of stops and checks; transnational police cooperation; and bans on rough sleeping; have a clear tendency to encourage policing that is not grounded in clear jurisdictions or reasonable suspicion. Although the interviewed police officers did not discuss the issue of begging in explicitly racialised terms, these practices increase the risk of ethnic profiling and discrimination. They can lead to institutionalised racism because, first, these practices concern a population that is discriminated against at a macro level and, second, while the policy is explicitly universalistic, in practice it targets a particular population: the street workers who are Bulgarian and Romanian nationals, and to a large extent belong to the Roma minority (Philips 2011; see also Reiner 2010, pp. 162–164).

This chapter has described policing of a rather exceptional population. However, the conditions that construct street workers as exceptional—unsecure legal position, poverty, and criminalised stigma—also describe other precarious minority groups such as asylum seekers and undocumented migrants. As Didier Fassin has remarked, aggressive policing tactics based on criminalising logics towards immigration do not serve to enforce the law, but instead perpetuate the current unequal social order (2013, pp. xv). In an apparent contradiction towards commitments to non-discrimination and the respect of the fundamental rights of all European citizens by the Finnish state, the current policing practices identified in this chapter have as their main only practical effect the increasing marginalisation of precarious migrants.

Notes

1 This chapter has gone through external blind review and was accepted by two reviewers. We thank the reviewers for their work with the chapter.
2 The main body of data collected by The Stopped project consists of 128 individual and group interviews conducted in the Helsinki metropolitan area and Turku between 2015 and 2017; 185 research participants, including 145 members of racialised minorities; and an additional 26 police officers and 14 other experts (Keskinen et al. 2018: 18).
3 Therefore, they were probably more acquainted with the existing, although limited, social services available for them than the street-worker population on average, and most of them had been in Helsinki at least once before the year of the interview for durations of some months.
4 The cooperation was enshrined in a 2012 agreement between the Finnish and Romanian governments, and later extended to Bulgaria. This transnational policing was coordinated by the Finnish National Police Board, and in practice, led by crime investigators of the Helsinki Police Department. The foreign officers spent between one and five months in Finland every summer.
5 According to Djuve et al., beggars and Romanian offenders in Oslo, Copenhagen, and Stockholm belong to different groups: based on self-reported crime, "those who beg for money are significantly less likely than non-beggars to have been fined for theft, drugs or violence in all three cities" (2015, p. 66).

References

Barker, V. (2013). 'Democracy and Deportation: Why Membership Matters Most', in K. Franko Aas and M. Bosworth (eds.), *Borders of Punishment: Citizenship, Crime Control and Social Exclusion*. Oxford: Oxford University Press, pp. 237–254.

Barker, V. (2017). 'Nordic Vagabonds: The Roma and the Logic of Benevolent Violence in the Swedish Welfare State'. *European Journal of Criminology*, 14(1), pp. 120–139.

Bradford, B. (2015). 'Unintended Consequences', in R. Delsol and M. Shiner (eds.), *Stop and Search*. UK: Palgrave Macmillan.

Cahn, C. and Guild, E. (2008). *Recent Migration of Roma in Europe*. OSCE High Commissioner on National Minorities. Available at: http://www.coe.int/t/commissioner/Activities/themes/RomaMigration_2009_en.pdf [Accessed 20 March 2018].

City of Helsinki (2011). *Linjauksia kerjäläisongelman käsittelemiseksi Helsingissä*. Helsinki: City of Helsinki.

Ciulinaru, D. (2017). 'The Justification of Harsh Treatment of Homeless Romanian Migrants in Sweden'. *Nordic Journal of Migration Research*, 7(4), pp. 243–250.

Clavé-Mercier, A. and Olivera, M. (2018). 'Inclusion and the "Arts of Resistance"'. *Intersections. East European Journal of Society and Politics*, 4(2), pp. 149–168.

Conant, L. (2006). 'Individuals, Courts, and the Development of European Social Rights'. *Comparative Political Studies*, 39(1), pp. 76–100.

Davis, M. F. and Ryan, N. (2017). 'Inconvenient Human Rights: Water and Sanitation in Sweden's Informal Roma Settlements'. *Health and Human Rights Journal*, 19(2), pp. 61–72.

Djuve, B. A., Friberg, J. H., Tyldum, G. and Zhang, H. (2015). *When Poverty Meets Affluence. Migrants from Romania on the Streets of the Scandinavian Capitals*. Fafo and The Rockwool Foundation. Available at: http://www.fafo.no/index.php?option=com_zoo&task=item&item_id=7974&Itemid=145&lang=nb [Accessed 8 October 2018].

Duval, L. and Wolff, F. (2016). 'Emigration Intentions of Roma: Evidence from Central and South-East Europe'. *Post-Communist Economies*, 28(1), pp. 87–107.
Engebrigtsen, A. I. (2017). 'Key Figure of Mobility: The Nomad'. *Social Anthropology*, 25, pp. 42–54.
Fassin, D. (2013). *Enforcing Order: An Ethnography of Urban Policing*. Cambridge: Polity Press.
Fekete, L. and Webber, F. (2010). 'Foreign Nationals, Enemy Penology and the Criminal Justice System'. *Race & Class*, 51(4), pp. 1–25.
Flyvbjerg, B. (2006). 'Five Misunderstandings about Case-Study Research'. *Qualitative Inquiry*, 12(2), pp. 219–245.
FRA [European Union Agency for Fundamental Rights] (2017). Second European Union Minorities and Discrimination Survey. Main Results. Available at: http://fra.europa.eu/en/publication/2017/eumidis-ii-main-results [Accessed 8 October 2018].
Franko Aas, K. (2011). 'Crimmigrant Bodies and Bona Fide Travelers: Surveillance, Citizenship and Governance'. *Theoretical Criminology*, 15(3), pp. 331–346.
Franko Aas, K. and Bosworth, M. (eds.), (2013). *Borders of Punishment: Citizenship, Crime Control and Social Exclusion*. Oxford: Oxford University Press.
Garland, J., Spalek, B. and Chakraborti, N. (2006). 'Hearing Lost Voices. Issues in Researching "Hidden" Minority Ethnic Communities'. *The British Journal of Criminology*, 46(3), pp. 423–437.
Granqvist, K., Enache, A. and Dorofte, M. M. (2016). 'Local Engagement for Roma Inclusion: Locality Study Helsinki (Finland). European Union Agency for Fundamental Rights'. Available at: http://fra.europa.eu/sites/default/files/fra_uploads/local-engagement-roma-finland-helsinki_en.pdf [Accessed 8 October 2018].
Grill, J. (2017). '"In England, They Don't Call You Black!" Migrating Racialisations and the Production of Roma Difference Across Europe'. *Journal of Ethnic and Migration Studies*, 44(7), pp. 1136–1155.
Guest, G., MacQueen, K. M. and Namey, E. E. (2012). *Applied Thematic Analysis*. Thousand Oaks, CA: SAGE Publications Ltd.
HE (2010). *Hallituksen esitys Eduskunnalle laiksi järjestyslain muuttamisesta*. HE 330/2010 vp.
Hepworth, D. K. (2012). 'Abject Citizens: Italian "Nomad Emergencies" and the Deportability of Romanian Roma'. *Citizenship Studies*, 16(3–4), pp. 431–449.
Himanen, M. and Könönen, J. (2013). 'Pukumiehiä ja kalliita autoja – ongelmakohtia ihmiskauppauutisoinnissa. Journalismikritiikin vuosikirja'. *Media & viestintä*, 36(1), pp. 121–127.
Ivasiuc, A. (2015). 'Watching Over the Neighbourhood: Vigilante Discourses and Practices in the Suburbs of Rome'. *Etnofoor*, 27(2), pp. 53–72.
Jokela, M. (2017). 'Kaupungin rajat. Sosiaalikeskus Satama, nuorisopolitiikka ja romanit'. *Sosiologia*, 54(1), pp. 63–78.
Keskinen, S. (2014). 'Re-constructing the Peaceful Nation: Negotiating Meanings of Whiteness, Immigration and Islam after a Shopping Mall Shooting'. *Social Identities*, 20(6), pp. 471–485.
Keskinen, S. (2016). 'From Welfare Nationalism to Welfare Chauvinism: Economic Rhetoric, the Welfare State and Changing Asylum Policies in Finland'. *Critical Social Policy*, 36(3), pp. 352–370.
Keskinen, S., Aminkeng Atabong, A., Himanen, M., Kivijärvi, A., Osazee, U., Rousku, V. and Pöyhölä, N. (2018). *The Stopped—Ethnic Profiling in Finland*. N. 3

Apr 2018, SSKH Notat. Helsinki: University of Helsinki, Swedish School of Social Science.
Ladányi, J. and Szelényi, I. (2001). 'The Social Construction of Roma Ethnicity in Bulgaria, Romania and Hungary During Market Transition'. *Review of Sociology*, 7(2), pp. 79–89.
Lee, J. A. (1981). 'Some Structural Aspects of Police Deviance in Relations with Minority Groups', in C. D. Shearing (ed.), *From Organizational Police Deviance— Its Structure and Control*. Toronto: Butterworths, pp. 49–82.
Leggio, D. V. and Matras, Y. (2018). 'How Open Borders Can Unlock Cultures: Concepts, Methods, and Procedures', in Y. Matras and D. V. Leggio (eds.), *Open Borders, Unlocked Cultures*. London and New York: Routledge, pp. 1–25.
Ministry of Interior (2010). *Kerjäämisen kieltämistä selvittävä työryhmä, loppuraportti. Sisäinen turvallisuus, sisäasiainministeriön julkaisuja 31/2010*. Helsinki: Ministry of Interior.
NIM [Norwegian Institute for Human Rights] (2015). *Criminalisation of Homelessness in Oslo: An Investigation*. Oslo: Nasjonal institusjon for menneskerettigheter ved Norsk senter for menneskerettigheter. Available at: http://m.nhri.no/getfile.php/13703/nim/Om%20NIM/NI/Thematic_Report%20Criminalisation%20of%20Homelessness%20in%20Oslo.pdf [Accessed 8 October 2018].
Nordberg, C. (2004). 'Legitimising Immigration Control: Romani Asylum-Seekers in the Finnish Debate'. *Journal of Ethnic and Migration Studies*, 30(4), pp. 717–735.
Phillips, C. (2011). 'Institutional Racism and Ethnic Inequalities: An Expanded Multilevel Framework'. *Journal of Social Policy*, 40(01), pp. 173–192.
Pulma, P. (2009). 'Kerjäläisyys, irtolaisuus, "mustalaisuus"'. In V. Mäkinen and A. B. Pessi (eds.), *Kerjääminen eilen ja tänään*. Tampere: Vastapaino, pp. 71–95.
Reiner, R. (2010). *The Politics of the Police*. 4th edition. Oxford: Oxford University Press.
Sigona. N. (2011). 'The Governance of Romani People in Italy: Discourse, Policy and Practice'. *Journal of Modern Italian Studies*, 16(5), pp. 590–606.
Sigona, N. and Trehan, N. (2011). 'The (re)Criminalization of Roma Communities in a Neoliberal Europe', in S. Palidda (ed.), *Racial Criminalization of Migrants in the 21st Century*. Farnham, Surrey, England; Burlington, VT, USA: Ashgate, pp. 119–132.
Solimene, M. (2013). 'Undressing the Gağé Clad in State Garb: Bosnian Xoraxané Romá Face to Face with the Italian Authorities'. *Romani Studies*, 23(2), pp. 161–186.
Tervonen, M. and Enache, A. (2017). 'Coping with Everyday Bordering: Roma Migrants and Gatekeepers in Helsinki'. *Ethnic and Racial Studies*, 40, pp. 1114–1131.
van Baar, H. (2011). 'Europe's Romaniphobia: Problematization, Securitization, Nomadization'. *Environment and Planning D: Society and Space*, 29(2), pp. 203–212.
van der Woude, M., van der Leun, J. P. and Nijland, J. A. (2014). 'Crimmigration in the Netherlands'. *Law & Social Inquiry*, 39(3), pp. 560–579.
van der Woude, M. and van der Leun, J. (2017). 'Crimmigration Checks in the Internal Border Areas of the EU: Finding the Discretion that Matters'. *European Journal of Criminology*, 14(1), pp. 27–45.
Waddington, P. A. J. (1999). *Policing citizens: Police, power and the state*. London: Routledge.
Weber, L. and Bowling, B. (2008). 'Valiant beggars and global vagabonds: Select, eject, immobilize'. *Theoretical Criminology*, 12(3), pp. 355–375.
Yuval-Davis, N., Varjú, V., Tervonen, M., Hakim, J., and Fathi, M. (2017). 'Press discourses on Roma in the UK, Finland and Hungary'. *Ethnic and Racial Studies*, 40(7), pp. 1151–1169.

11 A 'Muslim' response to the narrative of the enemy within

Sharam Alghasi

Introduction

Two personal experiences constitute the point of departure of this chapter. The first one goes back to 1989, when as a young refugee who had been in Norway for a couple of months, I accompanied a friend of mine to a party. Every guest had to pay a small contribution to help finance the party-related expenses. My friend said that I didn't need to pay my share. The host disagreed, asking my friend, "why do you care? Welfare pays for him anyway". The host was right. As a newly arrived refugee in Norway, I was dependent on welfare support. But the incident made a huge impact on me: it did something to my sense of pride and self-esteem. The second story happened years later in 2015, when I was hosting an Eastern European academic acquaintance who briefly visited Norway for research purposes. I prepared a nice dinner of pork chops and served him vodka. We were having quite a lot of fun when he suddenly started telling me about his anxiety about the future of Europe. He told me he was scared. I asked him, "what are you scared of?" His reply moved me greatly: "I am scared that people like you come to Europe". I went on to ask: "what do you mean by people like me?", to which he replied: "Muslims".

The intention with sharing these two stories is to emphasise the significant transformation of views—and how these views are articulated—with regards to the concept of the 'migrant', minority, Muslim, or whatever term one employs to differentiate oneself from those coming into *our* societies. I argue that these two stories capture the respective *zeitgeists* of their time within Norwegian debates on migration in general, particularly in relation to Islam and Muslims. While in 1989, I was viewed as a costly element for the Norwegian welfare state, in 2015, I was identified as a Muslim, and a potential threat towards the European 'way of life'. This current zeitgeist in Norway, which articulates its dominant views through distinguishing and proclaiming Islam as a major marker to divide societies into *us* and *them*, stands at the core of this chapter.

Obviously, it is sad to experience being considered an immediate danger to so many others, as I did in 2015. However, this should not be dismissed as a unique occurrence; elsewhere, the formation of a new narrative around Islam and the *Muslim figure* has been emphasised. In this new narrative, Muslim members of society are perceived to have the potential to become radicalised, and thus constitute a home-grown enemy—*the enemy within* (Kundnani 2017). The assumption of this article is that the narrative of *the enemy within* implicates the lives of Norwegian citizens with Muslim backgrounds. Accordingly, its focus is on how a group of individuals with Muslim backgrounds respond to this narrative—after all, it is about them, and their very existence within Norwegian society.

In grasping these individuals' views on the dominant narrative of *the enemy within*, this chapter takes a media–sociological point of departure, in the sense that its focus is on the interplay between media productions and lives of individuals, and not least on their reception and interpretation of media messages. For example, individual experiences, and pre-existing knowledges from different contexts, are vital in producing and receiving meaning in the interplay between media and individuals, or groups in a society (Alghasi 2011; Mcquail 2010). Accordingly, this chapter first focuses on *The Norwegian Islamist*, a documentary film that can be seen as a discursive representation of *the enemy within*, and second on how a group of formally "Muslim" individuals with Iranian and Turkish backgrounds respond to the documentary film, and relate its narrative of *the enemy within* to a wider range of sociocultural issues. Interviewees in this study watched the documentary and were individually interviewed thereafter about its content and related issues.

Islam and Muslims in the public sphere

Today, in public spheres across many societies, Islam and a constructed and established figure of the Muslim stand as a major marker in ongoing debates about who we are and who we are not. Said (1997) emphasises a perception of a historically constructed, culturally dangerous, threatening, and violent Islam in Western consciousness. However, since the 9/11 attacks, Islam and Muslims have gained new forms of visibility in our societies (Whitaker 2002). Recent geopolitical and geo-cultural conditions have led to the formation of new narratives about Islam and Muslims (Eide et al. 2008; Kundnani 2017). As a major marker between *us* and *them*, Muslims are often suggested to possess values and qualities opposite to *our* self-proclaimed values and qualities (Poole and Richardson 2006; Kundnani 2014). In Norway, the 22 July, 2011, right-wing extremist terrorist attack by Anders Breivik that left 77 people dead, is often presented as actions executed by a *lone wolf*. Bangstad, however, relates this terror attack to Islamophobic discourses in the country (Bangstad 2015).

The media is often recognised as vital in shaping our national memory of who we are; it guides us to identify what qualities 'we' possess, who our friends are, and who we consider as *outsiders* in relation to those understood as *insiders* (Hall 1992). Within many media representations, Islam is often considered as something strange and in opposition to an imagined normality and is subsequently framed as a source of conflict and unease (Poole 2006;

Said 1997). In recent years, the media's focus on Islam and Muslims has increased exponentially. This growth is exemplified in the coverage of terrorism and terrorist-related stories, Islamic extremism, and cultural difference (Moore, Mason, and Lewis 2008). In Norwegian media practices, there is a massive focus on Islam and Islam-related issues. According to *Retriever*—a media surveillance and analysis centre in Norway—in 2009 there were more news articles on Islam and Muslims than on the country's Prime Minister (Retriever 2016, p. 4). Furthermore, Islam is presented as "unchangeable" and as a "political religion". There is simply an obsession with Islam in Norwegian society.[1]

The enemy within

The dominant narrative of *the enemy within* is linked to the idea of Muslim members of our societies constituting a danger towards non-Muslims. It is presented as if some Muslim members of society can at any moment become radicalised (Kundnani 2017). Obviously, to deal with a radicalised enemy demands counter-radicalisation, a seemingly justifiable reason for a 'war' against this radicalised enemy within, whose purpose is stopping *them*, before they harm *us*. As someone with Muslim background, one runs the risk of being absorbed into a 'suspect' community in need of surveillance. Aistrop employs the term "the Muslim paranoia narrative" to describe the new narrative in which Muslims are a possible danger to societal peace and prosperity, and therefore impossible to cohabit with (Aistrop 2011).

The ruling condition in Norway is by no means an exception; radicalisation/counter-radicalisation are much debated issues, often linked to a possible inside enemy who could be a great danger to a society, its values, and ways of life. For instance, in recent years, the Norwegian Police Security Service (PST) has declared radical Islam as a prime suspect for possible terror acts on Norwegian soil. In March 2018, the Norwegian Minister of Justice—a member of the Progress Party (FRP), who are known for their critical and anti-migrant stance—had to resign due to controversial comments on Facebook in which she criticised the opposing Labour party for "defending terrorists against the interests of the nation". In her press conference after the resignation, she claims violence by Islamic radicals as the major threat for Norway in years to come. She said:

> Freedom of speech is very important to me. It's a Norwegian and Western value which we do everything in our power to protect. Therefore, I attempt to cherish my freedom of speech. Because I believe one of the main issues in Norway, in years to come, is Norwegian migration and integration politics.[2]

The political climate which led to the resignation of the Minister of Justice clearly illustrates the significant position radical Islam holds in the Norwegian political landscape. The recruitment of fighters for jihadist wars in Syria—more popularly called in Norwegian language "Syria-travellers" has during recent years been presented as a recurring issue in Norway (Fangen and Kolås 2016; Vestel 2016). According to *Retriever*, more than 60 percent of newspaper articles on foreign affairs in Norway deal with "Muslim terror, ISIS, foreign fighters, and radical Islam". The media coverage of the war in Syria—from encouraging and recruiting, to the development of the war in the country— was mentioned more than 53,000 times during 2016 (Retriever 2016, p. 4).

Relying on the aforementioned context, one may assume that there is an established narrative of *the enemy within* in the Norwegian context. A logical question to raise, is then to ask how a group of individuals with Muslim backgrounds make sense of the dominant context surrounding them. I will attempt to establish some understandings regarding this question within the rest of the chapter.

Media and identity

I attempt to extrapolate how the dominant narrative of *the enemy within* in Norwegian context—not least in Norwegian media—is interpreted by a group of individuals with Muslim backgrounds. This task, as I argue, highlights several fundamental and interconnected media–sociological issues.

The first issue is linked to the relation between social contexts and individual/group identities. Berger and Luckmann (1967), for instance, remind us that humans experience a sense of themselves in relation to how they are perceived and understood by others. In this regard, the media is recognised as a vital agent, since it is continuously involved in human processes of identification and classification; the media constantly comes up with suggestions about what is important around us, and how to think about the issues they frame as important (Hall 1992; Alghasi 2009). Furthermore, the impact of the media on identity formation among *the others/outsiders* is emphasised elsewhere (Madianou 2005; Alghasi 2009). Migrant interplay with the media may lead to varieties of identity formations, from reinforcing homeland identity, for instance, to diasporic, hybrid, or progressive identities. In their media use, migrants seem to have a particular focus on issues which deal with their conditions within the societies they are part of (Alghasi 2009). Accordingly, the assumption in this chapter is that media narratives—such as the narrative of *the enemy within*—do have an impact upon identity formation among individuals with Muslim backgrounds.

The second fundamental issue is—to employ Silverstone's term—about the ability of individuals to *work further* on media texts (Silverstone and Georgiou 2005, p. 434). This position indicates that media content does not have a single outcome. On the contrary, every media text can produce multiple meanings, and one's interpretation will be based on their individual context, culture, and world views. This is what the "reception" approach is about—to investigate how a receiver works further to create their own meaning and

A *'Muslim' response* 183

interpretation as to what a media message is about (Mcquail 2010). As Mcquail describes it, reception studies:

> emphasises media use as a reflection of a particular socio-cultural context and as a process of giving meaning to cultural products and experiences in everyday life. (Mcquail 2010, p. 338)

Accordingly, this research can be understood as a reception study into how a group of individuals with Muslim backgrounds produce meaning from a particular documentary's representation of Islam and Muslims.

A third and closely linked issue is the vital media–sociological distinction between the production and reception of meaning (Hall 1980). The idea that meaning-making, both on a production and reception level, are discursive constructions, means that they articulate certain ideas and beliefs of a given time. To elaborate further on these discursive constructions, I find narrative theories useful, since they may cast light on how a story is told in one way, and not in another (Grossberg et al. 2006).[3] In this regard, the distinction between *story* and *plot* is vital (Grossberg et al. 2006; Gillespie and Toynbee 2006). While the story is the actual development of events through time, the plot is the way in which a story is told. To produce meaning—for example in making a documentary or interpreting a documentary—you construct your plot out of an available repertoire of stories (Bordwell and Thompson 1990). This underlines the intertextual quality of a text in a context, in the sense that the story activates a series of different texts present in one's mental inventory (Hall 1973; Fiske 1987). It means that you choose your story, or construct your plot, based on surrounding cultural repertoires and pre-existing knowledges.

Accordingly, a film narrative with a plot that follows an extremist–Islamist recruiting for a jihadist war in Syria, is shaped and constructed by those available stories and ideologies about Islam. Stories about violence, terror, danger, and not least danger caused by someone from within, are obviously readily accessible stories about Islam. Furthermore, the same goes for the reception of a text—you construct a plot based on a pre-existing story or stories. Individuals with Muslim backgrounds then make sense of a media text or any other related texts in relation to cultural texts, and pre-existing repertoires of knowledge and history. Therefore, this chapter attempts to take a closer look at processes of meaning-making, and the articulation of ideas among respondents with Muslim backgrounds regarding the ruling narrative around Muslims and Islam in Norwegian society, which is the narrative of *the enemy within*.

Methodological design

To investigate the responses of individuals with Muslim backgrounds on the narrative of *the enemy within*, this study employs reception analysis, a type of analysis with a focus on the interplay between text and audience (Livingstone

1998, pp. 237–238). In reception analysis, the aim is to grasp how various media texts are perceived and interpreted by receivers (Mcquail 2010). Accordingly, a specific documentary film is chosen to investigate how this documentary is perceived and interpreted by 13 individuals with Muslim backgrounds. Both the documentary and the individuals involved in the study require further methodological elaboration.

In April 2017, the Norwegian public broadcasting channel (NRK) aired a 54-minute documentary programme called *The Norwegian Islamist*.[4] The title refers to Ubaydullah Hussain, a Norwegian man with Pakistani origins who is currently serving a nine-year sentence for recruiting fighters for the jihadist war in Syria.[5] As a spokesperson for a small group called Prophet's Umma, Hussain has been a frequently invoked figure in the media's coverage of Islamic fundamentalism and the recruitment of "Syria-travellers".[6] The documentary portrays Hussain as a fierce Islamic extremist, and a cynical recruiter of young Muslims—both ethnic and non-ethnic Norwegians—for ISIS' war in Syria and Iraq. The documentary crew accompany Hussain around Oslo, witnessing his views, and his missionary and recruitment efforts for ISIS' wars. The documentary narrative is unmistakable—one of *us*, born and raised in Norway, roams around *our* society inviting Norwegian citizens to join ISIS' jihadist war. Because of this explicit and unequivocal narrative, *The Norwegian Islamist* was chosen as the topic of discussion for the study.

All interviewees have Muslim backgrounds, which doesn't necessarily mean they are raised according to Muslim traditions, or that they identify as Muslims themselves. The criteria for choosing respondents was that they were born and raised by Muslim parents, either in Norway or in a predominantly Muslim country. I justify these criteria for choosing the respondents by reiterating the first issue raised in the section 'Media and identity': that humans experience a sense of themselves in relation to how they are perceived and understood by others (Berger and Luckmann 1967). Culturally and historically, there have been fixed and static understandings of "others", not least in regard to Muslims in Western societies (Said 1978; Bhabha 1994). In this way, the media operates as an important agent in the public sphere, and is continuously involved in the reproduction of a rigid understanding of Muslim identity, which often overshadows its other aspects (Said 1997); according to media logic, you are often defined as a Muslim if you are born into a Muslim family, and accordingly, you are associated with a range of qualities that run counter to cherished qualities in Western societies (Said 1978; Bhabha 1994; Alghasi 2009). Accordingly, one of the aims of this chapter is to examine how 13 individuals who bear the "Muslim label" respond to the media's narrative about *the enemy within*.

For the purpose of this study, Norwegian individuals with Iranian and Turkish backgrounds are perceived as analytically relevant. I understand Iranians as carrying the weight of a rather diverse history. Several ideological forces have shaped modern Iranian history. For instance, beside Islam, nationalism has been a major ideological force in Iranian modern history

(Dabashi 2008). Even today, the nationalist ideology in Iran seems to be more relevant than ever; for example, there is a renewal of nationalist symbols among Iranians both in Iran and its diaspora. There are also considerable conversion rates of followers of Islam turning to Zoroastrianism (Abdolmohammadi 2015) and Christianity (Alghasi 2011). Therefore, one may say that Iranian-Norwegians carry a paradox within—while they must bear the "Muslim label", they do not easily fit into clichéd representational categories, because they in fact represent an array of diverse and multi-layered identities, countering reductionist portraits of them as just "Muslims" (Alghasi 2009).

Similar to the complex and multi-layered Iranian identity, Turkish history also contributes to its citizens' marked identity struggle. As a young republic, it grapples with the secular quality of the Turkish state, and the Islamic dimension of Turkish identity is often emphasised (Baran 2010). The establishment of the Turkish republic was also an attempt to enable Turks to embrace Islam in the private sphere, while the organisation of the state and broader society was based on secular principles—in other words, a separation of religion and state. As the father of the young Turkish state, Atatürk's idea was to create a condition in which public life was characterised by secularism, and Islam remained a private matter (Baran 2010). To summarise, both Iranian-Norwegians and Turkish-Norwegians contend with a more multi-layered identity than what might be assumed, based on their presumed religious belonging. The histories of the societies they originate from indicates waves of secularisation and Islamisation. While in the 1920s and 1930s both societies moved towards secularisation, for the past 40 years, Iran has been ruled by religious forces, and in recent years Turkey has been increasingly influenced by Islamic perspectives (Dabashi 2008; Baran 2010). Subsequently, I make the assumption that the experiences of Norwegians with Iranian and Turkish backgrounds will be informed by these countries' historical contexts and may have an impact on how respondents "read" *The Norwegian Islamist*.

The respondents were selected through snowball sampling (Kristoffersen et al. 2015). Their age varied from 23 to 75, and six identified as male, and seven as female. All live in the Norwegian capital of Oslo, and its nearby suburbs. The majority of respondents moved to Norway and lived most of their lives there, while one was born in Norway. That they have spent many years living in Norway and have gained many societal experiences is an assumed important lens through which they read *The Norwegian Islamist*. They also represent different political, social, and ethnic backgrounds known to exist among Iranian-Norwegians and Turkish-Norwegians (Visdal-Johnsen 2005; Alghasi 2011). All interviews were conducted through Skype, then follow-up questions were sent via email. All names used in the study are pseudonyms.

Jihadist war—something distant

The message in the documentary is clear—an individual not from far away, but from right here—born and raised in our society—represents one of the most reactionary and violent versions of Islam. He is the established portrait of *the enemy within*. During the interviews, all respondents deeply distanced themselves from Hussain and associated figures. Huliya, for instance, insisted on having "never seen or been in contact with people like those in the documentary". Pari claims she could not initially watch the documentary because she believed that it was "free of charge PR for Islamists". Bagher reaffirmed Huliya's and Pari's stance, stating:

> I think the documentary was good, but to be honest, it didn't really give me new insights about Muslims. What I saw didn't represent what I believe (within my Muslim background), or the people I know. I know quite a few Muslims. They think differently and they act differently.

Fahri said that she did not understand the debate on Islam as represented in the documentary, since she takes it for granted that "religion should be treated as something private". Sudabeh shared Fahri's views, and emphasised her distance from the representations:

> Religion for me is the Ramadan of my childhood, when in the afternoon we had nice food, or when we had a religious gathering which I associated with playing with other relatives my age, or eating lots of sweets. Years later, I've been distanced from any religious beliefs. I think it may have something to do with my experience with religion, which is not good.

Other respondents also comprehend and practise their religion differently. Adil, for instance, partakes in Islamic festivities if they celebrate or commemorate the prophet Mohammed's birthday or death. It is important for him that his wife wears a hijab, and he insists on undergoing counselling with a religious priest to discuss important matters. But he still opposes the extremist interpretation of his religion, as represented in the documentary.

All respondents perceive the documentary's portrayal of Islam as a representation far away from how they comprehend or practise their religion. This was a consistent position amongst all respondents, regardless of whether they perceive themselves as religious or secular. To use Hall's term, respondents convey an *oppositional reading* of the documentary (Hall 1980). In representing an imagined reality throughout the documentary, these discursive constructions support the narrative of *the enemy within*. The respondents oppose their Muslim identity being constructed in this way, and instead present their own narratives; they reject the documentary's violent and reactionary portrayal of Islam, and of being Muslim. In doing so, they draw upon their experiences—such as their memories of childhood festivities and religious gatherings—pointing to a state of *becoming* religious or secular. By relaying their stories, they create representations of Muslim identity (or someone with Muslim background), which stands in opposition to the representations proffered by the documentary.

Islamophobia: A reality in everyday life?

As established, the respondents distance themselves from a violent and reactionary version of Islam. An appropriate question to raise, is why does the media—as a major force in the public sphere—focus on a radical, jihadist version of Islam, while there are in fact very few of its supporters in Norway. Following this question, there is another interrelated question to raise, and that is how this particular representation of Islam and Muslims affects the lives of Muslim respondents. Nasim believed that the persistent dissemination of this position through the media directly affected her life, stating:

> This documentary is really cliché. Nothing new, like I have seen [this a] 100 times before, but it does affect my life, even though I have no religious affiliation. I feel like in many social settings I have to defend myself that I am not a Muslim like we all the time talk about.

Nasim believes that even though she does not practise Islam, the visibility of her Muslim background nonetheless plays a major role in her everyday life. Nasim's statement may be linked to her intertextual surroundings, in which many other narratives are reminders and reproductions of the documentary's narrative. As Nasim described, one may argue that the dominant narratives that are put forward about Islam and Muslims lead to feelings of being stigmatised. Salar presented a different point of departure than Nasim, but with similar outcomes. He said:

> I don't think that this documentary increases the Islamophobia in society, since I believe that the question of *us* against *them*—that we might be a danger to society—is already there, so I don't think this programme in itself leads to Islamophobia. Islamophobia is already there.

Salar's statement, like Nasim's, reminds us of the intertextual quality of the message in the documentary; he employs the term *Islamophobia* to describe the condition he believes to exist in his surroundings.[7] In his *reading*, Salar seems to place the narrative in the documentary alongside narratives with similar ideas and articulations. His understanding is that because of the connotations Islam carries in Norway, it is inevitable that he'll constantly be negotiating Islamophobic positions. The paradox is that despite identifying as secular, he still faces the condition of Islamophobia in his everyday life. Pari faces similarly paradoxical receptions to her identity as Salar. She referred to an episode at a party, where the relatives of her girlfriend wondered aloud how her identity as a lesbian with Muslim background would be understood within the Islamic religion. She said:

> As I told them that I had Muslim background, they told me that it was not possible, since I was Norwegian. And when I asked, "why do you say

that?", they replied that what I represented contrasted with what they thought about Muslims. I think that I couldn't fit into their mind-boxes about the religion of Islam, and how a Muslim should be. It seemed that I disturbed their fixed ideas about Islam and Muslims. The rest of the night they tried to avoid me, like they did not know how to behave in my presence.

Despite understanding herself as secular, Pari articulates that what she believes to be the ruling ideology others use to approach Islam influences her relationship with, and capacity to engage with, her surroundings. The view that Islamophobia is ingrained in Norwegian society seems to be very present in respondents' descriptions of their everyday lives. Aida, who was born and raised in Norway, describes how Islamophobia materialises in her everyday interactions:

I am born here, and I don't wear a hijab. But my best girlfriend wears a hijab, and I know for a fact that she is really upset by the way she is treated. We always talk about it, and I'm really sad for the way she feels.

Respondents do not perceive the documentary as operating within a vacuum. On the contrary, they often reaffirm the intertextual quality of the documentary's message; they understand it as a reminder of a condition in which similar texts and narratives act as constant reminders that they are not considered to be 'ordinary' members of society. Despite their secularity, they are identified and classified as potential dangers to society. They articulate a condition in which they see themselves as victims of their society's ruling Islamophobic ideology; despite their distance from a violent Islamic mentality, they still seem to be marked by their assumed religious affiliation and associated with an orientation they do not possess.

The weight of history

So, to date we have learnt that respondents distanced themselves from the violent reactionary ideology articulated in the documentary, and that they believe their everyday life is marked by the "Muslim label" they oppose. A relevant question to then ask is: how do respondents deal with the labels and the stigmatised conditions they claim surround them? Bahman was asked about his views on how Norwegian society 'marks' those they perceive to practise Islam, and how he deals with this condition. He replied:

Why should this programme lead to Islamophobia while we already have problems with Islam as whole? I know what it means to have Islamic ruling, I don't want to have it here in Norway. I am part of this society, and I do everything in my power to expose Islam for what it is.

Bahman articulates a sharp and clear position, not only towards violent and reactionary Islam, but also in relation to Islam in general. By considering himself a part of Norwegian society, he rejects Islam as the marker between him and society. Sudabeh also somewhat shares Bahman's stance towards Islam, likewise relying on her experiences when talking about her position towards Islam, and at the same time providing a description of how she relates to Norwegian society:

> I admit that the reason I took refuge in Norway many years ago was because of religion. Islamists took over my country, and my life was never the same again. Now my life in Iran is a distant memory. I know what it means to be ruled by Islamists. I can understand the hysteria in Norway about Islam, but I always tell my friends, my Norwegian friends, that not all Muslims are Islamists.

Obviously, both Sudabeh and Bahman consider themselves to be a part of Norwegian society. One can also assume that in this process of becoming part of Norwegian society, they have rejected Islamic ideologies. Furthermore, despite sharing views with Bahman, Sudabeh proffers a more balanced position by distinguishing Islamists from Muslims, even though she does not consider herself a Muslim. Bahman's and Sudabeh's position towards Islam is not unknown among Iranian-Norwegians, or other Iranian diasporas for that matter (Alghasi, 2011)[8]. This position relies heavily on many Iranians' rather sad histories and experiences with Islamisation. Pari, another Iranian-Norwegian respondent, came to Norway at a very young age. She is very much preoccupied with the country's existing Islamophobia, and believes that "the problem is not Islam, the problem is Islamophobia". When I asked her what she meant by that, she replied: "Muslims are different, they are not all the same. Muslims are more than just being a Muslim". Pari does not see Islam as the problem—the problem is the reductionist view many individuals have about those with Muslim backgrounds.

The Iranian-Norwegian respondents views on how to deal with the narrative of *the enemy within* are splintered. While some seem to reject Islam totally, others consider existing practices towards Islam and Muslims in the Norwegian public sphere to be reductionist. Traces of history—signified by Islamists taking over their country—is vital in understanding their positions towards this documentary, and towards the religion of Islam in general (Alghasi 2009). In light of what Iranian-Norwegian respondents describe, one can conclude that while these respondents take an oppositional stance towards the message of the documentary, and are critical of Islamic politics, they are concurrently subject to certain reductionist classification approaches within Norwegian society, invoked by the narrative of *the enemy within*. To put it differently, they may feel they are accused of, and subjected to being stigmatised for something from which they have in fact been trying to disown or distance themselves.

Meanwhile, in the Turkish-Norwegian evaluations of the documentary, we can trace an interesting commonality—respondents often insist on the separation of Islam from the state. Derya articulates this position:

> All I heard in this documentary was this guy (Ubaydullah Hussain) spouting religious words, like *inshallah*,[9] or *mashallah*.[10] I can't understand that mentality. Religion and politics are two separate things.

Aida put forward a similar position:

> I have learnt that religion is something private. It has nothing to do with politics. I am born in Norway, but still I have seen the picture of Atatürk on the wall at our home, since I was a kid. This is someone my parents have always talked about.

Aida's reference to Atatürk seems to be common among the majority of respondents with Turkish backgrounds. Derya, for example, recounts moments from her childhood, and speaks warmly of Atatürk's impact upon Turkish society, which advocated for the separation of Islam and politics. Serdar is an enthusiastic supporter of what is known as *Kemalism*, which refers to Atatürk's doctrine that—among other things—supports a clear distinction between religion and state. However, not all Turkish-Norwegians are supporters of Atatürk and his ideology. For instance, Adil, a religious man, supports more recent developments that have increased the role of religion in Turkish politics. Nevertheless, he rejects the jihadist version of Islam, instead articulating how he thinks religion and politics should mix. He said:

> I really disliked Hussain in this film. I really disliked the Islam he represented. His Islam has for a long time been supported by non-Muslim powers, and I don't like that. We need to integrate Islam into democracy, something I think is about to happen in Turkey.

The positions of Aida, Derya, and Serdar on one hand, and Adil on the other, illustrate an existing division in which members of the Turkish-Norwegian community are distinguished by degrees of religious or secular beliefs and practices (Visdal-Johnsen 2005, pp. 26–27). This division seems to be embedded in Turkish identity, in which religion and secular orientations are purported to live side by side (Zubaida 1996) and is easily traceable through respondents' *readings* and evaluations of the documentary. Similar divisions can be identified when evaluating recent developments in Turkey—a number of respondents articulate a critical attitude towards religion gaining more power and influence in Turkish politics, while others support the very same developments.

Concluding remarks

This chapter has attempted to demonstrate what ideas and practices characterise the zeitgeist—the *spirit of this time*—regarding debates around *the Muslim figure* in Norway. It identified the dominant idea that Islam operates as a major marker in distinguishing between *us* and *them*. This chapter has focused on how individuals with Muslim backgrounds perceive their society's broader constructed portraits of "Islam" and "Muslims". These responses illustrate some interesting dimensions in the ongoing debate on Islam and Muslims that arguably need more attention.

First, without exception, all respondents distanced themselves from the documentary's portrayal of how Islam is practised, conflating this with a general Muslim identity. Obviously, the respondents cannot represent every Muslim's position, however, they do represent views that do not currently receive much space in the Norwegian public sphere, which continuously represents a violent and reactionary version of Islam through its media and other public forums. In other words, a reductionist approach is regularly put forward in the sense that the narrative of *the enemy within* is widely understood as the dominant narrative around Islam and Muslims.

Second, both the producers of the documentary as well as the receivers—in this case the respondents in this study—are involved in its construction practices. The producers rely on dominant knowledges and ideas about Islam and Muslims when encoding the narrative of *the enemy within*, while its respondents also rely on their repertoires of knowledges and ideas to decode, and make sense of, its narrative. This decoding process sees respondents associate the documentary's narrative with similar narratives and experiences they've had in relation to the media and society at large. They perceive media practices regarding Islam and Muslims as reductionist, and express being surrounded by states of stigmatisation and Islamophobia in their everyday lives.

Third, the respondents' views indicate a condition of in-betweenness among them, a condition that is beautifully illustrated in a Persian poem about a man standing between a mosque and a winery, saying: "I'm not allowed into the Mosque, because they tell me that I'm drunk. I'm not allowed into the winery, because they tell me that I don't know how to drink. O lord, [...] where is the way?" (Attar 2008, p. 70).[11] On the one hand, a discursive construction is at work, in which certain portraits of Islam and Muslims are continuously reproduced. There is a static and reductionist understanding of Islamic and Muslim identity; being a Muslim overshadows all other qualities one possesses. On the other hand, almost all respondents are opposed to Islamic ideologies infiltrating their societies of origin, since these ideologies—like the Norwegian context—reduces them to the *Muslim figure*, denying other dimensions of their identities. In one context, the idea of Islam and being a Muslim is associated with endangering the imagined "Norwegian" values and ways of life, while the other context constructs the idea of Islam and being a Muslim as a path to higher values and a better way of life. In both cases, the Islamic religion, and identifying as Muslim, dominates and overshadows the other layers within one's identity. The majority of respondents express a condition in which they are neither allowed into the Mosque, nor into the winery. In a time when Islam and Muslims are increasingly taking a major role in our societies, it is rather vital to reflect on this condition of unease—this condition of in-betweenness—that the respondents of this study express.

Fourth, to continue with the same analogy, respondents of this study oppose the manner in which they are perceived to be desired either at the winery or at the Mosque. This opposition may as well be a source of power; when you are not allowed into the winery or into the Mosque, and when you are opposed to how you are reduced to a Muslim subject in both places, then you have to move on towards new places and new people, new contexts and new relations. In a world where you are often either a Muslim with a set of values, or a non-Muslim with another set of values, this quest for alternative approaches in defining those perceived as *others,* not least Muslims, is often disregarded.

Notes

1 http://fritanke.no/reportasje/islam-den-misforstatte-religionen/19.7815
2 https://www.abcnyheter.no/nyheter/norge/2018/03/20/195381249/sylvi-listhaug-frp-gar-av-som-justisminister-jeg-vil-ikke-ga-stille-i-dorene
3 A narrative is "chain of events in a cause-effect relationship occurring in [a particular] time and space" (Bordwell and Thompson, 1990 p. 55).
4 The documentary was made by Adel Khan Farooq and Ulrik Imtiaz Rolfsen. During the making of the documentary, the material for the film was confiscated by the Norwegian secret police (PST), and later used in Hussain's 2017 trial. https://www.nrk.no/dokumentar/xl/den-norske-islamisten-1.13462081
5 Erlend Ofte Arntsen (2016) portrays Hussain as central in the recruitment of young Muslim Norwegians attracted to salafi-jihadism, and for grooming them for possible travel to Syria or Iraq as 'foreign fighters'. See also:
   https://www.dagbladet.no/nyheter/ubaydullah-hussain-32-domt-til-ni-ars-fengsel-i-lagmannsretten/69357186
6 Already in 2015, Hussain was a known figure in the Norwegian public sphere when he was charged for attempted murder with the intention "to create serious fear in the population". https://www.nrk.no/norge/ubaydullah-hussain-frifunnet-for-terroroppfordring-1.12422153
7 Islamophobia is a much debated term. My understanding of the term is:
   "Unfounded hostility towards Islam. It refers also to the practical consequences of such hostility in unfair discrimination against Muslim individuals and communities, and to the exclusion of Muslims from mainstream political and social affairs" (Runnymede Trust 1997, p. 4).
8 See also Alghasi 2018, available: https://www.dagbladet.no/kultur/paradoksale-talspersoner/69524017
9 God willing
10 Praise the lord
11 See also: https://www.amazon.com/Divan-Attar/dp/1535318686

References

Abdolmohammadi, P. (2015). 'The Revival of Nationalism and Secularism in Modern Iran'. *LSE Middle East Centre paper Series 11*, London: LSE Middle East Centre.

Aistrop, T. (2016). The Muslim paranoia narrative in counter-radicalisation policy. *Journal of Critical Studies on Terrorism*, 9(2), pp. 182–204.

Alghasi, S. (2009). *Iranians in Norway—Media Consumption and Identity Making*. PhD dissertation, Department for Sociology and Human Geography. Oslo: University of Oslo.

Alghasi, S. (2011). 'Irans diaspora og norsk utenrikspolitikk', in *Norges nye vi: Diasporaer som faktor i norsk utenrikspolitikk*, I.B. Neumann, M. Godzimirski and S. Alghasi (eds.) Rapport til Utenriksdepartementet. NUPI-rapport. Norsk Utenrikspolitisk Institutt/Norwegian Institute of International Affairs, pp. 55–86.

Arntsen, E.O. (2016). *Fremmedkrigerne. Fra en norsk småby til Den islamske staten*. Oslo: Kagge Forlag.

Attar, F. (2008). Divan-e ghasayed va ghazaliat. Sheik Farīd ud-Dīn Abū Ḥamīd Mohammed Aṭṭār Nishapuri. Collected by Cultural Sites of Torbat-e jam, Iran. https://fooji.ir/wp-content/uploads/2018/04/divan-ghasayed-va-ghazaliat-attar-fooji.ir_.pdf [Accessed 8 October, 2018].

Bangstad, S. (2015). *Anders Breivik and the Rise of Islamophobia*. London: Zed.

Baran, Z. (2010). *Torn Country: Turkey Between Secularism and Islamism*. Stanford: Hoover Institution Press.

Bordwell, D. and Thompson, K. (1990). *Narration in the Fiction Film*. Madison: The University of Wisconsin Press.

Berger, P.L. and Luckmann, T. (1967). *The Social Construction of Reality: A Treatise on the Sociology of Knowledge*. New York: Penguin Group.

Bhabha, H. (1994). *The Location of Culture*. New York: Routledge.

Dabashi, H. (2007). *Iran: A People Interrupted*. New York: The New Press.

Eide, E., Kunelius, R., and Phillips, A. (eds.) (2008). *Transnational Media Events: The Mohammed Cartoons and the Imagined Clash of Civilizations*. Goteborg: Nordicom.

Fangen, K. and Kolås, Å. (2016). '"The "Syria traveller": reintegration or legal sanctioning?'. *Critical Studies on Terrorism*, 9(3), pp 414–432.

Fiske, J. (1987). *Television Culture*. London: Methuen.

Gillespie, M. and Toynbee, J. (2006). *Analysing Media Texts*. Maidenhead: Open University Press.

Grossberg, L., Wartella, E., Whitney, D.C., and Macgregor, J.W. (2006). *Media Making. Mass Media in a Popular Culture*. 2nd edition. Thousand Oaks: SAGE Publications.

Hall, S. (1973/1980). 'Encoding/decoding', in Centre for Contemporary Culture Studies (eds.) *Culture, Media, Language: Working Papers in Cultural Studies 1972–79*London: Hutchinson, pp. 128–138.

Hall, S. (1992). 'The Question of Cultural Identity', in S. Hall, D. Held and T. McGrew (eds.) *Modernity and its Futures*. Cambridge: Polity Press and Open University Press, pp. 273–325.

Kristoffersen, L., Tufte, P.A., and Johannessen, A. (2015). *Introduksjon til samfunnsvitenskapelig metode*. Oslo: Abstrakt Forlag.

Kundnani, A. (2014). *Muslims are Coming*. London: Verso.

Kundnani, A. (2017). 'Extremism, Theirs and Ours: Britain's Generational Struggle', in G. Titley, D. Freedman, G. Khiabany, A. Mondon (eds.) *After Charlie Hebdo: Terror, Racism and Free Speech*. London: Zed Books.

Livingstone, S. (1998). *Making Sense of Television: The Psychology of Audience Interpretation*. London/New York: Routledge.

Madianou, M. (2005). *Meditating the Nation: News, Audiences and the Policy of Identity*. London: UCL Press.

Mcquail, D. (2010). *Mass Communication Theory*. 6th edition. London: SAGE Publications.

Moore, K., Mason, P., and Lewis, J. (2008). *Images of Islam in the UK. The Representation of British Muslims in the National Print News Media 2000–2008*. Cardiff: Cardiff University Press.

Pantazis, C. and Pemberton, S. (2009). 'From the "Old" to the "New" Suspect Community: Examining the Impacts of Recent UK Counter-Terrorist Legislation'. *British Journal of Criminology*, 49(5), pp. 646–666.

Poole, E. and Richardson, J.E. (2006). *Muslims and the News Media*. London: I.B.Tauris.

Retriever (2016). Islam og muslimer i norske medier i 2016. http://www.frittord.no/images/uploads/files/Muslimer_og_islam_i_mediene_2016.pdf [Accessed 8 October 2018].

Runnymede Trust (1997). *A Challenge for Us All. Report of the Runnymede Trust, Commissioned on British Muslims and Islamophobia*. London: The Runnymede Trust.

Said, E. (1978). *Orientalism*. New York: Vintage Books.

Said, E. (1997). *Covering Islam: How the Media and the Experts Determine How We See the Rest of the World*. London: Vintage Books.

Silverstone, R. and Georgiou, M. (2005). 'Editorial Introduction: Media and Minorities in Multicultural Europe'. *Journal of Ethnic and Migration Studies*, 31(3), pp. 433–441.

Vestel, J.V. (2016). *I gråsonen. Ungdom og politisk ekstremisme i det nye Norge*. Oslo: Universitetsforlaget.

Visdal-Johnsen, H. (2005). *Moderne Tyrkere i Norge. "Tyrkiskhet"—Grunnleggende og vedvarende. En studie av Tyrkiske kvinner og deres forhold til sin Tyrkiske bakgrunn*. Mastergrad avhandling. Institutt for sosialantropologi. Universitetet i Bergen.

Whitaker, B. (2002). 'Islam and the British Press After September 11'. Lecture at the conference Islam and the media. Central London Mosque. 20 June, 2002. Available at http://al-bab.com/special-topics/islam-and-british-press-after-september-11 [Accessed 8 October 2018].

Zubaida, S. (1996). 'Turkish Islam and National Identity'. *Middle East Report 199 (Summer 1996)*. p. 26. https://merip.org/1999/06/turkish-islam-and-national-identity/

12 Being unknown

The securitisation of asylum seekers in Iceland

Helga Katrin Tryggvadóttir

Introduction

As a child, I lived on a rural, Icelandic farm, next door to my grandparents who were both born in 1910. Their generation was raised with the view that hospitality to guests was not just polite, but essential in a country with volatile weather and harsh conditions. These old customs often resulted in guests coming and going, and I therefore experienced many afternoons sitting at the large table in the dining room, drinking hot chocolate and eating pastries, while listening with one ear to (what I thought was) endless conversations about genealogy. These conversations represented a general interest in who people's forefathers were, and to which farms they could be traced. This is probably not the only example of this generation tracing back the ancestry of themselves and their guests. In fact, most people from Iceland recognise the phrase *"hverra manna ertu?"* which translates as, "who are your ancestors", or literally, "whose people are you?". Subsequent generations, though, rather tend to ask "where are you from?"; once the origin has been established, conversations start to evolve around your common acquaintances or relatives.

Although not unique to Iceland (but common in many small-scale societies), the tracing of ancestry has continued to the present day, and can now be seen in the genealogical *Book of Icelanders,* which claims to be "the only genealogical database in the world that covers a whole nation"; it contains information about "more than 95 percent of all Icelanders since the first census in 1703" (Íslendingabók 2017). Skaptadóttir and Loftsdóttir (2009) have argued that this homogenous view of the nation is not to be taken at face value, and that migration to and from the country has been present throughout the ages, albeit on a small scale, until recent decades. These traditions, books, and projects on genealogy can all be seen to be founded on the premise of a specific 'us', a homogenous Icelandic nation that can trace its ancestry back to 1703. In stark contrast to this example is the uprooted and the newly arrived—the unknown 'Other'. While Icelandic genealogy is firmly enshrined, the arrival of the displaced is in stark contrast with it.

In this chapter, I will trace the securitising discourse on asylum seekers arriving in Iceland. The findings were based on three sets of data. First, they were based on discourse analysis of news and comments in online media on the topic of asylum seekers and refugees from 2009 to 2017. Second, on governmental discourse through parliamentary speeches from 2002 to 2017, and official reports of the State Police from 2015 to 2017. And third, on ethnographic material from six months of fieldwork and interviews with asylum seekers in Iceland. The findings revealed that securitisation discourses around asylum seekers in the Icelandic media and comments contained racialised and gendered elements, such as the construction of male asylum seekers as a threat, and female asylum seekers as suffering victims. In many ways, governmental discourse was also characterised by images of asylum seekers arriving in large numbers, and being undocumented and unknown, which was framed as a problem. Within the securitisation discourse, asylum seekers were subject to objectification and scrutiny, with calls in the media for access to personal and intrusive details about them. The asylum seekers who participated in the research, however, described how they were well known and documented within the asylum system. For asylum seekers, having their identity and whereabouts known can pose a risk. Despite that, in the context of small-scale Icelandic society, being known—through media or personal networks—could be helpful for some, when used as a strategy of survival and a way to become accepted in society. The small size of Icelandic society can therefore be of benefit to asylum seekers if they manage to become known but is simultaneously largely exclusionary for the unknown majority.

The securitisation of migration

The concept of securitisation is a useful tool to shed light on the discourse surrounding the arrival of asylum seekers in the EU. Here, the term securitisation refers to a discursive practice where threat is created by a securitising process, regardless of whether or not the particular issue represents a real security threat (Buzan, Wæver and de Wilde 1998).[1] According to Ibrahim (2005), securitisation of migration is racism in its most modern form. Within that discourse, 'cultural differences' are constructed as a threat and used as an exclusionary tool. The focus on 'cultural differences' is at the core of new racism (Balibar 2007) or cultural racism (Wren 2001. Increased securitisation is directly connected with racism when structural problems are reframed through blaming specific risk categories for them, resulting in everybody belonging to that category being perceived as a threat. In relation to asylum seekers, images and language used about them are often heavily associated with danger, criminality, and risk (Bigo 2002; Ibrahim 2005; Malloch and Stanley 2005). In Europe, the discussion about Muslims entering through the asylum system is in many ways signified by the image of an 'invading army', playing on fears about whether they are loyal to the new country or not. This discourse is both racialised and gendered, and constructs this group as the 'Other'. Since this security risk is mainly assumed to be connected with individuals and groups of certain origins and beliefs, it can be seen as a form of racism (Fekete 2001).

When it comes to securitisation discourses, refugees and asylum seekers are often spoken of in terms of welfare fraud and being a threat to society's cohesion (van Houtum 2010; Whitaker 1998). These types of discourses only focus on the supposed threat that asylum seekers pose to the society they move to. It turns the problem on its head—those who are fleeing threats by crossing borders instead become seen as a threat (Ibrahim 2005). Within these discourses, the number of asylum seekers is also posed as a danger in itself. This is what van Dijk calls the numbers game, or "the rhetorical manipulation of numbers of arrival" (van Dijk 1997, p. 46). Or as Appadurai (2006) points out, any threat to the national whole, even in small numbers, can bring out "ethnocidal" characteristics in the majority. It is therefore not the actual numbers that pose a threat, but the perception of these numbers by the majority.

The risk associated with asylum seekers also stems from perceived problems establishing their identity and origin, often because of a lack of identity documents (Malloch and Stanley 2005). As Griffiths (2012) points out, to be recognised as a refugee, asylum seekers need to be able to prove that they are threatened, and the assessment of that threat is often based upon their identity or origin. Second, it is seen as crucial for the claim of refugee status to be perceived as credible and trustworthy. However, Griffiths maintains that this assumption is based upon a simplistic view of identity and honesty. The requirement of identity documents can become a burden on refugees, where lack of documents can be used to exclude, marginalise, and criminalise them (Bhatia 2015; Griffiths 2012; Razack 2000). As Torpey (1997) points out, people are dependent on states for the possession of "identity". This can be problematic when individuals are trying to escape from states (Griffiths 2012). All of this is a way of examining individuals, making them an object of knowledge, and therefore an object of power (Foucault 1977).

In the Nordic countries, racism is often framed in terms of contrasting democracy and gender equality with the 'culture' of immigrant groups, who are seen as not possessing these qualities (Keskinen and Andreassen 2017). Mulinari and Neergaard (2017) have identified two modes of racism in Sweden—exclusionary, and exploitative racism. Exclusionary racism aims at protecting kin from supposedly threatening migration, by trying to exclude migrants from entering the country. In contrast, exploitative racism looks at migrants as a way to fill gaps in low-paid service-sector jobs. In the Icelandic context, Loftsdóttir (2017) has shown that racism is often directed at immigrants in general. There, as in the other Nordic countries, emphasis is put on the perceived homogeneity of the nation (Skaptadóttir and Loftsdóttir 2009; Keskinen and Andreassen 2017). Mulinari et al. (2009) have been critical of the idea that the Nordic countries are outsiders to the colonial project, which allows them to claim that they are not racist. The Nordic countries therefore never went through a clear critique of colonialism. This has allowed for the creation of Nordic "exceptionalism"—the idea of Nordic innocence of racism and colonialism (Loftsdóttir and Jensen 2012). Claims of advancing democratic traditions, welfare, and development—coupled with the idea of gender equality being nearly achieved—are all used to create an image of the Nordic countries as egalitarian and non-discriminatory. However, this image can also be used to exclude and marginalise groups that are seen as not belonging to the nation. That creates a dichotomy between the homogenous nation and its 'Others', who are not seen as fitting within this ideal (Mulinari et al. 2009).

Methods and material

The first set of data consists of a collection of online news and comments surrounding the topic of asylum seekers and refugees in Iceland from 2009 to 2017. News that contained the words 'asylum seeker' or 'refugee'—and comments attached to them from four online news outlets (visir.is, dv.is, eyjan.pressan.is, utvarpsaga.is)—were incorporated into a database. The result of this collection was a database of 11,843 comments and 3,386 news pieces. The text from the news and comments was first analysed through corpus analysis to identify keywords and phrases (Gabrielatos and Baker 2008), frequently used in connection with asylum seekers and refugees. Thereafter, the discourse in the media and comments was analysed more closely using critical discourse analysis (Blommaert and Bulcaen 2000).

The second dataset consisted of parliamentary speeches from 2002 to 2016 that contained references to asylum seekers and refugees; these were analysed using critical discourse analysis. The Act on Foreigners from 2002 and 2016, and its additional regulations from 2017 and 2018, were also analysed, as well as the official reports of the State Police. In both discourses, asylum seekers are spoken about, not to. As van Dijk (2008) asserts, access to discourse is essential in the reproduction of power and dominance. Access may determine who is written and spoken about. In this analysis, it is evident that asylum seekers and refugees are a topic of the discussion, but not active participants in it.

Third, the analysis also draws from six months of ethnographic fieldwork among asylum seekers and refugees in Iceland in 2016, and from in-depth interviews with 20 individuals who were asylum seekers, or had recently received refugee status in Iceland. The participants were recruited through snowball sampling. The interviewees all identified as male and came from nine countries. In this chapter, they are referred to anonymously. The interviews were recorded, transcribed, and thematically analysed. The fieldwork included visiting asylum seekers in their homes, and joining them in meetings with lawyers, in protests, and in various kinds of gatherings. The main focus in the interviews and fieldwork was to gain insight into asylum seekers' experiences of the asylum system in Iceland.

The fear of small numbers and of cultural clashes

One of the main themes surrounding the securitisation of asylum seekers in Iceland can be characterised as *the fear of small numbers* (Appadurai 2006). Iceland has traditionally received few refugees and asylum seekers, both in comparison with neighbouring countries, and in comparison with other groups of migrants in Iceland. Until 2015, the numbers barely exceeded 100 people a year, but increased in 2015 and 2016, in conjunction with increased numbers of asylum seekers elsewhere in Europe. In 2016, there was a record number of applications, when more than 1,000 people applied for asylum, although a vast majority of applications were rejected (Útlendingastofnun 2017). When numbers were mentioned in the news, they mostly referenced the increase in numbers of asylum seekers between 2015 and 2016. There were also references to politicians speaking about that increase. These politicians often framed their opinions in relation to the fear of increased numbers, using words such as an "explosion in numbers" and "applications will pour all over us". Already in 2012, there were claims made by the head of the Directorate of Immigration that asylum applicants were misusing the system, because the processing time was so long, and the applications so many. That year, applications stood at 115 (RÚV 2013). This discourse surrounding the fear of (small) numbers was present among politicians at both ends of the political spectrum, irrespective of how many asylum seekers were arriving. This was also a common topic in the comments sections, but it did not feature as heavily there as in the media discussion.

A common theme in the comment discussion evoked racialised and gendered images of asylum seekers, especially in regard to Muslim men being seen as a threat. Muslims in Iceland are few and not very visible, yet anti-Muslim discourse is common (Loftsdóttir 2012b). In the discourse analysis of the comments sections, the topic of Islam and its associated threats was recurring. There, arguments ranged from warnings against radical Islam taking a foothold, to fears of terrorism, and references to conspiracy theories of a Muslim takeover (see Fekete 2011). Analysis of the discourses in the comments also revealed that asylum seekers were generally assumed to be Muslims, and that Muslims were generally perceived as a threat. The media analysis showed that racialised discussions about Muslims were becoming more explicit within political discourse. It revealed that statements linking terrorism and Islam are often uncritically reported in the media.

Like elsewhere in Europe, the links between the terrorism discourse, and immigrants or foreigners, were present in public discourse in Iceland. In a speech introducing new immigrant laws in 2002, the then Minister of Justice made a strong association between terrorism threats and migration (Alþingi 2002). This discourse was also present in a risk report by the State Police (Greiningardeild ríkislögreglustjóra 2017). Under the subheading, 'Assessment of terrorism threats', there is a discussion around possible Islamic terrorist threats, directly followed by a discussion on the number and origin of asylum seekers. It is not clear if they as a group were assumed to be a terrorist threat or not, although the placement of the discussion in the document indicates that asylum seekers on the whole were associated with terrorism. The focus in the report is mainly on the risk *of* asylum seekers, but any risks *to* asylum seekers are not assessed in relation to Iceland.

Being unknown

Like elsewhere in Europe, people travelling without legal documents are met with suspicion in Iceland. Among politicians, there has been a noticeable fear of people entering the country undocumented or with false documents. Members of parliament have participated in that discussion, for instance, by expressing bewilderment over *why* people would use fake documents (DV 2014a). This view was echoed in the data from the comments sections, where the lack of identification was seen as a threat. In the comments, there was also a strong link made between travelling without documents, and dishonesty. Frequently, the commentators mentioned the possibilities of asylum seekers being thieves, murderers, criminals, and fanatics, indicating a conflation between being undocumented and being a criminal. There was little understanding of how asylum seekers commonly travel, and why they would need to use false documents. The 1951 Convention Relating to the Status of Refugees states that refugees should not be punished for entering countries illegally, as long as they make themselves known to the authorities after arrival (UNHCR 2010). Many asylum seekers in Europe experience problems of identity, such as being unable to access passports or birth certificates (Griffiths 2012). Asylum seekers therefore have many reasons for not being able to provide their official identity documents.

Many of the asylum seekers interviewed in this research came to Iceland without using their official identity documents. Often, they hadn't had the possibility of obtaining legal documents in their country of origin. However, others used false documents simply because they had never been allowed entry into the EU zone by using their real ones. The reason for using fake documents is, therefore, due to the EU effectively closing its routes to enter legally (van Houtum 2010). Authorities tend to view these offences as serious, since using a false passport undermines the immigration and border control system (Griffiths 2012). But, as Griffiths points out, using false documents, or destroying documents, are also strategies of survival. Those of the participants who had used fake documents to travel to Iceland wanted to stress that this was not their own, free choice:

> I am not criminal ... okay, this is not my passport, but I use it because I don't have no options, and I just use it because I want to save my life.

Yet even those who had official identity documents encountered problems of identity, such as losing these documents, or suspecting that they had been confused with other individuals.

In a society that is increasingly organised by managing identity, and where not knowing one's identity is associated with risk, identification techniques are becoming pervasive to such an extent that people who are beyond identification are seen as both threatening to the state, and at the same time, are very vulnerable in the face of the state apparatus (Griffiths 2012). From the state's viewpoint, the undocumented do not officially exist (Sigvardsdotter

2012). In Iceland, the impossibility of being undocumented is represented by the social security number, *kennitala,* which is used for just about everything, from library cards to rental agreements. Asylum seekers do not receive this *kennitala* when they arrive, but only if they have managed to apply for a temporary work visa, or after their refugee status is recognised. Not having this identification number led some interviewees to feel sub-human:

> I don't have *kennitala* ... Everywhere you go they ask you, and after many years they [asylum seekers] don't have this number, [it] makes you like a human and they don't have it.

Such emphasis on registration increases the exclusion that asylum seekers already face in society. They are therefore not only racialised and excluded in real-life situations, but also within the bureaucratic system.

It was a common theme in the media, comments, and governmental discourses that if asylum seekers were "allowed" to travel without documents, then it would become an easy way for criminals to enter. This does not take into account the scrutinisation that asylum seekers face when claiming asylum (Hammerstad 2008). Participants in this research discussed this scrutinisation, and how they were well known and documented in European databases, such as the Eurodac database, which contains fingerprints of those entering Europe. One of them said: "Even if it [a passport] is not valid, the police assesses you, they fingerprint you, check your face". It is becoming increasingly more common to emphasise establishing identity through using biometric data, and technology such as the Eurodac (Griffiths 2012). Fassin (2001) points out that in some cases, the body is seen to be more truthful than the words of asylum seekers, where scars and wounds are taken as proofs of torture or ill treatment. Bodies are seen as unchangeable and unable to lie. Therefore, identity is reduced to physical components by using DNA testing to prove nationality, and dental checks to prove age (although both techniques are contested); in other words, 'embodied identity' is privileged over testimony (Griffiths 2012).

In the public and governmental discourse analysed here, proving identity was assumed to be important. In the discourse in the comments sections, it was not only assumed necessary to prove identity for refugee status assessments, but also that problems with proving identity were signs of dishonesty, and even criminality. The comments discourse therefore constructs asylum seekers as a threat, because they were seen as unknown. In contrast, asylum seekers described how they were in fact registered in the European asylum system, which stored information about them and their biometric data. They were therefore both documented and known. However, they still lacked a social security number in Iceland, whose societal emphasis made them feel dehumanised and excluded.

Becoming known

Of the 3,386 news stories collected for this analysis, as many as 298 dealt with one case, which was by far the most discussed individual case within news coverage. It surrounded events relating to two Nigerian asylum seekers, beginning in late 2013 with an interview with one of them—a young, pregnant woman who was seeking asylum in Iceland. She was distressed since the father of her unborn child was due to be deported, and she could not get hold of him. A group called No Borders Iceland planned a protest in order to halt or cancel the deportation so the father could see his child. The same day as the protest was planned, the headlines of two major newspapers in Iceland stated: "Many unclear things in the asylum seeker case" (*Morgunblaðið* 2013) and: "Suspected of participating in human trafficking" with the subheading of: "Girlfriend thought to be pressured" (*Fréttablaðið* 2013). The two articles unanimously referenced a memo from the Ministry of Interior, stating personal details about the asylum seeker's case, such as his having three girlfriends, including the one who was pregnant. It also said that he had been suspected of being involved in a human trafficking case. In addition, the news claimed that the young woman who was carrying his child was a victim of human trafficking, and in one of the news articles, it was suggested that he had pressured her to claim he was the father, in order to halt his deportation. After nearly a year of relentless media coverage, charges and investigations resulted in the assistant to the Minister of the Interior admitting to having leaked the information. It was furthermore revealed that the assistant had added slanders to the memo, stating the asylum seeker pressured his former girlfriend, that he was not the father of her child, and that she was a victim of human trafficking (Magnússon 2014b; Kjartansson 2014). Therefore, it seemed that the purpose of leaking the memo was to tarnish the reputation of the asylum seeker by adding false and inflammatory information to the news. At the same time, the memo portrayed his former girlfriend as a helpless victim and a liar, although a reluctant one who was under pressure from her former boyfriend.

This whole case is interesting, not only because of its consequences, but also because of how it seems to reveal underlying racial and gendered prejudices of Nigerians in Iceland. This construction of the image of the dangerous male trafficker and the helpless female victim of trafficking brings to mind postcolonial feminist criticism, in which "Third World" women are portrayed one-dimensionally as victims of male violence (Mohanty 1988). This is highly connected with ideas about saving the female 'Other' from assumed patriarchal norms and exporting 'civilisation'. The idea that the Nordic countries are advanced when it comes to gender equality is used in this rhetoric to "construct dichotomous divisions between the 'nation' and its 'others'" and is linked to ideas about European superiority (Mulinari et al. 2009, p. 13).

When it became evident that personal information about the named asylum seekers had been leaked from the Ministry of the Interior, an editorial in one of the newspapers that published the original article, *Morgunblaðið*, questioned why the public should not be informed about the personal details of asylum seekers:

> It is a valid suggestion, that when attempts to pursue applications of official resolutions with pressure in the news or in the squares, is it not correct that the public gets the whole picture? That nothing is hidden. If the applicants are questionable people, should the public not have the right to be informed?[2]

In the aftermath, a number of politicians, including the Minister of the Interior, and politicians from the ruling parties of government, expressed the view that publishing information about asylum seekers would be a matter of transparency, and would serve both the public and the government, so everyone could assess decisions on asylum seekers (Magnússon 2014a). A municipal politician from one of the ruling parties also claimed that information about asylum seekers should be made available to the public. He suggested that a reception centre should be established, where police could assess criminal records, and medical examinations could be performed, including checking if female applicants had suffered female genital mutilation (DV 2014b). This reflects the discourse of how, presumably, 'African' bodies should be inspected and gazed upon by 'Western' experts, reminding us of the white gaze and images of colonial exhibitions (Fanon 1967; Loftsdóttir 2012a), as well as Mohanty's criticism of the stereotypical "Third World" female victim. It also suggests that the body be viewed as more truthful than an individual's words (Fassin 2001). The unknown should therefore be scrutinised in every possible way, until thoroughly inspected, examined, and documented.

In this light, it is interesting to note that this is not the only time that the personal data of asylum seekers has been leaked in Iceland, ostensibly to justify the decisions of the authorities. In 2009, an Algerian asylum seeker, claiming persecution because of his political opinions, had endured a hunger strike for more than three weeks, which sparked a protest about the treatment of asylum seekers. Incidentally, a day before the protest, his passport was found when searching the house in which he was staying. The passport revealed his real name, leading Icelandic authorities to discover that he was facing a prison sentence in Algeria. It was not revealed for what offence he had been sentenced (DV 2009). The information that was leaked was therefore used to discredit the asylum seeker and his story, and yet did not consider the possibility that he might be fleeing a prison sentence *and* political persecution.

In the media discussion, there was emphasis on the right of the public to know about, and scrutinise, those who want to settle in Iceland, even down to intimate details of their private lives. This was framed in relation to the security of knowing who might be undesirable or questionable individuals. The possibility of having valid reasons for concealing their identity, travelling on false papers, or being imprisoned, were generally not raised in the media discussion. It was barely brought to question that this 'transparency' may harm asylum seekers, who often feared that news of who and where they were could hurt them or their families. In the case of refugees, this is not only a matter of the right to privacy, but also a matter of their individual security. It is often in the interest of asylum seekers to be 'unknown.' As one of the participants stated, it would have been easier for him to go to a country closer to his origin, but he wanted "to go to some place that nobody knows me".

However, sometimes being 'known' could be beneficial for asylum seekers. A significant part of the media discussion on asylum seekers in Iceland was focussed on individual cases and personal interviews with asylum seekers. Some of the participants in this research hoped that media attention might have a beneficial influence on their case. Many of these interviewees spoke about Icelanders being friendly once they got to know them. They talked about it being hard to get to know Icelanders, "when you see someone like first time it's hard to get a connection", but once friendship was established, they generally received support. Having friends or colleagues seemed to help them during the asylum process: "Many people here in Iceland … try and do it to change the decision". Participants who had jobs spoke of their bosses or co-workers helping them out, and contesting deportations:

> When people know that you are very kind and you are very good, once they heard something for you is very bad, they support you, you know, it's not easy to get someone to support you until that person knows that you have a sound mind before he or she comes supporting you.
>
> I can say many people support us, for example my neighbour here [laughs]. Do you know after he see me in the newspaper he say: 'Hi, how are you, what has happened to you?' asking, you know, and I feel he cares about me.

In that regard, they assumed that it was not necessary to personally know people but being 'known' in society through media coverage was also important. Explaining his situation in an interview helped the second commentator to establish links with his neighbour which didn't exist prior. It seems that once they have become 'known' individuals, with links to the community and support of friends or employers, it was easier for the participants to contest negative decisions and fight deportations.

Asylum seeking is often framed in the context of hospitality. However, hospitality is a complex cultural practice, and is often conditional—inherent in it are rules, control, and supervision, which creates a hierarchical relationship between guest and host (Rozakou 2012). Theories of hospitality have mainly been divided between theories that address hospitality as a form of social and economic exchange, and as a form of social control, which manages the stranger as a potential for danger (Lynch et al. 2011). Hospitality and hostility, as Derrida has argued, represent two sides of the same coin, "control and management of strangers and the danger they embody" (Rozakou 2012, p. 585). This form of social control can be seen in the comments about asylum seekers, where it is assumed that they should become 'known' to the public. Hospitality is therefore conditional. Asylum seekers and refugees are supposed to be willing to be scrutinised and have their personal information shared in order to be accepted and welcomed. Both the tracing of ancestry, and the need to 'know' other members of society is not uncommon in small-scale societies. The myth that Iceland is a homogeneous nation furthermore creates the idea that 'knowing' individuals in society is possible, and those who are not 'known' remain excluded. On the other hand, knowledge about the 'Other' has been an integral part of the colonial project. Postcolonial feminists in Nordic countries have criticised how cultural differences are used to name, describe, and research those who are not European, white, or heterosexual (Mulinari et al. 2009). Therefore, the construction of knowledge about the 'Other' can be used as a tool for exclusion. This exclusion is further deepened with a securitisation discourse, which frames those who are not 'known' as a category of risk.

Conclusion

As Buzan, Wæver and de Wilde (1998) propose, securitisation entails a discourse that creates fear, whether there exists a real threat or not. This fear legitimises the breaking of rules in order to maintain security. As the specific cases of leaked information show, the securitisation of asylum seekers is used by both authorities and politicians to legitimise breaching privacy regulations. As demonstrated here, securitisation discourses around asylum seekers in Iceland seep into public and political discussion. It is represented in the fear of unknown masses arriving in unmanageable numbers and without documents. News coverage mainly focussed on how many asylum seekers there are today, and the degree to which this is an increase, while political discussion rather focuses on eliciting fear around even more people arriving.

A second paradigm of fear is the fear of criminality, cultural clashes, and terrorism. This type of securitisation discourse draws heavily on racialised and gendered images of asylum seekers. This type of fear seems to be characterised by racism and draws on ideas around the "clash of civilisations" that originated from the far right (Fekete 2001; Bigo 2002). Politicians and governmental actors seem to focus much more on the threat that asylum seekers might pose, instead of threats they could face, either in the case of deportation, or within the Icelandic context. Asylum seekers both embody and experience this threat. One iteration of that fear stems from the use of fake IDs, which was perceived as a survival strategy, and the only strategy that was available to asylum seekers if they were to come to the EU at all. In the comments sections, however, the dominant discourse was that this was a sign of dishonesty and fraudulent intentions.

If we look at security not as the absence of risk, but the absence of fear, one can say that the speech acts of politicians and the media discourses install fear in people. Part of the securitisation discourse surrounding asylum seekers legitimises intrusive measures to make them 'known', which can invoke racist and colonialist stereotypes. On the other hand, being 'known' is sometimes seen as a beneficial strategy for asylum seekers in order to contest negative decisions by the Directorate of Immigration, and to gather support and help from friends. The small society is therefore of help if one is known, but simultaneously exclusionary for the non-named, unknown masses. Knowledge of asylum seekers and the spread of that information is also used as a governmental tactic, both as a way to control the population, and to keep asylum seekers in place. There is therefore a narrow margin between hospitality and hostility, based on whether or not asylum seekers can become 'known' members of society.

Notes

1 This understanding of securitisation is attributed to the Copenhagen School. The central focus of this discourse has been criticised by Bigo (2002) and other proponents of the Paris School, who emphasise the need to look at more angles than just discourse when analysing securitisation, including bureaucratic practices.
2 Icelandic: "það er gild ábending að þegar reynt er að fylgja eftir umsóknum um opinbera úrlausn með þrýstingi í fjölmiðlum eða á torgum, er þá ekki rétt að almenningur fái alla myndina? Að ekki sé falið um hvað er að tefla? Ef umsækjendur eru vafasamir pappírar, á ekki almenningur í landinu rétt á að upplýst sé um það?" *Morgunblaðið* editorial, 12 February, 2014. http://www.mbl.is/greinasafn/grein/1497959/?item_num=10&searchid=57224b1ff62e3d90263b65dd1a9a59f52ea37c6e

References

Alþingi (2002). 'Útlendingar, 1. umr. Dómsmálaráðherra (Sólveig Pétursdóttir)', Parliament Debates, 5. February. Available at: http://www.althingi.is/altext/127/02/r05140314.sgml [Accessed 8 October 2018].
Appadurai, A. (2006). *Fear of Small Numbers: An Essay on the Geography of Anger*. Durham and London: Duke University Press.
Balibar, E. (2007). 'Is There a "Neo-Racism"?', in T. Das Gupta, C. James, R. Maaka, G-E. Galabuzi and C. Andersen, (eds.), *Race and Racialization: Essential Readings*. 1st ed. Toronto: Canadian Scholars' Press Inc, pp. 83–88.
Bhatia, M. (2015). 'Turning Asylum Seekers into "Dangerous Criminals": Experiences of the Criminal Justice System of Those Seeking Sanctuary'. *International Journal for Crime, Justice and Social Democracy*, 4(3), pp. 97–111.
Bigo, D. (2002). 'Security and Immigration: Toward a Critique of the Governmentality of Unease'. *Alternatives*, 27, pp. 63–92.
Blommaert, J., and Bulcaen, C. (2000). 'Critical Discourse Analysis'. *Annual Review of Anthropology*, 29, pp. 447–466.
Buzan, B., Wæver, O., and de Wilde, J. (1998). *Security: A New Framework for Analysis*. Boulder/ London: Lynne Rienner Publishers.
DV (2009). 'Hælisleitandi sagður bíða dóms', *DV*, 14 May, http://www.dv.is/frettir/2009/5/14/haelisleitandi-sagdur-bida-doms/ [Accessed 4 October 2017].
DV (2014a). 'Brynar svarar Helgu: "Til kallaðir sérfræðingar að sunnan í flóttamannarétti"', DV, 7 August, http://www.dv.is/frettir/2014/8/7/brynar-svarar-helgu-til-kalladir-serfraedingar-ad-sunnan-i-flottamannaretti/ [Accessed 4 October 2017].

DV (2014b). Elliði: "Staðreyndin er sú að málefni innflytjenda eru vandamál", 22 August, http://www.dv.is/frettir/2014/8/22/ellidi-segir-malefni-innflytjenda-vandamal/ [Accessed 4 October 2017].
Fanon, F. (1967). *Black Skin, White Masks.* London: Pluto Press.
Fassin, D. (2001). 'The Truth From the Body. Medical Certificates as Ultimate Evidence for Asylum Seekers'. *American Anthropologist*, 107(4), pp. 597–608.
Fekete, L. (2001). 'The Emergence of Xeno-Racism'. *Race and Class*, 43(2), pp. 23–40.
Fekete, L. (2011). 'The Muslim Conspiracy Theory and the Oslo Massacre'. *Race and Class*, 53(3), pp. 30–47.
Foucault, M. (1977). *Discipline and Punish. The Birth of the Prison.* Translated from French by Alan Sheridan. New York: Vintage Books.
Fréttablaðið (2013). 'Grunaður um aðild að mansali', *Fréttablaðið*, 20 November, p.1. http://www.visir.is/paper/fbl/131120.pdf [Accessed 8 October 2018].
Gabrielatos, C., and Baker, P. (2008). 'Fleeing, Sneaking, Flooding. A Corpus Analysis of Discursive Construction of Refugees and Asylum Seekers in the UK Press, 1996–2005'. *Journal of English Linguistics*, 36(1), pp. 5–38.
Greiningardeild ríkislögreglustjóra (2017). Mat ríkislögreglustjóra á hættu af hryðjuverkum. http://www.logreglan.is/wp-content/uploads/2017/01/Hry%C3%B0juverk-2017.pdf [Accessed 8 October 2018].
Griffiths, M. (2012). 'Anonymous Aliens? Questions of Identification in the Detention and Deportation of Failed Asylum Seekers'. *Population, Space and Place*, 18, pp. 715–727.
Hammerstad, A. (2008). 'Securitisation as a Self-Fulfilling Prophecy: Refugee Movements and the North-South Security Divide'. Draft Paper for the Political Science Association Annual Conference in Swansea, 1–3 April 2008.
Ibrahim, M. (2005). 'The Securitization of Migration: A Racial Discourse'. *International Migration*, 43(5), pp. 163–187.
Íslendingabók (2017). Um Íslendingabók. https://www.islendingabok.is/UmIslendingabok.jsp [Accessed 8 October 2018].
Keskinen, S., and Andreassen, R. (2017). 'Developing Theoretical Perspectives on Racialisation and Migration'. *Nordic Journal of Migration Research*, 7(2), pp. 64–69.
Kjartansson, A. (2014). 'Sigríður segir Gísla hafa beðið um upplýsingar um Omos', *Vísir*, 18 November, http://www.visir.is/g/2014141118869 [Accessed 8 October 2018].
Loftsdóttir, K. (2012a). 'Belonging and the Icelandic Others: Situating Icelandic Identity in a Postcolonial Context', in Loftsdóttir, K., and Jensen, L. (eds.), *Whiteness and Postcolonialism in the Nordic Region. Exceptionalism, Migrant Others and National Identities.* 1st ed. Surrey: Ashgate, pp. 57–72.
Loftsdóttir, K. (2012b). 'Whiteness is from Another World: Gender, Icelandic International Development and Multiculturalism'. *European Journal of Women's Studies*, 19(1), pp. 41–54.
Loftsdóttir, K. (2017). 'Being "The Damned Foreigner": Affective National Sentiments and Racialization of Lithuanians in Iceland'. *Nordic Journal of Migration Research*, 7(2), pp. 70–78.
Loftsdóttir, K., and Jensen, L. (2012). 'Introduction: Nordic Exceptionalism and the Nordic "Others"', in Loftsdóttir, K., and Jensen, L. (eds.), *Whiteness and Postcolonialism in the Nordic Region: Exceptionalism, Migrant Others and National Identities.* Farnham: Ashgate, pp. 1–13.
Lynch, P., Molz, J.G., McIntosh, A., Lugosi, P. and Lashley, C. (2011). 'Theorizing hospitality'. *Hospitality and Society*, 1(1), pp. 3–24.

Magnússon, J.B. (2014a). 'Enginn fótur fyrir staðhæfingum um hælisleitendamál', DV, 22 February, http://www.dv.is/frettir/2014/2/22/enginn-fotur-fyrir-stadhaefingum-um-haelisleitendamal/ [Accessed 4 October 2017].

Magnússon, J.B. (2014b). 'Málsvörn Hönnu Birnu stenst ekki skoðun', DV, 6 May, http://www.dv.is/frettir/2014/5/6/malsvorn-honnu-birnu-stenst-ekki-skodun/ [Accessed 4 October 2017].

Malloch, M., and Stanley, E. (2005). 'The Detention of Asylum Seekers in the UK. Representing Risk, Managing the Dangerous'. *Punishment and Society*, 7(1), pp. 53–71.

Mohanty, C. (1988). 'Under Western Eyes: Feminist Scholarship and Colonial Discourses'. *Feminist Review*, 30, pp. 61–88.

Morgunblaðið (2013). 'Margt óljóst í máli hælisleitanda', *Morgunblaðið*, 20 November, https://www.mbl.is/frettir/innlent/2013/11/20/margt_oljost_i_mali_haelisleitanda/ [Accessed 8 October 2018].

Mulinari, D., Keskinen, S., Irni, S. and Tuori, S. (2009). 'Introduction: Postcolonialism and the Nordic Models of Welfare and Gender', in S. Keskinen, S. Tuori, S. Irni and D. Mulinari (eds.), *Complying with Colonialism: Gender, Race and Ethnicity in the Nordic Region*. Farnham: Ashgate, pp. 1–18.

Mulinari, D., and Neergaard, A. (2017). 'Theorising Racism. Exploring the Swedish Racial Regime'. *Nordic Journal of Migration Research*, 7(2), pp. 88–96.

Razack, S. (2000). 'Simple Logic: Race, the Identity Documents Rule and the Story of a Nation Besieged and Betrayed'. *Journal of Law and Social Policy*, 15, pp. 181–210.

Rozakou, K. (2012). 'The Biopolitics of Hospitality in Greece: Humanitarianism and the Management of Refugees'. *American Ethnologist*, 39(3), pp. 562–577.

RÚV (2013). 'Sækja til Íslands til að fá frítt uppihald', RÚV, 17 January, http://www.ruv.is/frett/saekja-til-islands-til-ad-fa-fritt-uppihald [Accessed 8 October 2018].

Sigvardsdotter, E. (2012). 'Presenting Absent Bodies: Undocumented Persons Coping and Resisting in Sweden'. *Cultural Geographies*, 20(4), pp. 523–539.

Skaptadóttir, U.D., and Loftsdóttir, K. (2009). 'Cultivating Culture? Images of Iceland, Globalization and Multicultural Society', in S. Jakobsson (ed.), *Images of the North, Histories, Identities, Ideas*. Amsterdam, New York: Rodopi, pp. 205–216.

Torpey, J. (1997). 'Coming and Going: On the State Monopolization of the Legitimate "Means of Movement"'. *Sociological Theory*, 16(3), pp. 239–259.

UNHCR (2010). *Convention and Protocol Relating to the Status of Refugees*. Geneva: UNHCR. http://www.unhcr.org/protection/basic/3b66c2aa10/convention-protocol-relating-status-refugees.html. Retrieved 13 April 2017. [Accessed 8 October 2018]

Útlendingastofnun (2017). Tölfræði hælismála. http://utl.is/index.php/um-utlendingastofnun/toelfraedhi. [Accessed 8 October 2018].

van Dijk, T. (1997). 'Political Discourse and Racism: Describing Others in Western Parliaments', in Riggins, H. (ed.), *The Language and Politics of Exclusion: Others in Discourse*. 1st ed. London: Sage, pp. 31–64.

van Dijk, T. (2008). *Discourse and Power*. New York: Palgrave Macmillan.

van Houtum, H. (2010). 'Human Blacklisting: The Global Apartheid of the EU's External Border Regime'. *Environment and Planning D: Society and Space*, 28, pp. 957–976.

Whitaker, R. (1998). 'Refugees: The Security Dimension'. *Citizenship Studies*, 2(3), pp. 413–434.

Wren, K. (2001). 'Cultural Racism: Something Rotten in the State of Denmark?' *Social and Cultural Geography*, 2(2), pp. 141–162.

Index

Ahmed, S. 79
Assimilation 2, 4, 13, 22, 28, 30, 51, 52–54, 63, 72, 75,120, 121–123, 127, 128, 134–135
Asylum-seekers 113–114, 199–200
Austerity 8, 114

Begging 162, 165–167, 171–174
Berlant, L. 119, 122

Citizenship 11, 50, 59–60, 103, 121–123, 128, 135; neoliberal 104, 114; worker-citizenship 114
Class 3, 8–9, 13–14, 105, 114
Coercion, 128, 130
Colonialism 4–5, 14, 115
Copenhagen 41, 44
Criminalisation 163–164, 166, 172–175
Crimmigration 11

Denmark 36–38
Dependency 108, 115
Deservingness 103, 104, 106, 112
Discourse 102–105, 108–110, 112, 115–116
Diversity 29–30, 44; ethnic diversity, 44–46

Eldercare 120, 128, 131–134
Ethnicity 36, 105

Heterogeneity 3–4, 6–7, 21, 24, 35; notions of heterogeneity 29–30
Homogeneity, 1–4,119, 120, 121, 122, 134; ethnic homogeneity, 41; notions of homogeneity 21, 23
Husby 141

Identity 50, 182–183
Immigrant 151

Iran 184–185
Islam 180–181
Islamophobia 187

Kven, 119, 120, 123, 124, 126, 135

Labour activation 104

Marriage practices 128–129
Media 182–183
Mikkelsen, A. 120, 123–127, 134, 135
Militarisation, 143
Minority languages 121, 124, 135
Multiculturalism 1, 3
Muslim 180–181, 183

National identity 8, 37
National minority 71–72, 78
Nationality 50
Nation-state 3–4, 7–8, 10, 13; nation-state building 4, 72; narratives of 3, 78–81, 82
Neoliberal 18, 104
Nordic "exceptionalism" 4–5
Norway 21–23
Norwegianisation 120, 121, 123, 124, 126, 134,
Norwegian-Pakistani 120–121, 123, 127–129, 134, 135

Othering 69, 74

Police stops 167–170
Policing 163–165, 170, 172, 175
Politics of solidarity 1, 13–14
Precarity 104, 114
Privilege 106; white 104
Problematisation 102–104, 106–108, 114–115

Index

Race 1, 2–3, 110–111,
Racialisation 11, 45–46, 74–78, 81, 103, 106, 109
Racism 1, 11, 69, 70–71, 109, 123, 131, 134, 196–197
Representation 52, 58
Respectability 106, 109, 113–114
Rolfsen, U. I. 120, 128, 129, 131, 133, 135
Roma 4, 11, 13–14; Roma migration 162–164, 166–167

Sameness 121, 122, 126, 134
Sámi 4, 11, 13; Sámi Renaissance 51, 55–57
Securitisation 2, 10–11, 181, 196, 205
Social cohesion 6–8, 102, 104, 114
Social exclusion 11, 102–104, 108–109, 112–116
Social science research 23, 27–28

Social security 201
Stigmatisation 145
Suburb 141

Travellers 69–73
Turkey 184–185

Unemployment 103–104, 106; benefits 108

Warfare 143–144
Welfare: state 7, 8–9, 10, 13, 104; benefits 103, 108; chauvinism 103–104, 109; entitlements 103
Whiteness 103–108, 110; wages of 105
Work 104–105; ethic 111–112; worker-identity 112
Workfare 104

Youth 102–103, 105